BIBLICAL
INTERPRETATION

BIBLICAL INTERPRETATION

An Integrated Approach

REVISED EDITION

W. Randolph Tate

HENDRICKSON PUBLISHERS

ISBN 1–56563–252–4

Revised edition — April 1997

All Scripture quotations, unless otherwise noted, are from the New Revised Standard Version, © 1989, Division of Christian Education of the National Council of the Churches of Christ in the United States of America.

Excerpts and summarized material from Leland Ryken, *Words of Delight: A Literary Introduction to the Bible,* pp. 207–11, © 1987, Baker Book House. Used with permission.

Excerpts from Umberto Eco, *The Role of the Reader,* pp. 23–27, © 1979, Indiana University Press. Used with permission.

Library of Congress Cataloging-in-Publication Data

Tate, W. Randolph.
    Biblical interpretation: an integrated approach   /   W. Randolph
Tate. — Rev. ed.
    Includes bibliographical references and indexes.
    ISBN 1–56563–252–4 (cloth)
    1. Bible—Hermeneutics.   I. Title.
  BS476.T375   1996
220.6'01—dc20   96–35194
                                                                   CIP

To my wife, Elaine

Table of Contents

Abbreviations   xi
Acknowledgments   xiii
Preface to the Revised Edition   xv
Preface   xvii
Introduction: A Journey into Three Worlds   xix

Unit I: The World Behind the Text

CHAPTER ONE:
Why Study Backgrounds?
An Apology for Historical Research   3
Review and Study   11

CHAPTER TWO:
The Importance of Language:
The Grammatical Background   13
Phonology   14
Morphology   16
Lexicology   17
Syntax   21
Review and Study   27

CHAPTER THREE:
Reading and the World Behind the Text:
The Historical and Ideological Backgrounds   29
Historical and Cultural Background   30
Some Examples of Historical Background Studies   31
The Ideological Context   35
The Ideological World of the Old Testament   37
Examples of Comparative Study   39
The Ideological World of the New Testament   42
Review and Study   62

Unit II: The World Within the Text

CHAPTER FOUR:

The Bible as Literature and Literary Forms   67
Common Literary Sub-Genres   71
Archetypes   77
Review and Study   78

CHAPTER FIVE:

How the Hebrew Bible Communicates as Literature   80
Hebrew Narrative   80
Hebrew Poetry   106
Hebrew Prophecy   110
Review and Study   114

CHAPTER SIX:

How the New Testament Communicates as Literature   116
The Gospels and Acts   116
Sub-Genres in the Gospels   125
Epistolary Literature   132
Sub-Genres in the New Testament Epistolary Literature   141
Apocalyptic Literature   146
Review and Study   152

Unit III: The World in Front of the Text

CHAPTER SEVEN:

What Happens When We Read?   157
The Dialectics of Discourse   160
Review and Study   184

CHAPTER EIGHT:

What the Reader Brings to the Text:
The Role of Reader Presuppositions   187
The Role of Preunderstanding   187
Reader Presuppositions   188
Theological Presuppositions   189
Review and Study   193

CHAPTER NINE:

How Methods Affect Interpretation   195
Author-Centered Interpretation   196

Author-Centered Theories 198
Text-Centered Interpretation 208
Text-Centered Theories 209
Reader-Centered Interpretation 214
Review and Study 231

CHAPTER TEN:
Mark's Gospel and the Merging of Three Worlds 234
Mark's Use of Literary Allusion 235
Mark's Use of Intercalation 240
Jesus' Relationship to His Contemporary World View
According to Mark 242
Conclusion: The Ending of Mark and the Predicament
of the Reader 250
Review and Study 251

CHAPTER ELEVEN:
The Never-Ending Story 254

Select Bibliography 259
Index of Modern Authors 269
Index of Scripture References 271

Abbreviations

BAGD	W. Bauer, W. Arndt, F. Gingrich, and F. Danker, *A Greek-English Lexicon of the New Testament and Other Early Christian Literature*. 2d ed. 1979.
BDB	F. Brown, S. Driver, and C. Briggs, eds., *A Hebrew and English Lexicon of the Old Testament with an Appendix Containing the Biblical Aramaic*.
ExpT	*Expository Times*
IDB	*Interpreter's Dictionary of the Bible*
ISBE	*International Standard Bible Encyclopedia*
Int	*Interpretation*
JBL	*Journal of Biblical Literature*
JEPD	The Documentary Hypothesis
JSOT	*Journal for the Study of the Old Testament*
KJV	King James Version of the Bible (Authorized Version)
LXX	Septuagint (the Greek translation of the Hebrew Bible)
NASB	New American Standard Bible
NIDNTT	*New International Dictionary of New Testament Theology*
NIV	New International Version of the Bible
NRSV	New Revised Standard Version of the Bible
NTS	*New Testament Studies*
PMLA	Publication of the Modern Language Association
RSV	Revised Standard Version of the Bible
TDNT	*Theological Dictionary of the New Testament*
VT	*Vetus Testamentum*

Acknowledgments

I express special appreciation to Dr. Leon Golden of the Department of Humanities, the Florida State University for his catalytic role in the development of my interest in literary criticism. I also express gratitude to my colleagues in the Department of Biblical Studies and Philosophy at Evangel College for their scholarly criticism, liberal arts orientation, and professional nurture, and to Mr. Patrick Alexander of Hendrickson Publishers for his critical editorial eye that made this text better than it would have been.

Preface to the Revised Edition

I am more convinced than ever that the meaning of meaning is mean-ingless apart from the concept of intertextuality. By intertextuality I mean that human communication takes place within con-texts. An author is a complex of "texts"—social, religious, linguistic, etc. An author can no more free herself from the influences of these "texts" than a zebra can remove its stripes. It is reasonable, therefore, to retain as an integral part of the discipline of hermeneutics the focus on researching the world of the author. More informed readers make better readers.

When we get right down to it, however, we read not authors, but texts. We interpret texts, not authors. Hermeneutics is first and foremost a discipline concerned with how readers assemble understandings of texts. This means that the primary focus of hermeneutics is the relation-ship between the enabling structures of a text and the activities of a reader. Consequently, a responsible hermeneutic will give a large por-tion of its attention to the strategies and structures of texts.

But like an author, a reader is also a complex of "texts." A reader can never stand outside these texts and examine a particular literary text from a position of Cartesian purity. Necessarily, then, hermeneutics has a third focus: that of the role of the reader. Readers read for a variety of purposes and under a variety of influences, and these purposes and influences are partially constitutive of understanding.

The focus of this revised edition has not changed. The focus on the three worlds remains intact. But I have attempted to place additional emphasis upon the relationship between text and reader by lengthening the discussion in chapter 7, "What Happens when We Read?"

A legitimate criticism has been that while talking about integrating the three worlds, I actually never did it. In response I have included an additional chapter on the Gospel of Mark in which I attempt to demon-strate the thesis that meaning really is the result of a conversation between a text and a reader, a conversation that is enhanced by attention to the world of the author.

A final word. Integrity demands that any hermeneutic should remain tentative. Indeed, included in any hermeneutic should be a place for conversation between those involved in the discipline. What I offer in this text is an approach that seems to work well for me and my students in our particular academic and religious contexts. I am, however, constantly in conversation with other approaches that differ sharply from the one offered here. I do not think that it is a healthy practice to engage in ideological warfare, but in a field of study where it is extremely difficult to define "the reader" and "the genre," we should always attempt to inhabit that shadowy space between the thinkable and the thing thought, always eschewing an either/or world in favor of an "and + and" one. This encourages conversation, and the very heart of hermeneutics is the conversation.

Preface

This is a book about interpretation, not a book of interpretations. It concerns the poetics of the discipline of hermeneutics. The book is not primarily prescriptive, but rather descriptive. In other words, I have not intentionally prescribed *a* hermeneutic, but I have offered a general description of the task of hermeneutics. Nonetheless, where there is thought there is also presupposition and thus an unavoidable prescriptive element. Presupposition is to thought as Sancho is to Don Quixote, a constant companion. First, therefore, I disclaim total objectivity as characterizing this work. To claim total objectivity for any activity communicated through the rhetoricity of language is inexcusably presumptuous.

Second, as is to be expected of any introductory book, this work is not complete. Scholars have produced volumes on the various specialized areas of hermeneutics evidencing years of concentrated scholarly focus. In an introduction like this, limited treatment is necessarily the rule. It would be hoped, however, that this limited introduction to hermeneutics will have sufficient clarity and scope to hold the attention of its readers and be provocative enough to whet its readers' intellectual appetites.

Finally, I do not make the claim for definitiveness. A discipline as fluid as hermeneutics simply does not lend itself to this claim. Yet, those "who have ears to hear" will recognize that I have attempted to give audience to the range of interpretive voices presently jockeying for pole position. The implication is that all these voices deserve audience because they have valuable contributions to make to the discipline. Another implication is that hermeneutics cannot become a private exercise inseparably tied to systems of dogmas. Hermeneutics would become nothing more than individual hermeneutics of reduction. Part of hermeneutics is the art of conversation, a willingness to enter into a symposium of voices past and present. Hermeneutics in this sense becomes a hermeneutic of possibility, taking on the character of life itself, always adjusting itself to the fall of humankind into the solvency of time and history.

Introduction:
A Journey into Three Worlds

Hermeneutics has traditionally been defined as the study of the locus of meaning and the principles of interpretation. Biblical hermeneutics, then, studies the locus of meaning and principles of biblical interpretation. Hermeneutics in the broad sense is bipolar: exegesis and interpretation. **Exegesis** is the process of examining a text to ascertain what its first readers would have understood it to mean. The varied set of activities which the hermeneut performs upon a text in order to make meaningful inferences is *exegesis*. **Interpretation** is the task of explaining or drawing out the implications of that understanding for contemporary readers and hearers. Thus, the transformation of these inferences into application or significance for the hermeneut's world is interpretation. Combine *exegesis* and *interpretation* with an examination of the hermeneut's presuppositional repertoire and we may speak of hermeneutics. The terms *hermeneutics* and *interpretation*, however, are often used interchangeably to refer to the process of determining the meaning and significance of a text. Through usage the term *interpretation* has become a comprehensive one. Not only does it refer to the applications inferred from exegesis, but it also refers to the entire process and poetics of hermeneutics. Since words mean what they mean through common usage, I use the terms *hermeneutics* and *interpretation* interchangeably, just as I do the two terms **hermeneut** and *interpreter*.

Carl Braaten sees hermeneutics as "the science of reflecting on how a word or an event in the past time and culture may be understood and become existentially meaningful in our present situation."[1] E. D. Hirsch, Jr., assumes that hermeneutics involves explanation but is prefaced by understanding, while Gadamer and Ricoeur argue that interpretation of texts does not exhaust the responsibility of the hermeneutical enterprise.

---

[1] Carl Braaten, *History and Hermeneutics* (Philadelphia: Fortress, 1966), p. 131.

Hermeneutics assumes the responsibility to move beyond the scientific explication of the text's language to the search for ultimate truth that is incarnate in the language of the text. According to Gadamer and Ricoeur, the search for ultimate reality through the language of the text is the most important task of hermeneutics. Duncan Ferguson defines hermeneutics simply as "the task of hearing what an ancient text has to say."[2]

The common ground shared by these and most other definitions of hermeneutics is literary meaning. Whether reference is to explanation, exegesis, or understanding, the construction of literary meaning is absolutely central to hermeneutics. But where exactly is meaning to be found, and how is it to be actualized? In present scholarship, there are three different groups of theories regarding the locus and actualization of meaning: *Author-centered* (with attention directed to the world behind the text), *text-centered* (with the focus on the world within the text, or the textual world), and *reader-centered* (where the spotlight is trained upon the world in front of the text, or the reader's world). Since these three approaches are usually viewed as mutually exclusive in the articulation of meaning, and since one is often pitted against another, a brief canvas of each approach is not without value. (See chapter 9 for a more comprehensive discussion.)

Author-Centered Approaches to Meaning

Prior to the advent of New Criticism in the 1940s, hermeneutical interest converged on the author and the author's world. Meaning was assumed to lie in the author's intention, which was formulated in terms of the social, political, cultural, and ideological matrix of the author. Without an immersion into the author's world and the occasion which prompted the text, one could not attain meaning with any acceptable degree of plausibility. The text was seen as a shell with many layers. If the layers were appropriately peeled away, the scholar could discover the core and its original setting. This was the locus of meaning. What circumstances prompted the author to write? What sources were used? What was the geographical location of the author and the ecclesiastical tradition of that location? What was the history of the text's develop-

---

[2] Duncan Ferguson, *Biblical Hermeneutics: An Introduction* (Atlanta: John Knox, 1986), p. 6. Hans Georg Gadamer, *Truth and Method* (New York: Seabury, 1975). Paul Ricoeur, *Essays on Biblical Interpretation*, ed. Lewis S. Mudge (Philadelphia: Fortress, 1980).

ment? These are the questions usually associated with the historical-critical method. Since more attention will be given to the diversified criticisms making up the historical-critical method in unit III, only a cursory treatment is required here.

The three criticisms associated with the historical-critical method are *source* (often called literary-source), *form*, and *redaction* criticisms. Both source and form critics suppose that literary meaning rests in the original text and its *Sitz im Leben* (setting in life). Since these primal texts had been distorted through the church's subsequent use of them, these critics sought to salvage the original texts in their originating settings.

While source criticism seeks to discover the sources upon which the present texts rest, form critics desire to return to the oral phase of a particular literary form. The assumption is that the key to meaning lies in the original oral form, not in the final written form. Meaning is determined by the original form in its original sociological setting. Original form and setting are constitutive of meaning.

In its interest with the final form of the text, redaction criticism is more akin to present-day literary criticism than are source and form criticisms. Redaction criticism is dependent upon source and form criticism because of its stress upon the identification of the theological purpose which guided the author in the selection and organization of the individual, isolated forms.

Several points argue against the purely historical approach and its locus of meaning. First, there is an inevitable gap between the originating moment in the author's mind and the cultural specificity of the author's language. In other words, can there ever be a complete guarantee that the author has successfully transferred authorial intention to the written page? Is the text a foolproof and undistorted mirror of the author's mind? These types of questions led Wimsatt and Beardsley to formulate their famous statement of the "intentional fallacy."[3] Second, with the inordinate amount of attention given to the world behind the text, the text itself has suffered from too little attention. Historical criticism has relentlessly sought to focus its illuminating searchlight upon the world behind the text, the real historical world within which a work of literature was given birth. The understanding (i.e., an

---

[3] Warren Wimsatt and Monroe Beardsley, "The Intentional Fallacy," in W. K. Wimsatt, *The Verbal Icon: Studies in the Meaning of Poetry* (Lexington: University of Kentucky, 1954).

understanding with any degree of plausibility) of the literary work
hinges precariously upon a reconstruction of the work's historical milieu. It should be clear that the historical approach must ultimately lead
to a view of the text as an artifact that can and must be understood by
using the scientific tools of anthropology, archeology, and linguistics
just as one would employ for any other artifact. But due to the historical
method's exclusive focus on the world behind the text, the world within
the text has been unduly neglected.

Text-Centered Approaches to Meaning

Since the 1950s a reversal in the way interpreters approach the text
has occurred. With the modern emphasis on the autonomy of the text
and the role of the reader in the production of meaning, scholars have
dislodged the text from its historical mooring and set it adrift in a sea of
relativity, where there are as many meanings of the text as there are
waves of the sea. Rosenberg's assessment of the situation is extremely
insightful. In his evaluation of David Gunn's belief in the text's autonomy, he observes that the political (and by implication, the historical,
social, theological) dimensions of the text are made to be

> an incidental bonus in its unfolding as art, just as the historical investiga-
> tions of the story made its artistic brilliance an incidental bonus in its
> unfolding as history. This persistent blind spot shared by the two disci-
> plines (historical and literary criticism)—the absence of a sense of neces-
> sary connection between the story's historical knowledge and its literary
> mode—is curious and interesting.[4]

Textual autonomy is the springboard for text-centered theories of
meaning. This autonomy could not be stated more clearly than Abrams's
claim that the author's "intention is irrelevant to the literary critic,
because meaning and value reside within the text of the finished, free-
standing, and public work of literature itself."[5] The renewed interest in
the text itself instead of the world behind the text is the gift of what
scholars today refer to as New Criticism and Structuralism. New Criticism describes a trend in the meaning theory prominent especially in the
1940s and 1950s. The movement inherited its name from a book by

---

[4] Joel Rosenberg, *King and Kin: Political Allegory in the Hebrew Bible* (Bloomington: Indiana University, 1986), p. 108.
[5] M. H. Abrams, *A Glossary of Literary Terms* (New York: Holt, Rinehart &
Winston, 1981), p. 83.

John C. Ransom, *The New Criticism*. Only the major tenets of New Criticism are given here.

According to New Criticism, the author's intention and world are not important considerations for interpretation because the literary work itself is sufficient. The text is a literary entity which can stand on its own. Interpretation is limited to the text, meaning that the role of the author is for all practical purposes denied, or at least given no prominent role in interpretation. This, of course, demands an extremely close and careful reading of the text. The reader must give much attention to the various linguistic and literary relationships within the text.

Structuralism also focuses on the text. The author of a work is not an original creator, but simply uses certain literary devices already existing within contemporary culture. Since a work is conceived out of already existing literary conventions, the meaning of a text is located in the conventions, not in the intention of the author.[6] Again, neither the author nor the reader is very important. Since the authors have simply internalized the conventional system, they bring only that knowledge to the text. So the meaning resides in the conventional code and not in the author's intention or the reader's presuppositional world.

A text-centered approach is bittersweet. While it draws attention to the artistry of the text (New Criticism) and conventional literary codes (Structuralism), the author (and to a great extent the reader) has been pronounced dead. But as I argue in unit I, although the meaning of a text may not be found in the author's world, at least our understanding of the text improves when we immerse ourselves in its history.[7]

Reader-Centered Approaches to Meaning

Different readers interpret a text differently. The various and complex reasons for this tautology will be the concern of unit III. The reasons are, however, associated with what might be called the reader's repertoire. The reader brings to the text a vast world of experience, presuppositions, methodologies, interests, and competencies. The reader must actualize the meaning that is only potential in the text. Most reader-oriented theories hold that a text means nothing until someone means something by it. More radical proponents of reader-response

---

[6] Tremper Longman, III, *Literary Approaches to Biblical Interpretation* (Grand Rapids: Zondervan, 1987), p. 32.

[7] See Rosenberg, *King and Kin*, pp. 106–8.

criticism go further to say that the reader creates the meaning of the text. Others, like Edgar V. McKnight, hold that meaning is produced by the mutual interaction between the text and reader.[8] According to this view the text engages the reader as the reader engages the text. Meaning, then, is an invention by the reader in collaboration with the text rather than the intention of the author. The reader is constrained by the text, but is not divested of interests and presuppositions. The text is re-contextual-ized through the multicolored lenses of the reader.

An Integrated Approach to Meaning

To this point we have seen that author-centered approaches to meaning tend to neglect the world of the text and the world of the reader. Text-centered approaches, in claiming textual autonomy, down-play the boundaries imposed by the world of the author upon the text. Now we observe that reader-centered approaches generally find meaning in the interaction between the worlds of the text and the reader. The best we have here is the marriage of two worlds—the reader's and the text's or the author's and the text's. What I propose in this book is that meaning results from a conversation between the world of the text and the world of the reader, a conversation informed by the world of the author. Reverberations of the basic communication model are not accidental. Let me explain: In oral discourse, a speaker seeks to communicate some information to a hearer in such a way that it will be understandable. To accomplish this goal, the speaker makes primary use of language, a language which is generally shared by both parties. But there is another language which is also engaged, consisting of voice inflection, eye con-tact, physical gestures, etc. If for some reason the hearer fails to compre-hend all or part of the message, the hearer can request the speaker to repeat, elaborate, or modify the oral expression until the hearer's under-standing matches the speaker's intent.

In written discourse, an *author* intends to convey meaning through the *text* to a *reader*. Enlisting vehicles such as sound, voice inflection, gestures, and oral dialogue, however, is not possible here. Consequently, the authors must arm themselves with a whole arsenal of literary devices through which they attempt to transfer the message in the intellect to the written page. These literary devices are the woof and warp by which the

---

[8] Edgar V. McKnight, *The Bible and the Reader* (Philadelphia: Fortress, 1985), p. 128.

text communicates to the reader. Further, we may assume that the author has a particular type of reader or audience in mind, one at least familiar with the author's language and world. Otherwise, to speak of communication is absurd. The assumption here is that in the biblical texts, the subjective intention and discourse meaning overlap; that is, what the author intends and what the text says interact but are not identical. While the author is not available for questioning, some aspects of the author's world are. This assumption leaves sufficient room for the role of the reader in the production of meaning. Consequently, three realities converge: author's, text's, and reader's. We argue, therefore, that the locus of meaning is not to be found exclusively in either world or in a marriage of any two of the worlds, but in the interplay between all three worlds. Meaning resides in the conversation between the text and reader with the world behind the text informing that conversation. Interpretation is impaired when any world is given preeminence at the expense of neglecting the other two.

This model of communication sets the agenda for our discussion and for the basic structure of the book. Unit I is concerned with the world behind the text. Chapter 1 argues that the text is the result of an action performed by an author, and as such it is conditioned by the conventional codes that affect anything produced in that particular culture. This means not only that is it inseparably grounded in and influenced by that culture, but that it, in turn, influences its culture. I continue this argument in chapters 2 and 3 by discussing the indispensable adjunctive functions of grammatical, cultural, and ideological background studies within the discipline of hermeneutics.

Unit II deals with the world within the text. In chapter 4, I discuss the importance of genre and sub-genre. I define and illustrate several common sub-genres. Chapter 5 is limited to the broadest generic systems of the Hebrew Bible—narrative, poetry, and prophecy (apocalyptic is discussed in chapter 6). Chapter 6 presents an introduction to the generic systems of the New Testament, including gospel, letter, and apocalyptic. This unit argues that a plausible meaning is impossible without at least some competence in the literary systems of both the Hebrew Bible and New Testament literature.

If the discussion ceased at this point, this interpretive strategy might seem to place hermeneutics within parameters that would assure objective, definable, and communicable meaning. This is true as far as it goes, because as will be asserted in unit I, the text was birthed within a particular culture. I contend, therefore, that the text is an attempt to say something objective, definable, and communicable through conventions that reflect its culture. This recognizes, though, that interpretation has taken place over time, with each period influencing subsequent interpretations. In fact, any interpreter interprets a text over time. But time is not static and neither are interpreters or their worlds. Both the interpreter and the interpreter's world are constantly caught up in the continual flux of what John Caputo calls internal time. So any hermeneutical model must make allowances for a certain subjectivity, incompleteness, and open-endedness. Otherwise, how can we justify the ongoing, never-ending discipline of hermeneutics? Three chapters respond to this very question by addressing the role of the reader and the actual reading process. Thus unit III moves into the world in front of the text. In chapter 7, the reader is introduced to the dynamics of the reading process. The reader may come away with the notion that the process is so complex and has such a vast set of variables that meaning is ultimately unobtainable. However, if I have done my work well, the discussions in units I and II will have diminished this potential problem. In chapter 8, categories of presuppositions and preunderstandings are examined. These reader presuppositions are part of the reader's world and are just as constitutive of meaning as the presuppositions of the author. Since the category of methodological presuppositions is extensive, and since one's method dictates what questions will be put to the text, I give this category a chapter by itself—chapter 9. Chapter 10 offers an example of how the three worlds of author, text, reader intersect to produce meaning. Chapter 11 reflects on the nature of hermeneutics and the never-ending story.

UNIT I

THE WORLD
BEHIND THE TEXT

Why Study Backgrounds?
An Apology for Historical Research

E xegesis must never be swallowed up in application, but must always precede it. The exegetical questions must be answered before questions of application may be legitimately asked. In light of this, one of the cardinal rules of exegesis is that the interpreter must always approach and analyze a text in part or whole within **contexts:** historical, cultural, geographical, ecclesiastical, ideological, and literary. **Exegesis** is the spadework for **interpretation.** But exegesis without interpretation is similar to discovering a cure for the common cold and then not publicizing it. Exegesis alone has no power to produce change—the goal of interpretation. It is a heart without a beat. Interpretation that is uninformed by exegesis, however, has no foundation, like the house built upon the sand. In his discussion of the relationship between the text and the world behind the text, Clarence Walhout rightly observes that this relationship "forbids us to conceive of texts as linguistic objects cut loose from their mooring in an actual world and allowed to drift in some detached sea of aesthetic autonomy."[1]

The goal of this chapter is singular: to demonstrate that the pursuit of background studies (i.e., exegesis) is an indispensable prerequisite for the explication of plausible **textual meaning**; that is, historical, cultural, generic, grammatical, ideological, and even geographical studies are prerequisites for a successful interpretation of a **text.** While it is true that texts exist and are valued independently of their originating circumstances, a knowledge of those originating circumstances will inevitably increase the appreciation of a text. In the past few years, interpretive methodologies have focused on the text and the reader rather than on the author. This swing of the pendulum has produced some very healthy

---

[1] Clarence Walhout, "Texts and Actions," in *The Responsibility of Hermeneutics* (Grand Rapids: Eerdmans, 1985), p. 56.

results, not least of which has been a renewed interest in the biblical texts and the role that the responses of readers play in the creation of meaning. However, this refocusing of attention has tempted some scholars to push the world of the text so far into the background that it becomes relatively unimportant in determining the meaning of a text. For example, Roland Barthes claims that "writing is not the communication of a message which starts from the author and proceeds to the reader; it is specifically the voice of reading itself; *in the text, only the reader speaks.*"[2] While Donald Keesey rejects the idea of *the* meaning of a text, his is a less radical view than Barthes's:

> While we may agree that there is no complete, definitive, and absolutely correct interpretation of a poem, it does not necessarily follow that there are no better or worse interpretations, interpretations more or less complete, more or less accurate, more or less approximating a "best" reading.[3]

It is our contention that the most plausible interpretation or reading of a text cannot be realized apart from a consideration of the world that gave birth to the text. If we recognize that a text is a historical phenomenon in the sense that it originates at a specific time and place, under certain cultural, linguistic, political, and religious conditions, the validity of the above statement becomes more obvious. Literary works may communicate or at least address universal concepts, but they do so within cultural limits and by cultural conventions. A familiarity with these limits and conventions can be helpful in ascertaining from the text that which is universally applicable. Texts reflect their culture, and to read them apart from that culture is to invite a basic level of misunderstanding.

The reader may have noticed that I have consistently made reference to "the meaning of the text" and not to "the meaning of the author." This reference calls for some explanation, an explanation that will prevent an interpretive error. Most scholars today distinguish between authorial and textual meaning. Is the meaning of a literary work of art identical to what its creator meant in composing it? Without question an author purposes or intends to convey some message. Terry Eagleton observes that "every literary text is built out of a sense of its potential audience, includes an image of whom it is written *for*: every work encodes within itself what Iser calls an 'implied reader,' intimates

---

[2] Roland Barthes, *S/Z* (New York: Hill and Wang, 1974), p. 51.

[3] Donald Keesey, *Contexts for Criticism* (Mountain View, Calif.: Mayfield, 1987), p. 7.

in its every gesture the kind of 'addressee' it anticipates."[4] Does the author successfully incarnate this intention within the text and communicate it to the audience? The answer to this question is rather complex.

From a phenomenological perspective, an author perceives an **object of consciousness** (the mental formulation of the text). This object is not synonymous with the text. The text is the concrete literary product of the author's object of consciousness. For example, I have a perception of what this hermeneutics text should be. The perception is not the text; the perception is the intellectual or conscious origin of the text. For every literary text there must be an originating moment when the author conceives of the literary object and perceives it to be a certain way. On the one hand, since perception takes place through time (diachronically), the object of consciousness undergoes a perpetual redefinition from moment to moment. On the other hand, this object of consciousness (regardless of the author's literary purpose) receives concrete expression at a particular time (synchronically) in the form of an inscription (i.e., the text). There is absolutely no way to guarantee a one-to-one correspondence between the ever-changing, diachronic object of consciousness and the permanent, synchronic linguistic representation of it. Indeed, it is probably futile to argue for a one-to-one correspondence between the original intentional object and the text, because there is no way to objectively demonstrate the truth for such a relationship. How is it possible to enter into the consciousness of another, especially when that consciousness is unavailable for questioning? Complete **authorial meaning** is unobtainable, since it is the product of the author's individual consciousness; textual meaning is the cultural specificity of the author's original object of consciousness. There is no way to determine definitively just how accurately the text represents the object of intention.

The **hermeneut** might argue, then, that the text exists as an autonomous object in no way dependent upon the authorial consciousness that gave birth to the text. But intentionality in this sense is not the same as what is usually referred to as authorial intent or purpose. The general reason for writing is to communicate. A logical assumption, consequently, might be that communication resides within the text itself. Nonetheless, we might reasonably inquire whether or to what extent the author was successful in communicating the intended message. Two disparate assumptions are possible here: (1) the author was

---

[4] Terry Eagleton, *Literary Theory: An Introduction* (Minneapolis: University of Minnesota, 1983), p. 84.

not entirely successful in communicating intent but did communicate a message; or (2) the author was successful. In either case, it is presupposed that the author communicated *some* message to an audience through the medium of the written text. Since an author employs verbal symbols in communication, and since verbal symbols carry a wide semantic range of meaning, an author quite possibly (actually quite probably) communicates much more meaning than was consciously purposed. This possibility exists especially for writers who have unconsciously internalized symbols and concepts carrying unspoken, metaphorical usages that consequently have a tacit multivalency. By no stretch of the imagination may we classify this unconscious communication as authorially intended, but *it is in the text*. Therefore, a text does communicate; the author (consciously or unconsciously) communicates through the text, and the way readers actualize this communication is the primary concern of interpretation.

The above remarks bring us to the heart of the matter in this chapter: If the author's consciousness is private and ultimately inaccessible, wherein lies the need for historical research? Why should the hermeneut be concerned with the world behind the text? The answer is twofold.

First, an author perceives the object of consciousness (e.g., in literature, the object of consciousness is the text; in music, the symphony) within the context of a particular historical moment. This perception has its basis in all the various points of the author's culture and the author's unique assimilation of that culture; i.e., the original object of consciousness is at the same time grasped by the individual within a particular culture at a particular historical moment within that culture *and* filtered through an individual psychology.

Second, the literary representation of the object of consciousness has historical grounding. How can authors express themselves concretely apart from their contemporary matrix and their understanding of it? Even Dadaism found significance within a preestablished system of perception and reality. On a generic level, a literary text has meaning only upon the recognition that the author and reader share a body of literary conventions. If the author seeks to transform or modify these conventions, written discourse is possible only as far as the author and reader share the knowledge of conventional norms. Regardless of how much the author subverts conventional norms, understanding is possible solely against the backdrop of the accepted norm. Subversion is subversion only to the degree that the norms are transformed. The world of the text is in the real world while being outside of it. We define the world of the text exclusively in terms of the real world. Political satire, for instance, has no meaning apart from its contemporary political origin. Literature which makes a social statement loses its point if it is not interpreted within the light of those social issues being addressed. Therefore, we must approach the textual world in light of the real world in which it has its grounding. Without a sense of what the real world is like, it is impossible to imagine new ones. The same is also true for readers, even when the worlds presented to us are fictional ones. Clarence Walhout states this quite clearly:

> They [texts] become meaningful to us because we are able to compare their fictional worlds with the world that is already familiar to us. . . . We compare Huck Finn and Tom Sawyer to boys that we have known in actual life even though we have no doubt whatsoever which of the boys are fictional and which are actual.[5]

We can imagine new possibilities only against the backdrop of what we already know, of what in the real world is familiar to us. Outside of this relationship, communication is utterly impossible. The same can be said of an author. A text may be autonomous in relationship to the original intentional object, but the concretization of that object (the text) is conditioned by the real world of the author. How else does an individual communicate except through contemporary social, cultural, or literary conventions? For us to think that authors are not at least unconsciously marked in their thoughts and characters by their experiences in the real world is simply untenable. Behind every literary text, there lies a view of life, a view which has been conditioned by the author's real world. While an author may imagine a literary world with all sorts of new possibilities, the expression of such an imaginative world is impossible apart from the author's real world. An author can imagine a world and express it textually only through the real historical, cultural, literary, and ideological setting. For this reason, historical considerations are at once validated as an important adjunct to hermeneutics.

Since the text is historical in origin, having its birth within a complex of social, literary, linguistic, and ideological systems, certain limits are automatically placed upon the reader of the text. While these systems do not constitute meaning, they do serve as controls upon authorial literary expression. How does the author use or adapt available sources? What are the levels of tradition recognizable within the writings? Who is the author and under what circumstances did he or she

---

[5] Walhout, *Responsibility of Hermeneutics*, pp. 59–60.

write? What occasioned the writing and when? Because a text is historically conditioned, especially in its linguistic expression, these questions
will continue to be appropriate. Consequently, any reading must be
partially measured by the extent to which the reader shares the same
world-view as the author. Louise Rosenblatt offers a similar view:

> I am even ready to say that in most readings we seek the belief that a
> process of communication is going on, that one is participating in some-
> thing that reflects the author's intention. And especially if our experience
> has been vivid or stirring, we may wish to ascertain what manner of
> temperament, life-situation, social or intellectual or philosophic environ-
> ment, gave rise to this work. Especially if it is a text of the past, we may
> wish to discover to what degree our experience differs from that of the
> author's contemporaries. All of the approaches of the literary historian
> become potentially relevant—textual study, semantic history, literary, bio-
> graphical, and other types of history. All these may aid the reader to limit
> himself to the horizon of the author and his time.[6]

Biblical prophecy is an example. Frequently "historical" details are
ripped from their linguistic contexts and then applied to some contemporary situation or event in the reader's age. We may read of a commen-
tator's claims that "the north" and "the east" in the prophecy of Ezekiel
refer to the Soviet Union and China respectively. Observations of this
kind are independent of any interest in or consideration of the original
historical significance of such references. Regardless of the hermeneut's
religious tradition, interpretive methodology, or theological aims, there
must be sufficient focus on the author's historical frame of reference.
Attention to the author's historical circumstances supplies a valuable
safeguard against arbitrary interpretations like the one above.

I am not suggesting that we substitute information *about* authors or
their times for meaning. Meaning comes only through engaging the text.
Historical knowledge of authors and their age enables readers to engage
texts and to organize more plausibly the resulting experiences. Any
non-aesthetic information (biographical, cultural, literary, religious, etc.)
should be valued since it enhances the engagement experience. These
areas of information about the originating world behind the text are
heuristic adjuncts to the literary experience. In other words, understanding ancient texts requires a certain amount of historical spadework.
McKnight rightly observes:

---

[6] Louise Rosenblatt, "The Quest for 'The Poem Itself,' " in Keesey, *Contexts for
Criticism*, p. 144.

There is no need for denial of the fact that certain states of affairs or developments operated in some sense as sources for biblical writings and that biblical writings now reflect those enabling conditions. But attention is to be paid to the realities behind the text (as far as they can be ascertained or imaged) in order to understand the text as a pattern of meaning that continues to have an effect on readers.[7]

While it is true that readers usually value a literary text independently of its originating contexts, a fundamental knowledge of these contexts will certainly increase one's appreciation and understanding of the text. The grounding of a text in its historical dimension is an important aspect of hermeneutics, because biblical texts (any text for that matter) reflect the enabling sources and originating conditions and circumstances. Consequently, the modern hermeneut should not shun the great bulk of information which those craftsmen of the **historical-critical method** have supplied. Speaking of the New Testament writings, Luke Johnson makes a similar observation:

> The NT came to birth among social structures and symbols different from our own. The writings are conditioned linguistically by that historical setting. Their linguistic code is not only alien but also only partially available to us. Precisely the "things that go without saying" are not available to us. Every responsible reading therefore demands historical adjustment. The writings are very much conditioned by the times and places of their origin, by the settings and intentions of their authors. The more we can reconstruct those settings and intentions, the better readers we are.[8]

For example, an understanding of the debate between the schools of Hillel and Shammai concerning ritual cleanness is nothing less than essential to a plausible understanding of Matthew 15:10–12. The historical reference places certain restrictions on the possibilities of interpretation.

Nevertheless, this is not to argue that meaning is the domain of historical studies, because meaning is a function of the textual world. But this does insist that knowledge (as far as it is possible) of the world behind the text illuminates the world within the text. For any single author, we may have little or no information about educational background, literary sources, or even personal religious convictions; through historical research, however, we may discover a considerable amount of

---

[7] Edgar V. McKnight, *Post-Modern Use of the Bible: The Emergence of Reader-Oriented Criticism* (Nashville: Abingdon, 1988), p. 175.

[8] Luke T. Johnson, *The Writings of the New Testament: An Interpretation* (Philadelphia: Fortress, 1986), p. 6.

information about the educational systems of the author's time, the literary conventions in use, the political institutions under which the author lived, and the nature of orthodox and unorthodox religious views.

Summary

A text is the product of an author, and the author is a product of an age. Arguing for such a background study, Joel Rosenberg observes that because of an undercurrent of commentary by Shakespeare on contemporary political life and institutions, some Shakespearean scholars are sent to

> . . . the English constitutional histoires of Maitland and Elton as a way into *Henry IV*, or *Richard III* or even *Coriolanus* and *Julius Caesar*. This is not to suggest that a Tudor or Stuart audience needed to read such histoires in order to understand their poet, only that some members of those audiences possessed the political and institutional sophistication required to make full sense of Shakespeare's political themes, and that such understanding was a principal ingredient of the literary delight they certainly experienced.[9]

This knowledge would have been readily available to many of the contemporary readers, but such is not the case for the modern one. The same is true for readers of the biblical texts. The author could assume a certain body of knowledge on the part of at least some of the contemporary readers, and much of this knowledge is accessible to modern readers only through historical research. Therefore, we should welcome any available background knowledge if it increases our ability to organize into a meaningful whole the various levels of materials that we encounter in the text. **Hermeneutics** should ideally result in the articulation of the most plausible meaning. But there can be no hermeneutical ideal without some measurably competent reading of the text. If background studies enhance our chances of attaining to the hermeneutical ideal, we should welcome such studies with open arms. These non-aesthetic studies should never become substitutes for the aesthetic experience of the text itself. They are precursors, not ends.

Background studies may be divided into two areas—**semantics** and **pragmatics**. Semantics is the study of the language of a text, while pragmatics is the study of the circumstances surrounding the individual linguistic expressions. Exegesis must give equal weight to both areas. Peter Cotterell and Max Turner suggest that semantics and pragmatics should be divided more conveniently into the categories of **text**, **co-text**,

---

[9] Rosenberg, *King and Kin*, p. 108.

and **context**.[10] *Text* refers to the study of the actual words of the text; *co-text* is concerned with the relationships between words in sentences, paragraphs, and chapters; and *context* focuses on the historical and sociological setting of the text. The first two areas are the concern of semantics, while the latter is the domain of pragmatics. This observation by Cotterell and Turner is based upon their distinction between a sentence and an utterance. A sentence may occur repeatedly, while an utterance (which is the sentence within a particular *context*) can never occur more than once. Therefore, exegesis must be concerned with the explication of utterances, not sentences. This means that *pragmatics* must be an integral part of exegesis. When we begin to explore any text, we confront utterances instead of contextless sentences. When Paul wrote to the church at Corinth, he wrote within a particular context, a reconstruction of which yields a more informed reading of the text. In the remainder of unit I, I discuss the grammatical background (*text* and *co-text*) in chapter 2, and the *context* in chapter 3.

REVIEW & STUDY

Key Terms and Concepts

Object of consciousness	Textual meaning
Hermeneut	Authorial meaning
Semantics	Pragmatics
Text	Co-text
Context	Background studies
Exegesis	Historical-critical method
Interpretation	Hermeneutics

Study Questions

1. If an author's work unconsciously reflects his or her world, in what ways might a familiarity with that world assist in the interpretation of a text?

---

[10] Peter Cotterell and Max Turner, *Linguistics and Biblical Interpretation* (Downers Grove: InterVarsity, 1989), pp. 15–19.

2. Which do you feel is the final source of meaning, the author or the text? Why?

3. What advantage does oral discourse have over written discourse?

4. How does the distinction between "sentence" and "utterance" suggest the need for exegesis?

5. In what way might background studies inform interpretation even when the author of a text is anonymous?

6. What is the difference between authorial intention and textual meaning?

7. In what way do background studies offer a "check" on interpretation?

Suggestions for Further Reading

Braaten, Carl. *History and Hermeneutics*. Philadelphia: Fortress, 1966.

Fee, Gordon and Douglas Stuart. *How to Read the Bible for All Its Worth*. 2d ed. Grand Rapids: Zondervan, 1993.

Freyne, Sean. *Galilee, Jesus, and the Gospels: Literary Approaches and Historical Investigation*. Philadelphia: Fortress, 1988.

Hayes, John and Carl Holladay. *Biblical Exegesis: A Beginner's Handbook*. Atlanta: John Knox, 1987.

The Importance of Language:
The Grammatical Background

A fundamental truth: An author uses language in formulating a text. At the level of the text, the interpreter must give attention to the identification and description of details such as **phonology** (word sounds), **morphology** (word forms), **lexicology** (word meanings), and **syntax** (word relationships). Literature is the linguistic expression of a culture's entire symbolic world. The **symbolic world** refers to the infinite maze of interrelated customs, ideologies, religious expressions, and social relationships, within which a people finds its identity, its self-understanding, and its ultimate reason for being. We may reasonably assume, then, that if a culture's literature is the linguistic expression of this symbolic world, or at least the linguistic attempt to interpret the symbolic world, a study of that culture's linguistic expression—language in its many facets—should be an integral part of hermeneutics. We might also include more formal literary structures (such as genre, poetic subforms, and narrative sub-genres) within this context, but these pertain more to the world projected by the text (discussed in unit II). Our primary interest here is with the grammatical elements of the language of the text. This is a primary level of hermeneutics, incomplete within itself, but an absolutely necessary precondition for the other contexts which we consider.

That the languages of the biblical texts are not those of the modern reader is an inescapable hermeneutical consideration when dealing with the referential function of language. The world of the text is projected on the most elementary level of words. These words combine to form sentences, sentences form units, units form sections, and sections form entire texts. Since writers communicate meaning through combinations of words, phrases, sentences, linguistic units, and concepts, these are important hermeneutical considerations.

The **grammatical context** is concerned with the original thought-world of the author as it is expressed through the language of the text.

The most basic level of this concern is the single word. There will always exist the danger of overemphasizing the single word; while we must recognize, however, that a text communicates its message through the relationships of its phrases, sentences, and larger lexical units, the hermeneut cannot neglect single words.

Often we encounter words within the biblical texts whose references seem foreign to us. This is true whether we are using the original languages or a translation. These words may carry technical, cultic, or figurative meanings unparalleled in our culture. The biblical authors could assume that the original readers would understand these special concepts without any accompanying explanation. Terms such as "kingdom of God" in the Synoptics, "justification" as used by Paul in Romans and Galatians, "covenant" in the Hebrew Scriptures and the New Testament, and "Logos" in the Gospel of John are examples.

To summarize, grammatical study is concerned with the analysis of the language of the text. An author combines words and phrases to express certain ideas. These words and phrases carry meaning, simply because they are arranged into what we might call sense units. The importance of grammatical considerations is that they increase the probability of the reader's recognition of these sense units. Below are (1) some basic guidelines to assist the beginning hermeneut in developing competence in grammatical studies, and (2) some examples of how to apply these guidelines.

Phonology

Word sounds can best be appreciated when pronounced in the original languages (Hebrew, Aramaic, and Greek) of the Bible. As in most languages, the biblical writers used a range of sound combinations for a variety of purposes. Experienced writers employ word sounds for emphasis, aesthetic and lyric expression, irony, or for didactic purposes. With stylistic devices, authors call the reader's attention to some aspect of their message. The writers of Hebrew poetry extensively used word sounds.

Alliteration

Alliteration is the practice of beginning a series of words or syllables with the same or similar sounds. Psalm 119 is an example in which each line in a series of eight begins with the same Hebrew letter.

119:1	(א) 1.	אַשְׁרֵי תְמִימֵי דָרֶךְ הַהֹלְכִים בְּתוֹרַת יהוה
	2.	אַשְׁרֵי נֹצְרֵי עֵדֹתָיו בְּכָל לֵב יִדְרְשׁוּהוּ
· · · · ·	· · · · ·	· · · · · · · · · ·
	8.	אֶת חֻקֶּיךָ אֶשְׁמֹר אַל תַּעַזְבֵנִי עַד מְאֹד
119:9	(ב) 9.	בַּמֶּה יְזַכֶּה נַּעַר אֶת אָרְחוֹ לִשְׁמֹר צִדְקֶךָ
	10.	בְּכָל לִבִּי דְרַשְׁתִּיךָ אַל תַּשְׁגֵּנִי מִמִּצְוֹתֶיךָ
· · · · ·	· · · · ·	· · · · · · · · · ·
	16.	בְּחֻקֹּתֶיךָ אֶשְׁתַּעֲשָׁע לֹא אֶשְׁכַּח דְּבָרֶךְ
119:81	(כ) 81.	כָּלְתָה לִתְשׁוּעָתְךָ נַפְשִׁי לִדְבָרְךָ יִחָלְתִּי
	82.	כָּלוּ עֵינַי לְאִמְרָתֶךָ לֵאמֹר מָתַי תְּנַחֲמֵנִי
· · · · ·	· · · · ·	· · · · · · · · · ·
	88.	כְּחַסְדְּךָ חַיֵּנִי וְאֶשְׁמְרָה עֵדוּת פִּיךָ
119:153	(ר) 153.	רְאֵה עָנְיִי וְחַלְּצֵנִי כִּי תוֹרָתְךָ לֹא שָׁכָחְתִּי
	154.	רִיבָה רִיבִי וּגְאָלֵנִי לְאִמְרָתְךָ חַיֵּנִי
· · · · ·	· · · · ·	· · · · · · · · · ·
	160.	רֹאשׁ דְּבָרְךָ אֱמֶת וּלְעוֹלָם כָּל מִשְׁפַּט צִדְקֶךָ

Assonance

Assonance takes advantage of the same or similar sounds (usually vowels) within words. A good example is the hymn in 1 Timothy 3:16. A person who does not have a reading knowledge of Greek can still see that the first word in each line has the same final sound:

ephanerōthē en sarki	ἐφανερώθη ἐν σαρκί
edikaiōthē en pneumati	ἐδικαιώθη ἐν πνεύματι
ōphthē angelois	ὤφθη ἀγγέλοις
ekērychthē en ethnesin	ἐκηρύχθη ἐν ἔθνεσιν
episteuthē en kosmō	ἐπιστεύθη ἐν κόσμῳ
anelēmphthē en doxē.	ἀνελήμφθη ἐν δόξῃ.

Paronomasia

Paronomasia is a pun, a play on words that have the same or similar sounds but different meanings. In Amos 8:2, God asks, "What do you see?" to which Amos responds, "A basket of summer fruit." The expression "summer fruit" (qayits) sounds like the word for "end" (qets) in verse 2: "The end has come upon my people." The original readers would have appreciated the pun which is lost in translation. In 2 Corinthians

4:8 we see another illustration: *aporoumenoi all' ouk exaporoumenoi* ("Perplexed, but not driven to despair").

Onomatopoeia

Onomatopoeia involves using words whose sounds actually suggest the object or concept to which they are referring. For example, Richard Soulen suggests that "the Hebrew words *thohu wavohu* in Gen. 1:2 suggest to the ear what the English translation communicates only conceptually: 'without form and void.' "[1] Such word sounds and their beauty of expression are usually lost in translation. When dealing with poetic passages especially, the ideal is to work with the original languages. If this is not possible, however, the student should consult several modern translations; some will capture the phonological qualities of the original languages.

Morphology

Morphology is the study of the forms of words. The languages of the Bible are highly inflected languages. By "inflected" we mean that a word changes in form depending upon tense, voice, mood, person, number, case, and gender. In Koine Greek (the Greek of the New Testament) word order is much less significant than in an uninflected language like English. In English, the order is usually subject, verb, and direct object with prepositional phrases, adverbial clauses, and relative clauses occurring according to rules of syntax. In Greek, however, inflection is more crucial to meaning than word order.

Word forms influence meaning, and for this reason having the ability to recognize forms and their potential meanings is an essential part of interpretation. I may be able to ask a speaker of my language what is meant by an unusual statement or word or word form; the writers of the biblical texts, however, are not available for questioning. Therefore the best alternative is to equip ourselves with the knowledge necessary for recognizing forms and their possible meanings. For example, in 1 Corinthians 12:31 the word *zēloute* (translated as "strive for") may be either an indicative (a statement concerning a state of affairs) or an imperative (a command) in form. How is the interpreter to

---

[1] Richard Soulen, *Handbook of Biblical Criticism*, 2d ed. (Atlanta: John Knox, 1981), p. 132.

decide? Actually if the interpreter is not aware that there are two possibilities, there will be no choice except that one made by the translator. The point is that the statement assumes a different meaning if it is translated as an indicative rather than an imperative.

Lexicology

While single words do not comprise the hermeneut's primary point of concentration, we often encounter words seemingly unclear in meaning but potentially having special significance for understanding a passage. A plausible explication of a larger passage may hinge upon the meaning of a word which appears vague to us. When such a word is understood in the way in which it would have been understood by the original author or audience, the entire larger unit may assume a sharper focus. In reference to word studies, Hayes and Holladay observe:

> we gradually broaden our understanding of the term, the passage itself and the other biblical writings in which it occurs. It is through this process of interrogation and analysis that we begin to increase our own understanding of the passage by actually re-entering and re-creating the thought-world of the author or text itself.[2]

Key Words or Phrases

Isolate key words or phrases. Readers frequently encounter words appearing to have technical, cultic, cultural, or theological significance. The biblical writers shared a conceptual world with their contemporaries. When they set about putting the message of faith into coherent systems, defining and articulating its unique character, their only recourse was to exploit familiar concepts. The concepts may have been redefined and reinterpreted, but their new interpretation has significance only against the backdrop of the concept's original usage.

Reference Tools

Employ available reference tools to investigate the word or phrase. For the beginning student, there are basically three indispensable reference tools—Bible dictionaries and encyclopedias, lexicons or other word study books, and biblical concordances.

---

[2] John H. Hayes and Carl R. Holladay, *Biblical Exegesis: A Beginner's Handbook* (Atlanta: John Knox, 1987), p. 62.

Dictionaries and encyclopedias. These works offer the student an abundance of historical information on a variety of words and topics. For example, *The Zondervan Pictorial Encyclopedia of the Bible* (1977) provides a fifteen-page discussion of the word "righteousness." The discussion is divided into topics such as "The meaning of the term linguistically," "Righteousness in the OT," "Righteousness in the NT," and "Righteousness in the modern world." Other useful dictionaries and encyclopedias include the one-volume *New Bible Dictionary* (1962), the multivolume *Interpreter's Dictionary of the Bible* (*IDB*, 1962), the *International Standard Bible Encyclopedia* (*ISBE*, 1952), and the *Anchor Bible Dictionary* (*ABD*, 1992). All of these works are accessible to students unable to work with the original languages of the biblical texts. Any of these works provide the student with valuable background material for words, phrases, and concepts.

Word study books and lexicons. Word study books have a limited value for the student who does not know the biblical languages. When used with discrimination, they can supply useful information about specific words. These works can be single or multivolume. Generally the entries are arranged according to word families. The treatment may range from the earliest usage to the usage in the biblical text and beyond. Some of the better known word study works are John R. Kohlenberger, III, ed., *The Expanded Vine's Expository Dictionary of New Testament Words* (1984); Kenneth S. Wuest, *Word Studies in the Greek New Testament* (1975); Marvin Vincent, *Word Studies in the New Testament* (1973); and A. T. Robertson, *Word Pictures in the New Testament* (1930).

Lexicons have a more limited use for students unable to work with the original languages. But for those students who are able to use them, lexicons provide a distinct advantage. A useful **lexicon** provides the student with etymologies, an identification and discussion of irregular grammatical forms, possible meanings, and the usage of a word within a given context. The following are suggested lexicons: W. Bauer, W. Arndt, F. Gingrich, and F. Danker, *A Greek-English Lexicon of the New Testament and Other Early Christian Literature* (1979; BAGD); G. Lampe, ed., *A Patristic Greek Lexicon* (1961–1968); H. Liddell and R. Scott, *Greek-English Lexicon* (1940); J. Moulton and G. Milligan, *Vocabulary of the Greek Testament Illustrated from the Papyri and Other Non-Literary Sources* (1974); G. Kittel and G. Friedrich, eds., *Theological Dictionary of the New Testament* (1964–1976; *TDNT*); Colin Brown, ed., *The New International Dictionary of New Testament Theology* (1975–1978; *NIDNTT*); C. Spicq, *Theological Lexicon of the New Testament* (1994; keyed to Strong's)

F. Brown, S. Driver, and C. Briggs, eds., *A Hebrew and English Lexicon of the Old Testament with an Appendix Containing the Biblical Aramaic* (1907; BDB); E. Jenni and C. Westermann, *Theological Lexicon of the Old Testament* (1997; keyed to Strong's and other lexical resources); and W. Holladay, *A Concise Hebrew and Aramaic Lexicon of the Old Testament* (1971). There are aids available which make these tools accessible to the English student: John R. Alsop, *An Index to the Bauer-Arndt-Gingrich Greek Lexicon* (1968); George Wigram and Ralph Winter, *The Word Study Concordance* (1978; this particular work is keyed to BAGD, Moulton and Geden, and *TDNT*); George Wigram, *The Englishman's Hebrew Concordance* (1996; this work is coded to Strong's concordance numbering system); and *The Brown-Driver-Briggs-Gesenius Hebrew and English Lexicon with an Appendix Containing the Biblical Aramaic* (1996; this work is coded to Strong's concordance numbering system). *The New Analytical Greek Lexicon*, edited by W. J. Perschbacher (1990; keyed to Strong's and including variant readings) is an improvement over the older Wigram *Analytical*.

   Concordances.   There are different types of **concordances,** but the most useful for those lacking the original languages are the analytical ones. These concordances allow the student to find the Hebrew or Greek word translated by the English word. This can assist the student in using the lexicons listed above when a knowledge of the biblical languages is absent. Listed here are some of the better concordances: Gerhard Lisowsky, *Konkordanz zum hebräischen Alten Testament* (1958); William Moulton and A. S. Geden, *A Concordance to the Greek Testament According to the Texts of Westcott and Hort, Tischendorf and the English Revisers* (1978); Kurt Aland, *Vollständige Konkordanz zum griechischen Neuen Testament: unter Zugrundelegung aller modernen kritischen Textausgaben und des Textus receptus* (1975); and Eugene Nida and J. P. Louw, eds., *Greek-English Lexicon of the New Testament Based on Semantic Domains* (1988). Lisowsky, Moulton and Geden, and Aland list passages where a term is used in a similar sense. The reason for this arrangement springs from a recognition that the same word may be used in a variety of ways with a variety of meanings. In other words, the semantic range of a word is not limited to one definition. The most valuable concordances for those not acquainted with original languages are: James Strong, *The Exhaustive Concordance of the Bible* (1947) and Robert Young, *Analytical Concordance to the Bible*, 22d American edition (1955).

   A word of caution is needed here. While lexical tools are valuable for examining single words, there is a tendency of most of them to "over-exegete." For example, if I wish to examine the meaning of a word, normally I need to know how the word was used at a particular time. If I consult **BAGD** or *TDNT,* I am presented in some cases with pages of information tracing the meaning of the word back over centuries. As I have already pointed out, languages are not static, and words change meanings over time. For this reason, the study of words should generally be *synchronic* and not *diachronic.*

> A language has been compared with a river: take a cross-section here and the river can be described, or there and again it can be described, although the description will be different. If we see the length of the river as signifying time, then taking a cross-section at different points along the river, and comparing what is found, corresponds to *diachronic* linguistic study, while the examination of a single cross-section corresponds to *synchronic* study.[3]

For this reason, it is generally unacceptable to explain one writer's use of a word by that of another writer. It is also generally not wise to interpret an author's use of a word by that same author's use of the same word in a different text. Paul may not use the word *diakonos* (servant) in the same way that it is used in the Septuagint or in Matthew.[4]

Context

Contextualize.   The range of meaning of a word or phrase is deter-mined by its context. Word studies may supply a broad range of mean-ing for a word or phrase, i.e., ways it has been used in a variety of historical situations. This is helpful, of course, because an author often modifies the meaning of a word within a particular context; on the other hand, the author's modification may be set in relief by a knowledge of the word's historical uses. A word's range of meaning may aid in under-standing its meaning within a particular context. For example, *mystērion* (mystery) was used in the mystery religions to refer to a body of knowledge that was available only to the adherents of the particular mystery. Paul, however, uses the word to refer to the "good news" and to the fact that God has extended his grace to Jews and Gentiles alike. The mystery, thus, is no longer a mystery! Words such as *sōtēr* (savior), *logos* (word, message), and *hamartia* (sin) also had long histoires of secular

---

[3] Cotterell and Turner, *Linguistics and Biblical Interpretation,* p. 25.

[4] For an excellent discussion of the potential misuses of word studies, see James Barr, *The Semantics of Biblical Language* (Oxford: Oxford University, 1961).

usage but were modified within the context of Christianity. Christian writers employed the Koine Greek of their time. They did not develop a new religious language exclusively for their purposes. They may have modified the vocabulary, but we must understand this modification against the current uses of the time.

Syntax

If the student remains at the level of analyzing single words and phrases and their historical contexts, not much will ever be accomplished. A text is comprised of a series of sense units whose combination ideally results in a logical flow of thought or argument. For this reason, the interpreter must move beyond single words and phrases to sentences, sense units (usually paragraphs), larger lexical units, and finally to the text as a whole. For example, if I read the statement, "Santa is coming to town," the word "Santa" has meaning only in its relationship to the other words in the sentence. The sentence predicates something about "Santa." However, is "Santa" the slightly overweight bearer of gifts to children at Christmas? Or does "Santa" have some metaphorical or symbolic significance referring jokingly to some fat man in red with a long white beard? Is the force of the sentence a promise, an imperative, a concession (what linguists refer to as the elocutionary force of a sentence)? When is "Santa" coming to town? How will he arrive? These questions have answers only if we look beyond the sentence to the greater context of the sense unit and the text as a whole.

An effective method of ascertaining the logical flow of thought is to construct a **sentence flow** and/or a grammatical outline of a unit.[5] By identifying the coordinate and subordinate clauses, the student usually gains an initial sense of the thought flow. A grammatical outline will help the student identify adverbial clauses, prepositional phrases, relative clauses, infinitives, participial clauses, etc. and clarify their relationships with the main parts (subject, verb, direct object) of the various sentences. In constructing the sentence flow and grammatical diagram, the student will recognize associations not otherwise readily apparent. Also, figurative expressions, unusual grammatical constructions, and parenthetical excursions become recognizable.

---

[5] For an excellent discussion of the sentence flow, see Gordon Fee, *New Testament Exegesis: A Handbook for Students and Pastors*, 2d ed. (Philadelphia: Westminster, 1993).

Elements of syntax are best analyzed by working with the original languages, and a minimum competency in these languages should be a goal for any prospective Bible scholar. Until this goal is a reality, however, the student must combine two intermediate essentials: A mastery of English grammar and a rather literal translation of the Scriptures. This will allow the student to follow more correctly the thought flow of the text and will result in a more plausible interpretation.

Ideally, the student should move from one sense unit to another until the entire text has been covered. In this process, logical connectives such as premise and conclusion indicators should receive special attention. Words such as "therefore," "such that," "as a result," and "because," are red flags indicating a particular chain of thought or argument. Once the student has combed the entire text in this grammatical fashion, there will develop a tentative understanding of the central thrust of the text and the way in which the sense units are related to each other and to the whole. The following discussion of 1 Corinthians 13:8-12 illustrates the way a sense unit will be related to the larger context.

Paul's overarching reason for writing to the church at Corinth is to respond to a report of divisions which threatened the unity of the community (1:10-17).[6] Within this context Paul addresses the issue of spiritual matters in chapters 12-14. In chapter 12 he begins by stating, "Now concerning spiritual gifts, brothers and sisters, I do not want you to be uninformed" (12:1). The Greek word here for "spiritual gifts" is *pneumatikoi*. This word is different from the one normally used for spiritual gifts—*charismata*. Actually, *pneumatikoi* is better translated "spiritual matters" or "spiritual people." The translation "spiritual people" is one possibility. George Ladd writes: "In I Cor. 2:14-3:3, Paul describes three classes of people: Psychikos, the natural man (2:14); sarkikos, the fleshly man (3:3); and the pneumatikos, the spiritual man (3:1). In this passage . . . the 'spiritual man' is the man whose life is ruled by the Holy Spirit."[7]

The option "spiritual matters," however, has much to commend it. Since the form of the substantive is genitive plural (*pneumatikōn*), the substantive may be neuter ("matters") or masculine ("people"). Add to this the neuter form (*ta pneumatika*) in 14:1, and the most plausible choice for translating *tōn pneumatikōn* is "spiritual matters." If we accept

---

[6] See Johnson, *Writings of the New Testament*, pp. 272–90.

[7] George E. Ladd, *A Theology of the New Testament* (Grand Rapids: Eerdmans, 1974), p. 473.

this translation, then the *charismata* are only part of Paul's interest, and perhaps not his primary one. Paul is concerned here with "spiritual matters," and his discussion of the *charismata* is significant only as *charismata* relate to his primary concern with "spiritual matters."

After Paul moves through his list of gifts, services, and kinds of workings, he metaphorically compares these gifts and their operations to the unity and function of the parts of the human body (1 Cor. 12:12–26). His obvious purpose in this elaborate comparison is to show that, just as there are differences of function among the parts of the human body, there are likewise various charismatic functions within the body of Christ. The human body is made up of parts, and with one part missing, the body is incomplete. Furthermore, if one member, say the eye, is given preeminence to the neglect of the other parts, the body would not long survive ("If the whole body were an eye, where would the hearing be? If the whole body were hearing, where would the sense of smell be? But as it is, God arranged the members in the body, each one of them, as he chose. If all were a single member, where would the body be?" [1 Cor. 12:17–19]). The implication is obvious: If everyone within the community seeks after a gift because that gift is viewed as superior or impressive, then the unity of the charismatic body that God has ordained is jeopardized. Paul makes this explicit in 12:21–30, especially in verses 23b–25:

> And those members of the body that we think less honorable we clothe with greater honor, and our less respectable members are treated with greater respect; whereas our more respectable members do not need this. But God has so arranged the body, giving the greater honor to the inferior member, *that there may be no dissension within the body, but the members may have the same care for one another* [emphasis mine].

For a spiritually healthy body, all the members are necessary, regardless of their gifts. There is no hierarchy of the gifts on the basis of desirability. But how are we to understand Paul's statement in 12:31a ("But strive for the *greater* gifts")?

Based upon Paul's discussion in 1 Corinthians 12, we may be certain that the Corinthian believers were using what they considered to be the more desirable gifts as criteria for claiming spiritual maturity or elitism. Based upon our discussion above, we may also conclude that Paul goes out of his way to offer a corrective to this ranking of the *charismata*. Is it not then inconceivable that in his next breath Paul opts for just such a ranking by challenging these same readers to earnestly desire the "better" gifts? Certainly Paul is not suffering from doctrinal schizophrenia. The solution to this apparent dilemma is to be found in

the word *zēloute* (1 Cor. 12:31) translated as "earnestly desire" (imperative) in most versions of the New Testament (e.g., RSV, NIV, NASB).
Grammatically we may translate this form of the verb in either of two
ways: as a present tense indicative or a present tense imperative. I suggest
that in the present context, the former is the better translation. This
would then render the statement as an example of Pauline sarcasm Paul
is not bashful in using the literary device of sarcasm to get his point
across (e.g., 1 Cor. 4:10), and it would read: "you are striving for the
better gifts. And I will show you a still more excellent (*hyperbolē*) way"
(12:31). Paul thus proposes to the Corinthian believers the true measure
of spiritual adulthood or maturity.

In 1 Corinthians 13:1–8a, Paul selects representative gifts (three
from the list in ch. 12) and argues that they are for all practical purposes
functionally insignificant when manifested outside the umbrella of love.
Without the accompanying *agapē*, even generosity is functionally meaningless. In 13:4–8a, Paul describes love in lyrical prose form.

Then in 13:8b Paul again draws us to his original list by a second
sampling: "But as for prophecies, they will come to an end (*katar-
gēthēsontai*); as for tongues, they will cease (*pausontai*); as for knowledge,
it will come to an end (*katargēthēsetai*)." Note should be taken that Paul
uses the same verb to describe the fate of both prophecies and knowledge. The root verb is *katargeō*, which usually means "to make invalid,"
"to make ineffective," "to nullify," or "to abolish" (e.g., Rom. 3:3; 6:6;
1 Cor. 1:28; Eph. 2:15).[8] The verb *pauō* describes the fate of tongues and
can be translated "to end," "to subside," or "to stop" (e.g., Luke 8:24;
Acts 20:1; Eph. 1:16).[9]

In verses 9 and 10, Paul pursues two of the last three gifts even
further: "For we know only in part (*ek merous*), and we prophesy only in
part (*ek merous*); but when the complete comes, the partial (*to ek merous*)
will come to an end (*katargēthēsetai*)." Two things should be clear at this
point: First, Paul identifies the two gifts of prophecy and knowledge with
that which is imperfect, and all three are described as being partial (*ek
merous*); second, that which is imperfect suffers the identical fate of the
two gifts—*katargēthēsetai*. Consequently, within this context, Paul argues
that "that which is perfect" (*to teleion*) is set in juxtaposition to "that
which is *ek merous*." But what is "that which is perfect"? Since *to teleion* is
neuter in gender, we may rule out any reference to a person. Further-

---

[8] Gerhard Delling, "*katargeō*," *TDNT*, vol. 1, pp. 452–54.
[9] BAGD, "*pauō*."

more, since the New Testament canon was not even in its formative stage at this early period, we may also rule out the suggestion that *to teleion* refers to the canon. When used of things, the adjective *teleion* suggests completeness, or full measure (e.g., Rom. 12:2; Jas. 1:4a; 1 John 4:18).[10] The whole context is concerned with one thing—love. On the other hand, Paul's term for love (*agapē*) is feminine rather than neuter. Perhaps, then, Paul's "that which is perfect" refers to a state of completion or spiritual maturity whose hallmark is *agapē*.

This observation is supported by verses 11–13. In verse 11, Paul says that when he was a child (*nēpios*) he talked, thought, and reasoned as a child. This term *nēpios* occurs earlier in 1 Corinthians 3:1: "And so, brothers and sisters, I could not speak to you as spiritual (*pneumatikois*) people, but rather as people of the flesh (*sarkinois*), as infants (*nēpiois*) in Christ." Within this same context of 1 Corinthians 2:14–3:3 (referred to above), the worldly person (*sarkikos*) is in Christ, yet not a person of the Spirit (*pneumatikos*), for that one is only a child (*nēpios*). Ladd offers an excellent description of the *sarkikos*:

> [These are those] who are "fleshly" yet who are babes in Christ. They must therefore be "in the Spirit," yet they do not walk "according to the Spirit." Because they are babes in Christ, we must conclude that the Spirit of God dwells in them; yet the Holy Spirit does not exercise full control over their lives, and they are still walking "like men" (v. 3), manifesting the works of the flesh in jealousy and strife.[11]

In both 13:11 and 2:14–3:3, Paul is concerned with spiritual matters, not a literal child. After this reference to spiritual infancy, Paul claims that, when he became a man, he put childish things away. It is significant that the term Paul uses here for putting away is *katergēka*, a perfect form of the verb used in verses 8b and 10 in reference to the partials—prophecy and knowledge, and by implication the *charismata* inclusively.

Paul makes use of the metaphor of the mirror in 13:12 and offers a subsequent interpretation of the metaphor. Now in a state of spiritual infancy and immaturity, the Corinthians are using incompletes, partials (*ek merous*) by which to judge Christian maturity. Thus the Corinthians are misusing the charismata. Paul continues: "But then we will see face to face. Now I know only in part (*ek merous*); then I will know fully, even as I have been fully known." If the "now" refers to a state of spiritual childishness, we should expect the "then" to refer to

---

[10] Ibid., pp. 816–17.
[11] Ladd, *Theology of the New Testament*, p. 473.

that state of spiritual maturity or completeness marked by *agapē*—the "when that which is perfect comes." When Christians move into that state of spiritual maturity governed by love, with faith and hope running a close second, they will look upon fellow Christians through the clear glasses of love, rather than employing the incomplete gifts as the measuring rod of maturity.

The above discussion illustrates a hermeneutical paradox. Does the reader interpret the individual parts of a text in light of the whole or the whole in light of the individual parts? Once the student has analyzed the sense units and related them to each other, the sense of the whole may be ascertained. But then the student interprets each sense unit in light of the sense of the whole, which has been delineated only in conjunction with the parts. This is the hermeneutical circle, and I know of no escape from it. Actually, as a hermeneut continues to study, sense units may be modified, and this may result in the modification of the interpretation of the entire text. This modified interpretation of the entire text precipitates a reexamination of many of the individual parts. So the hermeneutical circle is actually a hermeneutical spiral where, after each subsequent modification, the hermeneut moves to a different plane of understanding. In this sense, the spiral is infinite. **Grammatical analysis** does not make the student a master of the text. Grammatical analysis is only the starting point. But the serious hermeneut must address this point, for it is foundational for other areas of study.

Summary

While it may be claimed that the text *is* a verbal icon, it *was* first and foremost an icon within its original language. Recognizing this requires that the interpreter give appropriate attention to the identification and description of linguistic details such as phonology, morphology, lexicology, and syntax. Since a people's language capsulizes that people's symbolic world (a world reflected in the text), grammatical concerns are an indispensable part of hermeneutics. Grammatical emphases range from single words to the entire book.

Ideally a passage of the text should be interpreted within the structure of the whole, and the whole must be brought to bear upon the individual parts. The dilemma of determining which comes first is called the hermeneutical circle. Grammatical studies constitute the starting point for dealing with this circle. Tools such as concordances, lexicons, word study books, dictionaries, and encyclopedias are essential adjunctive tools in interpreting the grammar of the text.

REVIEW & STUDY

Key Terms and Concepts

Phonology	Morphology
Lexicology	Syntax
Concordance	Lexicon
BAGD	*TDNT*
Grammatical analysis	Sentence flow
Symbolic world	Grammatical context

Study Questions

1. Do you feel that word studies constitute a part of exegesis? Why or why not?

2. In the Hebrew of Isaiah 17:12, the sound of the roaring of waves can be distinctly heard. Read this verse in the KJV, RSV, and NIV. Which do you think comes nearest to reproducing the sound of the roaring waves or the sound of a storm? Read Nahum 3:1–3 in the NIV. What sensation do you experience?

3. Read the parable of the "Friend at Midnight" in Luke 11:5–8 (KJV). The word "importunity" in verse 8 occurs only here in the New Testament. In the NIV, it is translated "boldness" with a note that it means "persistence." Do a word study on this word using some of the tools discussed in this chapter to see if you agree with either of the above translations. If the word means something else, how does this affect your understanding of the entire parable?

4. Read the short epistle of 1 Peter. The section 2:11–4:11 is a call to acceptable conduct in a variety of settings, even during times of unjust suffering. In light of this context, how should we interpret 2:24b ("by his wounds you have been healed")?

Suggestions for Further Reading

Barr, James. *The Semantics of Biblical Language*. Oxford: Oxford University Press, 1961.

Cotterell, Peter and Max Turner. *Linguistics and Biblical Interpretation*. Downers Grove: InterVarsity, 1989.

Fee, Gordon. *New Testament Exegesis: A Handbook for Students and Pastors*. 2d ed. Louisville: Westminster, 1993.

Kennedy, George A. *New Testament Interpretation Through Rhetorical Criticism*. Chapel Hill: University of North Carolina Press, 1984.

Reading and the World Behind the Text:
The Historical and Ideological Backgrounds

Every text is created within some context. According to Paul Ricoeur, at least three developmental stages of a text must be considered in the interpretive process. First there is the event, second the recording of the event in a text, and third the reading of the text.[1] Each stage is separated by a time gap. In the case of the biblical text, the gap between the recording of the event in the text and the reading of the text is centuries. During this time the text does not change, but languages and cultures do. The distinct possibility exists, therefore, that the interpreter will impose the understanding of his or her contemporary world upon that of the text. As will be seen in unit III, this imposition is inevitable; it need not, however, be wholesale. The most effective safeguard against a wholesale imposition of the interpreter's world upon the world of the text is the diligent study of the world that produced the text. Thus, what did it mean to be slapped on the face in an ancient Near Eastern culture? This knowledge is essential for interpreting Matthew 5:39. Understanding the practice of purchasing fields and animals is significant for the interpretation of Luke 14:15–24. In the world of the New Testament, both reader and writer would have shared this common knowledge. The task of *pragmatics* (context studies such as historical and ideological ones) is to narrow the gap between the original readers and modern ones.

As the title of this chapter indicates, we will explore two major areas relating to background studies. The first area concentrates on general historical and cultural concerns and examines why a knowledge of these makes the difference between just a reading and an informed reading of a text. The second area of discussion focuses on the ideological contexts of both the Hebrew Bible and the New Testament. Since the

---

[1] See Paul Ricoeur, *The Conflict of Interpretation* (Evanston: Northwestern University, 1974).

second area may be less familiar to most readers, it necessarily will require more detail and attention.

Historical and Cultural Background

The preferred reading of any text is the one in which the interpreter establishes the most probable historical and cultural contexts. Simply put, the best reading of any text is informed by the interpreter's concern for date, place, originating circumstances, audience, and authorship of a text. Other cultural information, such as marriage practices, systems of taxation, architectural practices, home furnishings, implements of warfare, means of transportation, agricultural practices, geographical concerns, or political systems, may be the deciding factor between a more or less plausible reading. Why? Communication (whether written or oral) is colored by behavior patterns, which are themselves culturally grounded. Consequently, communication is not possible apart from the influences of culture. This means that the biblical authors communicate through their cultural filters, speaking to people within the same culture and to people who would understand the communication within the same cultural patterns. The biblical authors were not consciously communicating to readers in a twentieth-century Western culture. Therefore, since the biblical authors stood within a particular culture proclaiming a culturally conditioned message to a culturally identified audience, does it not seem logical that the modern hermeneut must, to as great a degree as possible, return to that world? Perhaps E. D. Hirsch is correct when he says, "the interpreter's primary task is to reproduce in himself the author's 'logic,' his attitudes, his cultural givens, in short his world."[2] Mickelsen also supports this claim:

> The interpreter . . . stands in a modern culture, whether this be Western or another. He must understand the particular biblical culture which influenced the original source, message, and receptors. He must note both how it differs and how it resembles his own. Only then can he effectively communicate the message from one culture pattern to another.[3]

Historical and socio-cultural research is not just an addendum to literary considerations, but it is both an intellectual and a practical necessity, because conscious or unconscious ignorance of the historical and cultural *Sitz im Leben* of a text most often results in vague and convoluted

---

[2] E. D. Hirsch, Jr., "Objective Interpretation," *PMLA* 75 (1960), p. 478.
[3] A. Berkeley Mickelsen, *Interpreting the Bible* (Grand Rapids: Eerdmans, 1963), p. 170.

interpretation. This is usually the case when readers/interpreters remain prisoners of their own culture, imposing it upon the text, which is a product of another culture.

Historical and cultural information may be internal (information found within the text) or external (information found outside the text). While some texts virtually stand alone as far as background information is concerned, these are the exception. Most often the hermeneut must use both internal and external information in the reconstruction of the text's life situation. The internal information is primary, while external information serves a supportive and verifying role. Some examples of how historical and cultural reconstruction aid in interpretive plausibility should illustrate its importance.

Some Examples of Historical Background Studies

Example 1: Gehenna

In Matthew 5:22, we read, "But I say to you that if you are angry with a brother or sister, you will be liable to judgment; and if you insult a brother or sister, you will be liable to the council; and if you say, 'You fool,' you will be liable to the hell of fire." The word used here for "hell" is *gehenna* and is found elsewhere in Matthew 5:29, 30; 23:15, 33; and James 3:6. In the Authorized Version of the Bible the word "hell" also translates *hades*. While *hades* is consistently used to name the place of abode after death, *gehenna* refers to a place of punishment usually associated with a perpetual fire. The Valley of Hinnom was the place where Ahaz sacrificed his sons and burned incense to idols. It also seems that prior to the Israelite conquest, this valley was a place of human sacrifice. Therefore, to later generations of Jews it represented a place of extreme abomination towards Yahweh. In fact, the sight now called in Greek *gehenna* became the place for dumping garbage that was consumed by a perpetual fire. As a result, whereas *gehenna* originally referred metaphorically to the place of punishment after death, it eventually became a technical term for such a place. Since *gehenna* was an actual physical place, it was ideal for this metaphorical application. The original readers or listeners would automatically make associations between *gehenna* and the more abstract concept of a future place of punishment. Interpreters should keep this metaphorical character in mind when exegeting and applying any passage containing *gehenna*.

Example 2: Revelation 3:14-21

In his book *The Letters to the Seven Churches of Asia in Their Local Settings*,[4] C. J. Hemer illustrates the importance of background information in interpreting Revelation 3:14-21.

> And to the angel of the church in Laodicea write: The words of the Amen, the faithful and true witness, the origin of God's creation: I know your works; you are neither cold nor hot. I wish that you were either cold or hot. So, because you are lukewarm, and neither cold nor hot, I am about to spit you out of my mouth. For you say, "I am rich, I have prospered, and I need nothing." You do not realize that you are wretched, pitiable, poor, blind, and naked. Therefore I counsel you to buy from me gold refined by fire so that you may be rich; and white robes to clothe you and to keep the shame of your nakedness from being seen; and salve to anoint your eyes so that you may see. I reprove and discipline those whom I love. Be earnest, therefore, and repent. Listen! I am standing at the door, knocking; if you hear my voice and open the door, I will come in to you and eat with you, and you with me. To the one who conquers I will give a place with me on my throne, just as I myself conquered and sat down with my Father on his throne.

The church at Laodicea was famous for three things: its banking facilities, its textile industry, and its medical school—which produced "Phrygian powder," an eye-salve. When Laodicea suffered almost total destruction by an earthquake around A.D. 60, assistance from Rome was refused, and the city was rebuilt from "her own resources." The prophetic utterance must be understood in the context of these facts, because the church had apparently assimilated the city's sense of pride and self-sufficiency in these things. Jesus then addresses the church in opposite terms; the church at Laodicea was actually poor, blind, and naked. They were in need of the spiritual correlates of those material things of which the Laodicean church was so proud.

In verses 15-16, we hear Jesus describing the Laodicean church as neither hot nor cold, but lukewarm. This passage has always been somewhat of a thorn in the flesh because theologians have not known what to do with being coldly antagonistic towards Jesus. Through an interesting geographical study, however, Rudwick and Green[5] have suggested a promising interpretation: the church at Laodicea is being com-

---

[4] C. J. Hemer, *The Letters to the Seven Churches of Asia in Their Local Settings* (Sheffield: JSOT, 1986).

[5] M. J. S. Rudwick and E. M. B. Green, "The Laodicean Lukewarmness," *ExpT* 69 (1957-58), pp. 176-78.

pared with the strengths and weakness of the city. Hierapolis was located within sight of Laodicea and was well-known for its hot calcium salt waters, which were prized for their healing properties. Also close to Laodicea was the city of Colossae, which was famous for its cold, refreshing stream. As the city of Laodicea outgrew its water supply, it was forced to pipe water in from a long distance through stone pipes. When the water arrived, it was warm and contained a sludgy deposit, making it almost undrinkable. While the hot water of Hierapolis healed and the cold water of Colossae refreshed, the Laodicean church brought neither spiritual healing nor refreshment. Like their water supply, the works of the Laodicean church were fit only to be spit out.

Example 3: Prophecy and the Exile

The prophetic writings offer another example of the importance of placing a text within its historical context. This context is both general and specific. The general context refers to developments in the Mediterranean world from the eighth to the fourth centuries B.C. Around 760 B.C. the nation of Israel was divided by civil war into two independent nations—Israel, the northern kingdom, and Judah, the southern kingdom. In 722 B.C. the northern kingdom of Israel fell to Assyria. Prior to this date, prophets such as Amos and Hosea preached to the northern kingdom, proclaiming its impending destruction and calling its people to repentance. The southern kingdom of Judah was defeated by Babylon in 587 B.C. The voices of the prophets Isaiah, Jeremiah, Joel, Micah, Nahum, Habakkuk, and Zephaniah can be heard pronouncing judgment upon Judah prior to this date. During the exile of Judah, the prophets Ezekiel, Haggai, Zechariah, and Malachi begin to announce Yahweh's future plans for his people.

The exile of Judah in 587 B.C. is the most critical historical event for interpreting the prophets because it has rendered a threefold division of prophecy—usually referred to as pre-exilic, exilic, and post-exilic. Each of these periods is characterized by a particular emphasis. The primary concern of pre-exilic prophecy was the announcement of impending judgment upon the nations of Israel and Judah. For instance, in Isaiah 1–40 the primary thought is the destruction of a nation, and this dominates Isaiah's preaching from beginning to end. During the exilic period, because of the change of the historical situation, the message of wrath diminishes and the message of hope prevails. The return of the exiles and the establishment of a new state in the homeland become the chief themes of the exilic prophets. The prophets describe these events in miraculous terms. The actual circumstances of the return did not match the glory which the exilic prophets had anticipated, and the arrival of the exiles in Jerusalem was not greeted by any universal homage to Israel. So the disappointment of difficult times produced a problem with the eschatological hope of the exilic prophets. This gave way to a more patient anticipation of the coming day of Yahweh (which could obviously now not be seen as the return of the exiles), and the post-exilic prophets pushed it further into the future. An eschatological hope of the new Israel, with a new Jerusalem, blessed by the presence of Yahweh, became a prominent feature of post-exilic prophecy. The last of the canonical prophets still points toward the expectation of Yahweh's triumphant coming to his people. During this time highly imaginative language was used to describe the perfect age to come (e.g., Isa. 65:17–25; Zech. 14:1–9; Mal. 4:1–6).

As might be expected, the events of the prophet's time influenced his message. Stuart rightly observes: "Unless you know these events and others within this era, . . . you probably will not be able to follow very well what the prophets are saying. God spoke in history and about history. To understand His Word we must know something of that history."[6]

Example 4: Philippians 3:2

When exegeting the New Testament epistles, it is desirable to know the author, place of writing, destination, and occasion for writing; moreover, the hermeneut must do additional historical research for small units or even for a sentence or word. An example of the latter is found in Philippians 3:2: "Beware of the dogs, beware of the evil workers, beware of those who mutilate the flesh!" With biting sarcasm, Paul describes a group of opponents of the Philippian church. Three expressions describe metaphorically the opponents. Paul's choice of words reveals to whom he is referring and what they represent. He is speaking of only one group, the Judaizers, describing them in three ways.

The first term Paul uses to describe the opponents is "dogs." This term must have had tremendous impact. First of all, being compared to a dog was "insulting and dishonoring" (1 Sam. 17:43).[7] To be called a

---

[6] Gordon D. Fee and Douglas Stuart, *How to Read the Bible for All Its Worth*, 2d ed. (Grand Rapids: Zondervan, 1993), p. 157.

[7] Otto Michel, "*kyōn*," *TDNT*, vol. 3, p. 1101.

dead dog was the worst insult one could receive. It was considered a special judgment from God to be eaten by dogs in the street (1 Kings 14:11; 16:4). Second, Deuteronomy 23:18 in the KJV forbids a person from bringing the "hire of a whore, or the price of a dog," into the sanctuary. Here, "dog" refers to a male prostitute (as the NRSV makes explicit). Therefore, to call a Jew a dog meant he was unfit for temple worship and thus excluded from the true worship of God. Third, the Jews felt they were superior to the Gentiles because they had the Torah. The Jews despised Gentiles and referred to them as dogs. Jesus refers to Gentiles outside the law as dogs in Mark 7:27–28. Fourth, Revelation 22:15 speaks of dogs metaphorically as those outside of fellowship with the Lord when he sets up his final reign. Fifth, Paul's metaphor may also have brought thoughts of yelping animals (Judaizers) following him around and harassing him. Sixth, the possibility exists also that Paul may have been referring to Cynics along with Judaizers, because the word "cynic" comes from the same root as dog (*kyōn*). The founder of Cynic philosophy, Diogenes of Sinope, was called "the Dog" due to his impudence.

Any of these—Jews who want to prostitute the gospel, Gentiles, or Cynics—is a possibility. Due to the other descriptions of this group of opponents in the immediate context, however, the best choice here is that Paul wanted his readers to recall the male prostitute as referred to in the Old Testament.

The Ideological Context

As we mentioned above, writers can exercise no alternative but to express themselves in the conceptual and ideological categories of their own time. For authors to express themselves in a future ideological framework is impossible, while to express themselves in a conceptual milieu of the past would be anachronistic. A people's conceptual framework is especially evident in its religious and philosophical expressions, and these expressions most often are interrelated. An understanding of the ideological world which makes a text possible is essential to a critical reading of that text. This is not to suggest that an author is a prisoner of a particular ideological world. An author may modify certain philosophical and religious concepts through reapplication or redefinition, but in order to appreciate the meaning resulting from such a modification, readers must understand the "normal" or accepted meaning or usage.

A literary work of art may transform the ideological structure of which it is a part, but it is still a part of that structure. People live their lives in accordance with societal roles in which ideas, values, and images tie them to particular social functions. Therefore, any literary expression bears the imprint of its historical epoch, and the most plausible reading is a critical one which takes into account this ideological imprint. Terry Eagleton underscores this point when he suggests that understanding literature "means understanding the total process of which it is a part."[8] He goes on to say:

> Literary works are not mysteriously inspired or explicable simply in terms of their author's psychology. They are forms of perception, particular ways of seeing the world; and as such they have a relation to that dominant way of seeing the world which is the "social mentality" or ideology of an age. That ideology, in turn, is the product of the concrete social relations into which men enter at a particular time and place. . . . To understand *King Lear, The Dunciad* or *Ulysses* is therefore to do more than interpret their symbolism, study their literary history and add footnotes about sociological facts which enter into them. It is first of all to understand the complex, indirect relations between those works and the ideological worlds they inhabit.[9]

Every writer has an individual psychology *and* is a product of society; every writer responds individually to a general history from a particular standpoint. But it is an individual response defined by a common ideological world. Furthermore, an author's current ideological world did not spring up overnight, but was formed over a period of time, having a continuity with its pre-history (i.e., each phase of a society's cultural development is influenced by previous phases). Consequently, to study the ideological world of a text one must have a wide vision. For example, to interpret the Genesis account of creation the interpreter must ask how that account relates to other earlier accounts within the Mediterranean world, for the society that produced the Genesis account was itself the product of a long history, a history which helped shape its ideological world. Ideally, the student of biblical literature should become acquainted with the history of literature, the history of religion, and the philosophy of religious texts.

Since there are numerous excellent works on the ideological worlds of both the Old and New Testaments,[10] we offer only an introductory

---

[8] Terry Eagleton, "Literature and History," in Keesey, *Contexts for Criticism*, p. 41.
[9] Ibid.
[10] For the New Testament, see Helmut Koester, *Introduction to the New Testament*, 2 vols. (New York: Walter de Gruyter, 1982), vol. 1; and Everett Ferguson, *Backgrounds of Early Christianity*, 2d ed. (Grand Rapids: Eerdmans, 1993). For the

treatment here in hope that we might convince the student of the indispensable nature of background studies.

The Ideological World of the Old Testament

The literature of the Old Testament has close and meaningful links to Mesopotamian, Canaanite, and Egyptian literature. Though there are differences between certain world-view elements, there are also similarities between the ideological worlds of the Hebrew authors and their counterparts. The literary productions of the Hebrew writers had as their sources the literary traditions and productions of the surrounding Near Eastern world, the most immediate contact being with Canaanite culture. The ideological elements within the Hebrew world-view were thus both continuous and non-continuous with those of their Near Eastern neighbors and ancestors. The ideological framework of the Hebrew authors is continuous in the sense that some formal literary practices and terminology are similar. The ideological framework is discontinuous because the Hebrew writers at various times consciously or unconsciously reshape literary materials or tradition in order to expound a differing ideological element within a world-view. As Jonas Greenfield observes: "The Hebrew writers have been called 'good students' of their Canaanite predecessors, but it is more accurate to designate them as active participants in a broader literary culture: they were participants and also innovators."[11] The links between the literary expressions of the respective ideologies go a long way in showing both the origins of biblical literature and its particular individuality. A comparative study of Mesopotamian, Canaanite, and Egyptian literature constitutes the best source for discovering the literary norms from which and against which Hebrew literature developed.

Comparative Literature

David Damrosch offers a convincing argument for a comparative study of Hebrew literature and other ancient literature. He argues that at least Hebrew narrative "is the product of a rich mixture of direct use, thorough adaptation, and outright polemical rejection of earlier narrative

---

Old Testament, see David Damrosch. *The Narrative Covenant: Transformations of Genre in the Growth of Biblical Literature* (San Francisco: Harper & Row, 1987).

[11] Jonas C. Greenfield, "The Hebrew Bible and Canaanite Literature," in *The Literary Guide to the Bible*, ed. Robert Alter and Frank Kermode (Cambridge: Harvard University, 1987), p. 560.

practices."[12] Hebrew literature thus reveals a history of conscious generic adaptation, modification, and transformation; and these changes are significant for determining meaning. Damrosch outlines a process in Mesopotamian and Hebrew literary development in which there was a metamorphosis of genres over a period of time. During this process two or more literary genres were combined to form a new genre, which in turn reflected ideological peculiarities of the author's age. For example, poetic epic, characterized by an internal search for meaning within the brevity of life, was combined with historiography to produce a historicized mythology. Mirroring the *Gilgamesh Epic*, the Hebrew writers transformed this genre into historical prose narrative. Referring to this "cross-fertilization" of genres, Damrosch concludes:

> The origins of Hebrew historical prose can be traced in Mesopotamian literature of the second millennium, but not through a direct comparison of historical writings alone. Rather, the Bible's historical writing can best be understood as the result of a far-reaching transformation of earlier genres, resulting in a combination of many of the values, themes, and formal properties of historical chronicle with that of poetic epic. Scholars who have sharply separated epic from chronicle, and myth from history, have thus unduly restricted the Near Eastern evidence that can, and should, be used in assessing this movement, since the background to the confluence of epic and history can already be shown within Mesopotamian literature itself.[13]

Because innovation witnesses to a particular ideology, the student of the Old Testament should become acquainted with the ideological worlds of civilizations such as Mesopotamian, Egyptian, Hittite, and Canaanite. Below are some suggested sources that will familiarize the student with the ideological framework within which the Hebrew Bible was produced.

For an English translation of some of these texts see J. B. Pritchard, ed., *Ancient Near Eastern Texts Relating to the Old Testament* (1969) and idem, *The Ancient Near East: Supplementary Texts and Pictures Relating to the Old Testament* (1955 and 1969; 1958). Also see J. H. Breasted, *Ancient Records of Egypt* (1906–7), vols. 2 and 3; J. Simons, *Handbook for the Study of Egyptian Topographical Lists Relating to Western Asia* (1937); W. F. Edgerton and J. A. Wilson, *Historical Records of Rameses III, Studies in Ancient Oriental Civilization* 12 (1936); D. D. Luckenbill, *Ancient Records of Assyria and Babylonia* (1926–27); D. W. Thomas, *Documents from Old*

---

[12] Damrosch, *Narrative Covenant*, p. 41.
[13] Ibid.

Testament Times (1958); Michael David Coogan, *Stories from Ancient Canaan* (1978); Barbara C. Sproul, *Primal Myths: Creating the World* (1979); and Joan O'Brien and Wilfred Major, *In the Beginning, Creation Myths from Ancient Mesopotamia, Israel and Judah* (1986); V. Matthews and D. Benjamin, *Old Testament Parallels* (2d ed., 1997).

Ras Shamra Texts. These texts were discovered in 1929 in the ruins of ancient Ugarit, a Phoenician city on the Syrian coast. They are of utmost importance for understanding Canaanite culture and the ideological milieu within which Hebrew culture grew during the second millennium B.C. They also provide the modern hermeneut with a knowledge of the Canaanite pantheon along with the religious cult surrounding it.

Mari Tablets. Found in the palace archives at Tell el-Hariri, a city of Mari on the Euphrates, these tablets aid in the reconstruction of the Amorite culture of the second millennium B.C., which is the period of the Old Testament patriarchs.

Amarna Tablets. These tablets come from El-Amarna in Egypt and are written in Akkadian. Most of these tablets are correspondences between the Egyptian court and the rulers of city-states in Syria, Phoenicia, and Palestine. Their usefulness lies in the insight they give into the social and political situations in Palestine during the first half of the fourteenth century B.C., which is the period just prior to the birth of the nation of Israel.

Royal Egyptian Inscriptions. These Egyptian reports of military campaigns and lists of conquered cities offer a glimpse of the social conditions in Syria-Palestine. They are of limited import, however, because the conquests to which these inscriptions refer were history by the time the Hebrews settled in Palestine.

Royal Assyrian Inscriptions. Valuable information concerning Israel's history is contained in these inscriptions. The practice of dating the beginning of a ruler's reign and certain natural phenomena (like a solar eclipse) is of great value in establishing the chronology of Assyrian Israelite rulers.

The Babylonian Chronicles. These chronicles assist in reconstructing the final days of Judah and the Exile.

Examples of Comparative Study

Perhaps some examples of the manner in which an author modifies or generally reacts to sources will demonstrate how crucial a comparative approach is to interpretation. A considerable amount of light can be shed on a text if it is interpreted against the backdrop of its written sources and/or its ideological framework. We will look at three such cases, from Job, Genesis, and the Prophets respectively.

Example 1: Job and the God El

The Ras Shamra texts portray El as the god who presides over the assembly of the gods and connect him with wisdom. El is also credited with two offspring, Yam (Sea) and Mot (Death). In Job 27, Job accuses God (El) of being unjust to him while blessing the wicked. Job 28 is a description of humankind's effort to uncover the earth's mineral wealth. Job says: "The sources of the rivers they probe; hidden things they bring to light" (v. 11). The source of the rivers is the dwelling place of El according to the Ras Shamra texts. Job asks, "But where shall wisdom be found? And where is the place of understanding?" (28:12). The Deep (Yam) responds: "It is not in me" (v. 14), followed by Death's (Mot) response: "We have heard a rumor of it with our ears" (v. 22). Job finally gives the answer in verse 23: "God understands the way to it, and he knows its place." It appears that Job's ancient source or tradition has already associated wisdom with El.[14]

Example 2: Genesis 1–11 and the Gilgamesh Epic

When a **comparative study** is made, differences in emphasis, deemphasis, exclusion, or combination of sources suggest specific interests, and as such they are clues to literary meaning. Our second example, involving a comparison of Genesis 1–11 and the *Gilgamesh Epic*, illustrates this point. The *Gilgamesh Epic* and Genesis 1–11 are both "the epic story of primordial times from the creation of human beings to the Flood."[15] In each story, four basic elements appear: the creation of the world, the creation of human beings, the Flood, and the establishment of the human order following the Flood. The *Gilgamesh Epic* moves towards a meditation on the limits of human culture, while the Genesis account of creation takes up the theme of separation between Yahweh

---

[14] For an excellent and somewhat detailed discussion of the relationship between certain Hebrew cosmological concepts and those found within the Ras Shamra texts, see the article by Jonas C. Greenfield, "Hebrew Bible and Canaanite Literature," in Alter and Kermode, *Literary Guide to the Bible*, pp. 545–60.

[15] Damrosch, *Narrative Covenant*, p. 91.

and humans. Damrosch demonstrates how the opening section of Genesis transforms the older creation and flood stories in order to reflect on the nature of human culture. Every event in Genesis 1–11 has a direct parallel in the *Gilgamesh Epic*.[16] Damrosch observes:

> Each of these parallels shows considerable differences as well as similarities (though the flood story shows a particularly close resemblance), and there is no need to suppose a direct dependence of Genesis on the *Gilgamesh Epic*; but it is evident that the two texts are parallel efforts, from roughly the same period, to rework the old mythic material of the creation and Flood. The many similarities between these texts, and their far-reaching differences both in form and theme will, I believe, suggest much about the theological and literary forces at work in the early phase of the composition of biblical literature and will set the stage for a better understanding of the relations of the Yahwistic legendary material to the fully developed epic historiography of the story of King David.[17]

For example, the Genesis epic parallels the old Babylonian predecessors, where the story of creation, far from being the central point of the story, is merely a prologue to the flood story.

When we read the Genesis epic against the comparative backdrop of its earlier models, each similarity and subtle change becomes significant for meaning. Further, if these changes are due to ideological considerations, they may continue to be operative in other portions of the Hebrew Scriptures. The ideological lessons expressed in Genesis 1–11 may be developed even further in the stories of the patriarchs and monarchs. If this is indeed the case, as Damrosch suggests,[18] then the development of the themes of separation, exile, and revolt are primary ideological concerns, and consequently thematic controls, throughout other portions of the Hebrew canon.

Example 3: The Prophets and Egyptian Wisdom Literature

Another area where a comparative study of ideological literature is essential is the association between the Egyptian wisdom literature and the ethical concerns found in the Hebrew prophets. Many consider the Hebrew prophets to have been the first to place moral concerns above cultic ritual in Israel. Moral behavior is the desire of God rather than sacrifice (Isa. 1:11–17; Jer. 6:20; 7:22; Mic. 6:6–8; Amos 5:21–25). The

---

[16] Ibid., pp. 118–35.
[17] Ibid., p. 120.
[18] Ibid.

same concept, however, is found in the Egyptian wisdom literature. In "The Teaching of Merikare" the following instruction is given to King Merikare:

> Make firm your place with uprightness and just dealing for it is on that which their hearts rely; more acceptable is a loaf (perhaps "character") of the upright than the ox of the wrongdoer.[19]

To summarize, the Old Testament writers were not working or living in a vacuum, but were sensitive to their culture and its traditions, as well the cultures around them. The writers imitated numerous alien types of speech and utilized them for their own purposes. They took over and adapted a wide range of traditions to make themselves clearly understandable to their audiences. They borrowed foreign and older traditions and adapted them to new situations, giving them fresh significance. A familiarity with these various traditions will put the reader in a more favorable position to offer the most plausible explication of a text or any portion of it. This is necessarily true because any adaptation, modification, or reapplication of any portion of a tradition is most accurately understood when the reader has some knowledge of the original tradition itself.

The Ideological World of the New Testament

The ideological world of the New Testament writings is especially that of first-century Judaism. But the symbols of first-century Judaism were transformed by the infusion of Greco-Roman culture. Consequently, it is more appropriate to speak of the ideological worlds of these writings. For this reason, the student of the Bible should have some background knowledge of the elements which constitute first-century **Judaism** and **Hellenism** and the ancient Mediterranean world. As Johnson observes, "the way humans organize themselves in the world depends little on biology and less on instinct but a great deal on humans' ideas about themselves and the world."[20] These ideas are most concretely expressed through a people's religious and philosophical productions. Since literary productions of a segment of a society are influenced by and have meaning in relationship to other literary productions within the larger society, students are better equipped to interpret the New Testament

---

[19] Moshe Weinfeld, "Ancient Near Eastern Patterns in Prophetic Literature," *VT* 27 (April 1977), p. 180.

[20] Johnson, *Writings of the New Testament*, p. 12.

writings if they have a familiarity with the literature contemporary with the New Testament. Therefore, we will look briefly at what is meant by Hellenism, the philosophical and religious milieu of the hellenistic period, the make-up of first-century Judaism, and comparative literature.

Hellenism

In 334 B.C., a young Alexander the Great set out to conquer the Persian Empire in the east. Traveling with him were poets, philosophers, and historians. He himself was a student of Aristotle and was convinced that the Greek mode of life was unexcelled. Alexander's successors were generally of the same opinion and continued in the attempt to establish a hellenistic world. For the most part, when Greek culture came into contact with oriental influences, the Greek element predominated; there was, however, a process of religious and philosophical interpenetration and mutual influence. This process of interpenetration of cultures in which the Greek element predominated is usually referred to as hellenization, while the period of such cultural confluence, beginning with Alexander the Great and continuing into the Roman imperial period, is referred to as the hellenistic period. This does not mean that Hellenism ceased to be influential during the Roman imperial period. On the contrary, Hellenism continued to be effective throughout the Roman imperial period. By the first century B.C., a distinctively universal culture (an amalgamation of Greek and oriental) had emerged under the umbrella of a single political entity—Rome. Because Christianity had its birth during the Roman imperial period, we might rightly expect it to exhibit hellenistic traits. Christianity was the heir of a hellenized Judaism. For the most part, the earliest Christians were people whose lives and thoughts were formed and molded by Hellenism. The earliest Christians used the **Septuagint** (the Greek translation of the Old Testament) as their Bible. This is significant when we recognize that religious and philosophical concepts are modified when writings are translated from one language to another.

Hellenism is characterized by **syncretism** (the mixture of worldviews and ideologies), especially in the area of philosophy and religion, where there is an obvious mixture of Greek and oriental elements. Even where local or territorial religious expressions remained the same in essence, these expressions appeared in Greek dress. The Septuagint is an example of this syncretism. The syncretistic tendency of hellenization resulted in a sort of universalization. When the local deities of the East came into contact with the Greek pantheon, the equating of these two was inevitable. This eventually led to the idea of the existence of a single divine power with multiple manifestations. But the sacrifice of local deities on the altar of universalism produced a view of the universe as one governed by Chance and Fate. This in turn resulted in a search for a more profound, individual religious experience. The universalization of Hellenism presented a universe where the individual had no control over his or her existence. A spirit of fatalism characterized the period. When the ideal of individual citizen participation in the community was frustrated by the decline of the *polis*, the citizens lost their social identity. When the local deity became identical with other gods of other people (i.e., when individual religious experience gave way to religious universalism or monotheism), people lost their religious identity, and their lives became meaningless, governed by *tychē* (Chance) and *heimarmenē* (Fate). Since human life was predestined by these powers, humans had little or no control over their existence. In the wake of such losses, a need of individual salvation became paramount. This attitude characterizes the hellenistic period, especially during the period of Roman rule when individual identity was expected to give way to the welfare of the state. As a result, both religious and philosophical expression in the hellenistic period placed increased importance upon the individual and the salvation of the individual from the control of a universe governed by Chance or Fate. It was to this matter of individual salvation that all the philosophical and religious expressions spoke.

The Philosophical and Religious Milieu of the Hellenistic Period

Hellenistic Philosophies.[21]   Prior to the hellenistic period Greek philosophies were primarily concerned with creating a world in which there was some rational system of meaning, a universe governed by some

---

[21] For information about the hellenistic philosophies see Ferguson, *Backgrounds of Early Christianity*, pp. 299–371; Koester, *Introduction to the New Testament*, vol. 1, pp. 141–63; E. Bevan, "Hellenistic Popular Philosophy," in *The Hellenistic Age*, ed. J. B. Bury et al. (London: Cambridge University, 1925), pp. 79–107; J. Dillon, *The Middle Platonists, 80 B.C. to A.D. 220* (Ithaca: Cornell University, 1977); P. Merlan, *From Platonism to Neoplatonism*, 2d ed. (Hague: Nijhoff, 1960); R. D. Hicks, *Stoic and Epicurean* (New York: Russell and Russell, 1962); A. Malherbe ed., *The Cynic Epistles* (Missoula: Scholars Press, 1977); and Wayne A. Meeks, *The Moral World of the First Christians* (Philadelphia: Westminster, 1986), pp. 40–64.

ontological reality, against which everything has its meaning and significance. But when the universal ideal of the hellenistic period failed, a sense of skepticism became prevalent. Therefore, the **hellenistic philosophies** (Stoicism, Epicureanism, Neopythagoreanism, and Neoplatonism) contained an element of skepticism.

Hellenistic philosophical schools were half religious and half philosophical. Members of such schools tended to live according to the teachings of their founding masters. The schools placed emphasis on ethics and offered their members a world-view and suggested practical ways for adherents to conduct themselves in everyday living. In a world where individuals were on their own, many were looking for such guidance within a group of friends that would supply a sense of community. The hellenistic philosophies spoke to the individual and his or her place in the universe. Paul Tillich offers the following insight:

> During this period when the skeptical mood permeated the ancient world, they wanted certainty above all; they demanded it in order to live. Their answer was that their great teachers, Plato, Aristotle, Zeno, Epicurus, Plotinus, were not merely thinkers or professors, but they were inspired men.[22]

Stories about the founders of these philosophical communities resemble accounts Christians related about their founder. For instance, Epicurus was called *sōtēr* (savior) by his followers. Commenting on this, Tillich goes on to say, "What does this mean? He was called *sōtēr* because he did the greatest thing anyone could do for his followers: he liberated them from anxiety."[23] The hellenistic philosophies in one way or another offered freedom from the anxiety of the age by offering the individual a pattern of living that afforded at least a measure of control. These philosophical schools constitute one of the immediate sources for a great deal of early Christian thought. Therefore, a brief look at each is in order, but we must encourage students to take the time to plunge deeper into the philosophical and religious expressions of the hellenistic age.

Stoicism. Stoicism was one of the most influential philosophical systems of the hellenistic period. Founded in Athens by Zeno of Citium (332–260 B.C.), Stoicism acquired its name from the painted porch (stoa) in the Agora where its proponents taught. Stoicism was introduced in Rome (161 B.C.) by Panaetius who made Stoicism more practical.

---

[22] Paul Tillich, *A History of Christian Thought* (New York: Simon and Schuster, 1968), p. 5.

[23] Ibid.

Seneca (ca. 4 B.C.–A.D. 65), a contemporary of Paul, did much to popularize the ethical teachings of Stoicism by his writings.

Resting on a religious basis, Stoicism made a strong appeal to the Roman character. For the Stoic, the universe itself was God, and the ultimate substance of the universe was a "fiery breath" or "spirit" which was distributed throughout in varying degrees.[24] This spirit was considered to be alive and rational, and in its manifestation as reason (*logos*) it introduced order into the world. Since humanity possessed in reason a particle of the divine breath, the individual was capable of entering into communion with the supreme reason. **Logos** refers to the reasonable structure indicated by a word, thus meaning the universal law of reality. The *logos* is also the law which determines the movement of all reality. According to the Stoics, the *logos* is in everything. (Compare John's comment, "The true light, which enlightens everyone, was coming into the world" [John 1:9].) This idea of the *logos* is one of the major influences of Stoicism upon early Christianity.[25]

The fundamental tenet of Stoicism is that virtue is the only good, and vice the only evil. The wise person is not mastered by pain and pleasure, wealth and poverty, or success and misfortune. Self-control or contentment (*enkrateia*) is the hallmark of the wise person.

There are similarities between the teachings of the New Testament and those of Stoicism. This is especially true of the writings of Paul. Paul's Judaism was itself influenced by hellenistic concepts and modes of expression. Paul adapts the religious views of the Hebrew Bible and Palestinian Judaism along with the style and views of hellenistic popular philosophy.[26] Paul read a Greek Bible, which bore the impressions of the hellenistic society, wrote in Greek, and labored among Gentile people.

We must understand that Paul was concerned about communicating to his contemporaries and would not have ignored the jargon of the day or the meaning of established terms and concepts. Along with other New Testament literature, Paul's writings took shape within and were addressed primarily to the hellenistic world. Consequently, we should interpret them in terms of their meaning for that world.

---

[24] Ralph P. Martin, *New Testament Foundations*, 2 vols. (Grand Rapids: Eerdmans, 1978), vol. 1, p. 42.

[25] The discussion of *logos* is adapted from Tillich, *History of Christian Thought*.

[26] Victor P. Furnish, *Theology and Ethics of Paul* (Nashville: Abingdon, 1968), p. 46.

Paul's ethical teaching is indebted to hellenistic sources in a general way. Scholars have pointed out the numerous Pauline phrases, metaphors, and terms which were familiar in Stoicism. These include: metaphors of life as warfare (2 Cor. 10:3; 1 Thess. 5:8) or as an athletic competition (1 Cor. 9:25); descriptions of God as "all in all" (1 Cor. 15:28) and as the one of, through, and to whom all things are (Rom. 11:36); the term "your duty" (Philemon 8); the concept of "spending" and "being spent" for others (2 Cor. 12:15); and disregard for the external circumstances of one's life (2 Cor. 6:8ff.; Phil. 4:11–12).[27] Philippians 4:8 also contains clear Stoic influence. Paul commends two qualities in this verse that are not mentioned elsewhere in the New Testament: "pleasing" and "commendable." Other terms in this verse having a significant place in Stoic ethics are "excellence" and "worthy of praise."

The moral teachings of Seneca exhibit many parallels to the teachings of Jesus on the mount. Examples include Seneca's statements that "the mind, unless it is pure and holy, comprehends not God" and that "a man is a robber even before he stains his hands; for he is already armed to slay, and has the desire to spoil and to kill."[28] There are also echoes of the parable of the sower, of the mustard seed, and of the forgiven debtor.

Other New Testament writings also reflect Stoic concepts, such as John's Gospel and his portrayal of the *logos*. The metaphor that instructs the readers to "gird up the loins" of their minds (cf. 1 Pet. 1:13, KJV) also appears in Seneca's writings as an instruction to let the mind stand ready.

The New Testament did enlist Stoic terminology and style. But its writers also altered Stoic patterns and used the major concepts with different meanings. Whether the concepts were modified or not, any reading and understanding of a text is enhanced by a familiarity with the text's ideological matrix.

Epicureanism. Epicureanism advocated the higher pleasures of the mind along with an emphasis on friendship and contentment. Like Paul, Epicurus was a father figure to his followers; he founded communities of followers and instructed these communities through letters. Unlike Paul, his birthday was celebrated annually, and his followers bestowed divine honors upon him.

---

[27] Ibid.
[28] See J. B. Lightfoot, *St. Paul's Epistle to the Philippians* (reprint; Peabody: Hendrickson, 1993), p. 287f.

It is through Lucretius (94–55 B.C.), though, that we have most of our knowledge about Epicureanism. According to Lucretius, nature is made up of matter and space, which he calls "the void." Matter is divisible, but it cannot be divided indefinitely because this would result in nothing. Eventually one arrives at the atom (Gk. "indivisible"). Atoms are the fundamental substance of everything in the universe. They can be neither created nor destroyed, but they can be arranged in different configurations.

Atoms and space constitute the universe, which is itself without limits, infinite. The physical world is comprised of atoms and exists and moves according to the dictates of law. As a result, nature is without purpose, having neither beginning nor end. If atoms—the building-blocks of the universe—are indestructible and non-creatable, then the world must be eternal.

Epicurus sought to deliver his followers from what he perceived to be the darkness of religion. He accomplished this through his materialistic approach to the universe. If the soul itself is a type of physical object composed of atoms, it will die when the body dies. Therefore, since the soul does not survive the death of the body, there is no future life of bliss or punishment to worry about now. This absence of any future life was intended to relieve the followers of any fear of punishment after death. If there is no future life to be concerned about, we should live with our attention directed squarely toward this life, of which the highest good is tranquillity, the absence of agitation.

In the wake of the devaluating effects of the universalization of Hellenism, Epicurus succeeded in substituting a community or circle of close friends and associates for the loss of the sense of community so prevalent in Hellenism. Within this circle of friends, one finds the greatest pleasure of the soul. This idea of friendship is basic, for the individual is a stranger in the world. Each person needs friends who offer shelter and give pleasure.[29]

Some similarities between Epicureanism and the early Christian communities exist, but they seem to be only superficial. Yet, the Epicureans and Christians were responding to the same loss precipitated by Hellenism—the devaluation of the individual. The founding of a community where all were equal, whether slave, free, woman, or man, and where the community was insulated and separated from the world and bonded together by worship and reverence, is characteristic of both

---

[29] Ibid., pp. 298–301.

Epicureans and Christians. The following passage in 1 Thessalonians 4:9–12 illustrates this point:

> Now concerning love of the brothers and sisters, you do not need to have anyone write to you, for you yourselves have been taught by God to love one another; and indeed you do love all the brothers and sisters throughout Macedonia. But we urge you, beloved, to do so more and more, to aspire to live quietly, to mind your own affairs, and to work with your hands, as we directed you, so that you may behave properly toward outsiders and be dependent on no one.

Paul is describing a quiet, separated life of tranquility. Gilbert Murray has suggested that the early Christian communities were patterned after the Epicurean communities, even down to the use of the title "friends" in John 15:15 and 3 John 15.[30]

Neopythagoreanism. In the first century B.C. there was a revival of the ideas of Pythagoras. The Neopythagoreans were interested in astrology and in the stellar space between God and the material world. This space is inhabited by intermediary demons arranged in a descending order. The Neopythagoreans also conceived of the material world as evil, since it is so far removed from a transcendent god. This negative view of the material world became one of the primary tenets of Gnosticism and Neoplatonism.

The best known adherent of Neopythagoreanism is Apollonius of Tyana, who is known through his biographer, Philostratus. Apparently Apollonius lived during the first century A.D. Philostratus portrays him as an itinerant teacher traveling to the major cities of the Roman Empire. He is a wise man with miraculous powers to heal the sick. He rejected marriage (at least for himself), was able to see into the past and future, and taught a substitution of prayer and meditation for animal sacrifice. The following parallels exist between Philostratus' account of the life of Apollonius and that of Jesus:[31]

(1) His miraculous birth

(2) The gathering of a circle of disciples

(3) Itinerant teaching

(4) Collection of miracle stories (demon-possessed boy, lame man, blind man, paralytic)

---

[30] Gilbert Murray, *Five Stages of Greek Religion* (Garden City: Doubleday, 1955), pp. 204–5.

[31] See Ferguson, *Backgrounds of Early Christianity*, pp. 361–63.

(5) Disappearance at his trial

(6) The charge that Apollonius was a magician

The writings of earliest Christianity primarily took shape within and were addressed to the hellenistic world. Therefore, we must interpret them in terms of their meaning for that world. The hermeneut should give due weight to the positive influence of hellenistic philosophical thought upon these New Testament writings. But the influence of hellenistic philosophical categories and ideas upon the New Testament writers is not the only one. There was a veritable plethora of interest in the oriental **mystery religions** during the hellenistic period. Any study of the New Testament must consider the influence of these religions or at least the conditions which gave rise to the unquestionably renewed religious sensitivity. There was also rabbinic influence upon both the form and content of the NT authors. But we must also underscore that the Jewish influence upon the New Testament writers was a Judaism that had been modified by Hellenism.

The Mystery Religions

During the hellenistic period, there was a loss of confidence in the established gods/goddesses, religions, and philosophies. Many people sought help to live meaningful lives within an impersonal world. The classical gods of Greece were impersonal and capricious, state religions were irrelevant to the immediate needs of the common person, and emperor worship was a political tool rather than an intimate faith.[32] The time was ripe for the rise and success of the mystery religions.

The object of the mysteries was to secure salvation for people who were subject to moral and physical evil, dominated by destiny, and unable to free themselves from the corruption that beset the material side of nature.[33] By participating in mystery rites and dramas of the cult, the adherents believed that they could share in the life of their deity. The mysteries allowed the worshippers to commune with their god/goddess and to enjoy a better life, confident of immortality. The mysteries offered emotional release for the participants through

---

[32] Merrill C. Tenney, *New Testament Times* (Grand Rapids: Eerdmans, 1975), p. 117.

[33] C. K. Barrett, *The New Testament Background: Selected Documents,* rev. ed. (San Francisco: Harper & Row, 1987), p. 120.

rituals, communal meals, pageantry, ecstatic ceremonies, festivals, and in some cases orgiastic rites.[34]

Initiation usually involved purification of the initiate (*katharsis*), the assembling of the initiates for a ceremonial procession (*systasis*), the procession of the initiates (*mystae*) into the mystery's sacred precincts (*temenos*), and the encounter with the mystery's deity.[35] Following the initiation the initiate stood outside of a fate-dominated world and was reborn into the cult's deity.

Purification was symbolized through animal sacrifice, application of water and/or blood, eating sacred meals, or a combination of these. Some of the mysteries included fasting, sacrifice, frenzied dancing and colorful processions, reenactments of the drama of their deity's wanderings, life, or entrance into immortality, orgiastic rites, and communal meals.

The gods of the mystery religions were originally fertility gods of agriculture, and the rites which initially secured crop and livestock productivity evolved into a personal religion. "In the myths of the mysteries, the deities are represented as wanderers whose journeys lead them from an existence of humanlike suffering to a transformed existence as celestial saviors."[36] Some myths were based upon a wife (or mother) who grieves for her lost husband (or child), and after a period of suffering, the lost family member is restored to the seeker—usually from the dead—and begins a new life.[37] The story of the wanderings, sufferings, and homecoming of the god or goddess offered the possibility that one's own suffering and wandering might come to an end through a personal soteriological relationship under the god's providential protection.

Although each mystery religion possessed its own rituals, symbolism, and interpretation of its rites, all of them shared several of the following common characteristics:

(1) a firm organization to which all members were subject

(2) membership through rites of initiation

(3) participation in regular meetings in which sacramental ceremonies were celebrated

---

[34] Cyril Bailey, *Phases in the Religion of Ancient Rome* (Westport: Greenwood, 1972), p. 177.

[35] Ibid., pp. 61–62.

[36] Luther Martin, *Hellenistic Religions* (New York: Oxford University, 1987), p. 59.

[37] Howard Clark Kee, *Understanding the New Testament*, 4th ed. (Englewood Cliffs: Prentice-Hall, 1983), p. 33.

(4) obligation to observe moral or ascetic precepts

(5) mutual support of all members

(6) obedience to the cult leader and the community of adherents

(7) cultivation of secret traditions[38]

The mysteries became a primary institution in many hellenized cities prior to, during, and after the birth of Christianity.

When Paul and other New Testament writers penned their works, they employed many words, concepts, and categories that were current in the mysteries. Such concepts include divine instruction through dreams and visions, baptism, fasting, regeneration, rebirth, communion, heaven, hell, conquest of evil, the savior-god as the mediator between deity and the individual, and the shedding of blood. In Revelation 12, there is reference to the woman and the dragon. Isis and Horus were also persecuted by a dragon named Typhon. The image in Revelation 12 depicts a woman attired in royal clothes, clothed with power, and giving birth to a child. These symbols parallel Isis, her power, her birth, and persecution. Mithras was believed to have life-giving power: "You have rescued us, too, by shedding the blood that makes us immortal."[39] The evangelist Mark tells his readers that Jesus gave his blood for humanity's sins because he "came to give his life a ransom for many" (Mark 10:45). Mithras was both the mediator between good and evil, and the representative of deity on earth. In his struggle with the bull, Mithras portrays the human struggle of those in pursuit of good; and by slaying the bull for humanity's benefit, he brought life and victory over evil.

This mystery also held that the initiate should strive for perfect unity and freedom from sensuality. Adherents were to show perfect loyalty to their god and companionship toward their comrades. They were also to live a good life because they were giving the right service to god. The similarities between Mithraism and Christianity were so close that some of the early church fathers were amazed.[40] Yet, while some of the terminology and concepts were identical, the interpretations were often quite different. A case in point is the reinterpretation of the pivotal

---

[38] Koester, *Introduction to the New Testament*, vol. 1, p. 198.

[39] Kurt Rudolph, "Mystery Religions," in *The Encyclopedia of Religion*, ed. Mircea Eliade (New York: Macmillan 1987), vol. 7, p. 236.

[40] George Gilmore, "Mithraism," in *The New Schaff-Herzog Encyclopedia of Religious Knowledge,* ed. Samuel Macaulty Jackson (Grand Rapids: Baker, 1977), vol. 7, p. 419.

term in the mysteries—"mystery." In the ordinary sense of the word, mystery refers to knowledge that is withheld. According to the author of Ephesians, a mystery is truth revealed. In Ephesians 1:9, there is reference to the mystery, and in 3:6 it is defined. The mystery is that the Gentiles are also included in God's promises. Then the author goes on to say, "this grace was given to me . . . to make everyone see what is the plan of the mystery" (3:8–9). The mysteries sought to keep their rites secret from all but a select few. The writer of Ephesians took a term that was common to his audience and radically redefined it in order to declare the not-so-secret plan of God.

We emphasize again that the writers of the New Testament (or any document for that matter) could exercise no alternative but to express themselves in the ideological milieu of their times. To borrow terms and ideas from other religious, philosophical, or literary traditions and then reapply, modify, or redefine them is probably the surest way that writers can make themselves both heard and understood. The reason for this is that such terms and concepts already carry with them a range of meanings that the reader can then adjust when the terms and concepts are placed in a new contextual setting.

Judaism

Christianity was conceived at least partially in the womb of Judaism. But Judaism of the first century was anything but a monolithic religious tradition. There were numerous ideological threads running through it—Messianism, apocalypticism, legalism, Hellenism. Many times these threads were intertwined. To complicate matters, Judaism existed in two general forms—Palestinian Judaism and Judaism of the Greek Diaspora.

The historical trek that eventually produced first-century Judaism, or what some call Pharisaic Judaism, is a long and complex one. A reconstruction of that history should begin with the Exile, proceed to the Persian period (538–332 B.C.), continue through the Greek period (332–167 B.C.) and the Maccabean period (167–63 B.C.), until finally it arrives at the Roman period (from 63 B.C.). But such a journey is not feasible for an introductory hermeneutics text. There are excellent New Testament introductions and texts on backgrounds which the hermeneutics student should consult, because there simply is no substitute for a knowledge of the long and complicated history which spawned the Judaism of the first century. This is the Judaism that passed on a variety of ideological and pedagogical factors to early Christianity and its literary productions we call the New Testament. It was a Judaism that revolved around monotheism, national feasts, temple, synagogue, a sense of destiny, and most of all the Torah. What we do propose to do here is offer the student a brief introduction to the various parties within first-century Judaism having significance for New Testament interpretation.

The Pharisees.   After the Maccabean revolt of 167 B.C., there were at least three courses which a person could follow: One could drop out of the mainstream of religious and political life into a private community; the religious tradition could be perpetually reinterpreted in the light of new circumstances; or a person could view the new circumstances apart from the religious tradition. The Essenes choose the first course, the **Pharisees** chose the second, and the Sadducees followed the last.[41]

Although their power was limited primarily to their own fellowships, and their influence was concentrated upon the common people, the Pharisees were instrumental in giving Judaism its distinct character and definition after the fall of Jerusalem in A.D. 70. Judaism after this time was primarily Pharisaic Judaism.

The religious program of the Pharisees was supported by two primary underpinnings—the written Torah and the oral Torah. The Pharisees believed that the written Torah stood in constant need of interpretation and application to new and changing circumstances. They believed that God had given Moses both the written Torah and an oral one that interpreted and explained the written one. This oral Torah (interpretation) became as authoritative for the Pharisees as the written Torah. The interpretive applications which the Pharisees gave to the written Torah were as binding as the written Torah itself. Because of this openness to the interpretation of the Torah, the Pharisees were susceptible to doctrines that were unacceptable to the Sadducees (e.g., bodily resurrection, final judgment, and rewards and punishment after death).

Not usually recognized by the casual readers of the New Testament is the amazing amount of doctrinal agreement among the Pharisees and Jesus and the early Christians. A substantial amount of Jesus' ethical teaching is paralleled in the rabbinic writings. Even where there is disagreement, the meaning of Jesus' teaching or that of the early church must be understood in the light of the Pharisaic difference. For example, the practice of summarizing the Torah by the use of a few principles

---

[41] Ferguson, *Backgrounds of Early Christianity*, pp. 480–85.

(Matt. 22:36) was a rabbinic practice. Separation from the world meant to the Pharisee that the pious individual must avoid contact with those people who neglected the Torah (both written and oral); but for Jesus and the early Christians, separation from the world was a matter of attitude. When Jesus reinterprets the Torah in Matthew's Sermon on the Mount, he offers six antitheses whose premises are drawn from the written and oral Torah. Another example where a comparison with rabbinic material is crucial for interpreting a remark by Jesus occurs in Matthew 18:20: "For where two or three are gathered in my name, I am there among them." This is a reapplication of a rabbinic teaching that claims where two or three are together studying the Torah, God is with them (*Pirqe ʾAbot* 3:2). As will be shown in unit II, Matthew is using this and similar sayings of Jesus to present Jesus as the personification of the Torah. Jesus also rejected the Pharisees' practice of giving priority to the oral tradition over the written Torah. As Ferguson observes, for Jesus, "The written word is authoritative, but the great fundamental principles therein take precedence and provide the standard by which it is to be interpreted and applied."[42] Jesus agreed with the Pharisees' desire to make the Torah applicable, but he disagreed with aspects of their methodology. This method of interpretation, *midrash*, was used extensively by the New Testament writers. Since we will discuss this in the next unit, suffice it here to say that in many instances a familiarity with this interpretive method is a definite plus for the modern interpreter.

The Sadducees. Whereas the Pharisees were connected with the synagogue, the **Sadducees** were affiliated with the temple. They were more open to hellenization and Roman rule than the other parties within Judaism. Acceptance of Roman rule ensured their power and influence. However, after the destruction of the temple and Jerusalem in A.D. 70, resulting in the loss of their seat of authority, the Sadducees never again exerted any influence upon Judaism.

As mentioned above, the Pharisees eventually accepted not only the books of Moses (Genesis–Deuteronomy) as authoritative, but also the Prophets and the Writings. They also placed the oral Torah on a par with the written Torah. The Sadducees would have no part of this, accepting as authoritative only the written law of Moses (Pentateuch) and rejecting as authoritative the Prophets, the Writings, and the oral Torah. Therefore, when Jesus responded to the Sadducees' questions concerning the resurrection (Matt. 22:23–33), he answered them by

---

[42] Ibid., p. 485.

appealing to a passage in the Pentateuch (Exod. 3:6). The Sadducees' acceptance only of the Pentateuch as authoritative explains why Jesus did not quote a passage from a text which would have more clearly dealt with the resurrection (e.g., Dan. 12:1ff.).[43]

The Essenes. The distinguishing characteristic of this group was their strict observance of the law. When Jonathan, a Hasmonean, became high priest in 161 B.C., the leader (referred to as the Teacher of Righteousness) of the **Essenes** along with his followers left Jerusalem and settled near the Dead Sea. This settlement was actually a community of scribes (legal experts) who, along with the Zadokite high priest, waited for the end of the age. During this interim period, the scribes of the community spent time interpreting the Scriptures, especially the Prophets, using a method called *pesher.* According to this method of interpretation, the Essenes interpreted prophecies as if their own circumstances were their fulfillment. The **Dead Sea Scrolls** produced by the Qumran community give evidence of a group that lived according to a strict order of discipline. Activity within the community included a common meal, water baptism, copying of texts, and strict observance of the Sabbath. New members faced a three-year probationary period. The initiate was required to follow the strict habits, rules, and regulations. Furthermore, the newcomer was forbidden to share any information with outsiders as to the practices and beliefs of the sect. In regards to marriage, the majority of the Essenes did not marry. They saw women as selfish and unstable. Women, they felt, would cause their sect to become weak. If a man was bound to a woman, he was a slave and would not be a productive part of the sect. This sounds remotely like the Apostle Paul in 1 Corinthians 7.

Much like the early Christians, the Essenes felt they were living in the last days. They saw themselves as the righteous remnant of Israel. This is the main reason they withdrew into the wilderness of Judea—to prepare themselves for the coming events. They pictured their present world as coming to an end and wickedness being defeated; following this would be the inauguration of the kingdom of God. Naturally, their literature had a strong eschatological thrust.

One of the prominent features in Essene eschatology is a messianic hope. Hippolytus states that "all the Essenes were looking for the Messiah."[44] This messianic hope is evident in the form of three figures

---

[43] Ibid., p. 486.

[44] J. E. H. Thompson, "Essenes," *ISBE*, vol. 1, pp. 997–1005, citing Hippolytus, *Refutation of Heresies.*

foretold in the Prophets: the prophet like Moses of Deuteronomy 18:15ff., the Davidic Messiah, and a great priest of Aaron's lineage.

There are many similarities between Essene literature and the New Testament, but nowhere in the New Testament is this similarity so prominent as in the Gospel of John. For example, John writes, "In the beginning was the Word, and the Word was with God, and the Word was God. He was in the beginning with God. All things came into being through him, and without him not one thing came into being" (John 1:1-3). The *Manual of Discipline*, which is part of the Qumran literature, states:

> From the God of knowledge exists all that is and will be . . . and by his knowledge everything has been brought into being. And everything that is, he established by his purpose; and apart from him, nothing is done (1QS 3.15 and 1QS 11.11).[45]

Other similarities between Essene writings and the Gospel of John include eschatological views, expectations regarding a messiah, and a strongly dualistic outlook (e.g., light vs. darkness, truth vs. error, death vs. life). Without question a study of the Qumran documents casts light upon numerous New Testament terms and concepts.

Other groups with which the interpreter should become familiar are the Zealots, the Herodians, and the Therapeutae. The customs and actions associated with these groups can illuminate a passage which might otherwise remain vague.

Comparative Literature

The writings of any period most often reflect ideas or forces shaping all aspects of a culture. As we have already argued, a knowledge of and and a willingness to consult such literature in a comparative sense can greatly enhance a person's understanding of a particular text or a portion of it.

For an English translation of some of these texts see David R. Cartlidge and David L. Dungan, *Documents for the Study of the Gospels* (1980); A. Dupont-Sommer, *The Essene Writings from Qumran*, translated by G. Vermes from the 1961 ed. (1973); G. Vermes, *The Dead Sea Scrolls in English*, revised ed. (1968); H. Danby, *The Mishnah* (1933);

---

[45] Raymond E. Brown, "The Qumran Scrolls and the Johannine Gospel and Epistles," in *The Scrolls and the New Testament*, ed. Krister Stendahl (Westport: Greenwood, 1975), p. 186.

I. Epstein, ed., *The Babylonian Talmud*, 35 vols. (1951); G. H. Clark, *Selections from Hellenistic Philosophy* (1940); J. Ferguson, *Greek and Roman Religion: A Source Book* rev. ed., (1980); C. K. Barrett, *The New Testament Background: Selected Documents* (1987); Flavius Josephus, *The Works of Josephus,* translated by William Whiston (repr., 1987); Philo Judaeus, *The Works of Philo,* translated by C. D. Yonge (repr., 1993); Claude J. Montefiore, ed. and trans., *A Rabbinic Anthology* (1974); Ron Cameron, *The Other Gospels* (1982); Edgar Hennecke, *New Testament Apocrypha,* ed. Wilhelm Schneemelcher, revised ed. (1990); Marvin M. Meyer, *The Secret Teachings of Jesus* (1984); and Cyril C. Richardson, ed. and trans., *Early Christian Fathers* (1953). Among the writings with which the student should become acquainted are the following:

The Writings of Josephus.   **Flavius Josephus** is an important source for the history of the Jewish people during the first century A.D. His extant writings include four major works, the *Jewish War*, the *Jewish Antiquities*, *Against Apion*, and the *Life*. While Josephus' interpretations of historical events (some of which he himself witnessed) may be questionable, his writings constitute a valuable record of a turbulent period in Jewish history, a period which parallels the developing years of early Christianity.

Philo of Alexandria.   A Jewish scholar during the first century A.D., **Philo of Alexandria** in Egypt attempted to reconcile the Greek rationality with the Hebrew Scriptures. Employing the Greek term *logos*, for instance, Philo identified the concept of Wisdom as the creative intermediary between God and the material universe. In his writings, Philo shows himself to be a product of Hellenism—an eclectic. In his fascination with numbers, Philo evidences the influence of the Pythagoreans; in his sense of human ignorance and evil, the Skeptics; in his idea of the body as the prison of the soul, the Platonists; and in his concern for freedom from passion, living according to nature and *adiaphora* (indifferent things), the Stoics. Philo's conceptions of the Conscience as the internal judge, of the Spirit, of faith, of immortality, and other concepts are so similar to concepts in the New Testament epistles as to demand comparison. His allegorical method of interpreting the Hebrew Scriptures also serves as a model for New Testament writers such as the author of Hebrews, Matthew, and Paul.

The Dead Sea Scrolls.   The Dead Sea Scrolls constitute a collection of writings used and preserved by an Essene community at Qumran. As well as copies of the Hebrew Scriptures, this collection also contains writings which were presumably composed by the Qumran community itself. Works such as the *War of the Sons of Light Against the Sons of Darkness* and the *Manual of Discipline* reveal a number of similarities between the Qumranians and early Christians (e.g., both groups felt that Israel had broken its covenant with Yahweh, both regarded themselves as the new Israel, both observed a communal meal of bread and wine, both advocated holding all things in common, both evidence a cosmic dualism).

Rabbinic Literature. Within Judaism there developed a need to interpret the Hebrew sacred writings in order to make them meaningful for different and new circumstances. This "tradition of the elders" (Mark 7:3) became known as the oral Torah and consisted of a body of legalistic interpretations which rabbis made over many centuries. These interpretations were eventually compiled and codified into the Mishnah around A.D. 200. The rabbinic method of interpretation called **midrash** is used by New Testament writers such as Matthew, Paul, and the author of Hebrews.

The Apostolic Fathers. Several writings (some of which may date prior to the canonical Catholic epistles) enjoyed a position of quasi-authority in early Christianity. These works offer valuable glimpses into the developing liturgy, episcopate, and world-view of a church on its way to becoming an institution. The writings normally designated "Apostolic Fathers" are the Didache, the Shepherd of Hermas, the epistles of Clement, the epistles of Ignatius, the epistle of Barnabas, the epistle of Polycarp to the Philippians, and the Martyrdom of Polycarp.

The New Testament Apocrypha. Early Christians produced an extensive corpus of writings which became known as **apocrypha**, either because they were thought to contain secret or hidden meanings or because the works remained hidden from ordinary Christians. Many of these writings have their origin in Gnosticism. Thus they were naturally shunned by orthodox Christianity. These works vary in genre—gospels, epistles, apocalypses, and acts. The value of these works for New Testament studies is that they offer insight into some of the concepts and teachings which orthodox Christianity had to battle in its struggle for identity and survival.

Other sources that will aid in interpretation include extant hellenistic biographies, histoires, and romances, Greek and Jewish epistolary writings, and the Old Testament Apocrypha.

Social Science Criticism

On the one hand, the Bible was produced by individual members of faith communities, and it consequently reflects the historical perspective and cultural patterns of those communities. On the other hand, modern readers tend to interpret the Bible in terms of their historical perspective and cultural patterns. Bridging the gap introduced by these two truisms is the domain of a critical method known as social science criticism.

Social science criticism attempts to narrow this gap by providing methods that explain what a text meant in its original historical and social context. By applying the constructs provided by sociologists and social anthropologists, social science critics employ cross-cultural models of human interaction and methods of analyzing data regarding social organizations, politics, structures of authority, and social institutions. For example, social scientists have found that the Greco-Roman world was characterized by an intractable hierarchical structure that guarded and maintained a stable social order. The family was the microcosm of this structure with its tripartite relational organization founded on a pattern of dominance and subordination: parent/child, husband/wife, and master/servant. If the state was the macrocosm structurally of the family, and if the state's existence depended upon this family pattern, any deviation from the structure on the level of the family would have been viewed as a threat to the state's well-being. After experimenting with a new egalitarian structure, the church realized that such an experiment threatened its existence. It thus adopted the pattern of dominance and subordination as its internal structure at both ecclesiastical and family levels. Based upon such an insight from social science criticism, the interpretation and application of passages such as Ephesians 5:21–6:9, Colossians 3:18–4:1, and 1 Peter 2:13–3:8 take on new significance.

Since this method of criticism offers such important assistance in interpreting the Bible, I list here some of the important sources for the interested student.

For the Hebrew Bible: Norman K. Gottwald, "Sociological Method in the Study of Ancient Israel," in *Encounter with the Text*, ed. Martin J. Buss (1979), pp. 69–81; Robert R. Wilson, *Genealogy and History in the Biblical World* (1977); idem, *Sociological Approaches to the Old Testament* (1984); idem, *Prophecy and Society in Ancient Israel* (1980); Cyril S. Rodd, "On Applying a Sociological Theory to Biblical Studies," *JSOT* 19 (1981):

95–106; Burke O. Long, "The Social World of Ancient Israel," *Int* 37 (1982): 243–55; V. Matthews and D. Benjamin, *The Social World of Ancient Israel 1250–587 BCE* (1993).

For the New Testament: Sean Freyne, *The World of the New Testament* (1980); John G. Gager, *Kingdom and Community: The Social World of Early Christianity* (1975); Martin Hengel, *Property and Riches in the Early Church: Aspects of a Social History of Early Christianity* (1974); Abraham J. Malherbe, *Social Aspects of Early Christianity* (2d ed., 1983); Bruce J. Malina, *The New Testament World: Insights from Cultural Anthropology* (1981); Wayne Meeks, *The First Urban Christians: The Social World of the Apostle Paul* (1983); Carolyn Osiek, R.S.C.J., *What Are They Saying about the Social Setting of the New Testament?* (1984); Gerd Theissen, *The Social Setting of Pauline Christianity: Essays on Corinth* (1982); Jerome H. Neyrey, ed., *The Social World of Luke–Acts* (1991); Richard Rohrbaugh, ed., *The Social Sciences and New Testament Interpretation* (1996).

In the last chapter, I referred to the idea of a people's symbolic world and to that people's practice of offering literary interpretations of experiences within that world. Literary productions look the way they do and say what they say because they interpret experiences within the symbols of the world that gives the text birth. For this reason, the interpreter must develop both an interest in and an acquaintance with the originating symbolic world. The religious experiences of the biblical writers necessitated that they reshape, modify, redefine (i.e., reinterpret) their symbolic worlds. An understanding of the way each writer accomplished this reinterpretation is greatly facilitated by a familiarity with the symbolic world.

Summary

A visit to the world behind the text is indispensable for the interpreter. Any literary work of art (at least any good literary work of art) will extend to the reader an open invitation to discover something about reality. By what is said *in* texts, there will be communicated something *through* texts. But the content of the text and its message are clothed in the terms, ideas, symbols, concepts, and categories which are current in the author's world. If the interpreters do not give serious attention to that world *behind* the text, whatever they say about the world *within* the text—the literary context—will be less than it should be.

REVIEW & STUDY

Key Terms and Concepts

Sitz im Leben	Comparative study
Hellenism	*Logos*
Mystery religions	Hellenistic philosophies
Judaism	Pharisees
Sadducees	Essenes
Pesher	Dead Sea Scrolls
Apocrypha	Flavius Josephus
Philo of Alexandria	Midrash
Septuagint	Syncretism

Study Questions

1. Read the first paragraph in this chapter again. Draw a simple diagram illustrating the two gaps that are introduced. What do you consider to be the best way to lessen the size of these gaps?

2. Read the section in this chapter entitled "Historical and Cultural Background" and then explain the following diagram:

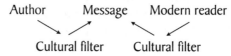

3. In a New Testament introduction or some other source (e.g., Carolyn Osiek, *What Are They Saying about the Social Setting of the New Testament?* [New York: Paulist Press, 1984], pp. 73–83), read the section on the "household code." Then read Ephesians 5:21–6:9 and Colossians 3:18–4:1. How does an understanding of the social phenomenon of the structure of the household in the Greco-Roman world affect your interpretation of these passages?

4. Do you feel that the reading of a biblical text is enhanced by a familiarity with other literature contemporary with the biblical text? Why or why not? Read the *Manual of Discipline* from a translation of the Dead Sea Scrolls and then read the Gospel of John. Make a list of similar terms, concepts, and views (e.g., the dualistic outlook in both).

Suggestions for Further Reading

Damrosch, David. *The Narrative Covenant: Transformations of Genre in the Growth of Biblical Literature*. San Francisco: Harper & Row, 1987.

Ferguson, John. *Greek and Roman Religion: A Source Book*. Park Ridge, N.J.: Noyes, 1980.

Gager, John G. *Kingdom and Community: The Social World of Early Christianity*. Englewood Cliffs: Prentice-Hall, 1975.

Kennedy, George A. *Classical Rhetoric and Its Christian and Secular Tradition from Ancient to Modern Times*. Chapel Hill: University of North Carolina Press, 1980.

Malina, Bruce J. *The New Testament World: Insights from Cultural Anthropology*. Atlanta: John Knox, 1981.

Meeks, Wayne. *The Moral World of the First Christians*. Philadelphia: Westminster, 1986.

Sanders, James A. *Canon and Community*. Philadelphia: Fortress, 1984.

Stambaugh, John and David Balch. *The New Testament in Its Social Environment*. Philadelphia: Westminster, 1986.

Van der Woude, A. S. *The World of the Old Testament*. Grand Rapids: Eerdmans, 1989.

UNIT II

THE WORLD WITHIN THE TEXT

The Bible as Literature
and Literary Forms

When a hermeneutic includes in part or whole the text as a locus of meaning, the hermeneutic is literary in nature. Central to our integrated approach is the text as a literary creation. The mainspring of any literary approach is the view that the Bible is literature; thus, the Bible as literature is *the* basic presupposition for literary criticism. But, as McKnight questions, "are the nature and content of the Bible consistent with a literary approach or orientation? Is the Bible as sacred scripture compromised by a literary approach?"[1] McKnight thinks not, and I concur. While God might be the author of sacred poetry and narrative, he used the verse and prose forms native to Hebrew and hellenistic cultures. While the Bible may be part of God's revelation and self-disclosure to humanity, it is a revelation expressed in human language. In one sense the authors of the biblical texts employ the finiteness of written discourse to say something about an infinite God. Further, the written discourse is a special case of language—literary. By literary I mean creative and imaginative language, language adorned with artistic devices that transform and intensify ordinary language or everyday speech. This literary quality requires interpretation, and of central importance in interpretation are the concepts of genre and sub-genre.

The **natural languages** of the biblical texts, Hebrew, Aramaic, and Greek, are governed by grammatical, syntactical, and lexical codes. But literature also uses secondary languages called **literary languages.** These languages also have codes. These literary languages with their codes enable a reader to move beyond what the text *says* in its natural language to what the text is *about*. This distinction is the mimetic character of literature. In other words, literature has a **referential quality** and a **mimetic quality**. The referential quality is the relationship

---

[1] McKnight, *Post-Modern Use of the Bible*, p. 168.

between the language of the text and the world projected by that language. The mimetic quality is the relationship between the real world and the world of the text. On the one hand, by means of the referential quality of literature, an author is able to use language to create the world of the text. This world may or may not be similar to the real world of the author (e.g., science fiction). In this textual world, words refer to objects which may or may not be recognizable in the real world. The referential quality enables the world of the text to have a story line and plot. On the other hand, the mimetic function enables the author to challenge the reader to discover some truth, message, or insight to which the textual world points. The following chart should make the distinction between the referential quality and mimetic quality clearer.

LANGUAGE

⟵—— Referential quality

TEXTUAL WORLD

⟵—— Mimetic quality

REAL WORLD

TRUTH, MESSAGE, INSIGHT

DIAGRAM 4-1

Any hermeneutic that takes seriously the text must give attention to both of these qualities. Traditional hermeneutics (by which I mean primarily the historical-critical and historical-grammatical approaches) has demonstrated a remarkable tenacity in its unwillingness to place as much importance upon the mimetic function of biblical literature as upon its referential function. Characteristic of this hermeneutic has been the persistent tendency to divert attention away from the text itself to the world which produced the text. This tendency has perpetuated an attitude towards the biblical texts which views them as distorted historical records at best and poor substitutes for more veritable originals at worst. One has only to recall the hypothetical Aramaic original for Matthew's Gospel, the sayings source "Q" used by Luke and Matthew, and the original documents from which Genesis was redacted. Recent literary approaches have come a long way in demonstrating that the biblical texts in their final forms are works of tremendous literary power and aesthetic quality. These approaches have not only shown that the biblical texts employ the syntactical, grammatical, and linguistic codes of the natural languages in creatively pleasing ways; they have also succeeded in spotlighting the Bible's equally creative use of the literary languages of the different genres and subgenres. These may include a whole range of literary devices, such as style, point of view, characterization, plot, thematic organization, and dynamics of reticence. Hermeneutics can no longer be content only with the historical-critical attempts at a reconstruction of the original document, oral traditions, and *Sitz im Leben*. Nor can it be completely satisfied with the historical-grammatical method's parsing of the natural languages. While each of these approaches offers valuable heuristic background information often indispensable for interpretation (as we saw in unit I), hermeneutics must be equally, if not more, concerned with parsing the literary languages of a document's generic systems. Meaning is conveyed through both the natural and literary languages. Grammatical content cannot be separated from the form through which it is communicated. Inattention to genre ultimately precipitates an inattention to meaning. This means that a consideration of genre is an absolute must for hermeneutics.

We are constantly faced with the necessity of distinguishing between literary **genres.** Within a single week many students will read a short story, a poem, a tragic play, labels on food containers, a newspaper, a letter, a telephone directory, or a recipe. All of these "forms" communicate differently and represent different literary types or genres. When a reader approaches a text, a conscious or unconscious identification of genre is made. Even the casual reader knows that a poem must be read and interpreted differently from a recipe. John Hayes and Carl Holladay describe the issue as follows:

> The required effort and means necessary for the exegesis and interpretation of texts thus vary greatly, depending upon the nature of the texts and their relationship to normal communication. Some texts merely need to be read to be understood. Others require very detailed analysis. Some use normal, everyday language, grammar, and sentence structure. Others use a very specialized vocabulary, involved grammatical and sentence structure and distinctive forms of expression. Some texts employ symbolic and metaphoric language. Others seek to employ language and words so as to limit severely the range of meaning and the potential to persuade. Others seek

to merely inform. Some texts are produced to entertain. Others seek to produce some particular response and action.[2]

There is an intimate relationship and interconnectedness between form and content. Hermeneutics must concern itself not only with the content, but also with the form of the text. This concern entails understanding the conventions of the generic systems. This is true because different genres involve different literary codes and conventions. Perhaps a couple of illustrations will clarify this. In most cultures, unspoken rules govern what is worn and when it is worn. Rules of dress dictate that a person not wear a ski suit to a formal wedding. Also, within a given society, rules or principles dictate family relationships. On the basis of these rules, persons within a particular social group will relate to other members of the group, making decisions such as whom they can or cannot marry.

Similarly, in language, rules of grammatical construction and syntax govern the way we group words or symbols. This ensures communication. Furthermore, rules govern or identify literary genres and subgenres. Consequently, we read different genres with different expectations and interpret them differently by recognizing the relationship between what is said (content) and how it is said (genre, form). Different kinds of genres are capable of different kinds of meaning and offer different kinds of information to a reader. Knowing the genre of a text or the sub-genre of a literary unit allows us to know what type of questions can sensibly be asked of the material.[3]

The most plausible understanding of a text and its subsequent explication is best actualized when the reader has an adequate grasp of the literary genres and sub-genres by which the author operates. Robert Alter puts it well:

> A coherent reading of any art work, whatever the medium, requires some detailed awareness of the grid of conventions upon which, and against which, the individual work operates. . . . Through our awareness of convention we can recognize significant or simply pleasing patterns of repetition, symmetry, contrast; we can discriminate between the verisimilar and the fabulous, pick up directional clues in a narrative and see what is innovative and what is deliberately traditional at each nexus of the artistic creation.[4]

---

[2] Hayes and Holladay, *Biblical Exegesis*, p. 7.

[3] Ibid., p. 83.

[4] Robert Alter, *The Art of Biblical Narrative* (New York: Basic Books, 1981), p. 47.

Biblical texts are not simply conglomerates of disjointed and unsophisticated religious tradition, but carefully crafted works of great artistic accomplishment which we should study as unified wholes.

In the Bible, poetry has its own set of codes centering in the concept of parallelism, in which "the poet makes a statement and arouses expectation. To meet that expectation, the poet goes back to the beginning and says the same thing or follows a line of thought parallel to that already laid down."[5] Like narrative in general, biblical narrative utilizes plot; in plot, events are arranged so that the action is a unified whole. The fodder for narrative consists of characters, settings, and conflicts. Embedded within the two Hebrew genres of poetry and narrative are literary forms (which we will call sub-genres) such as simile, metaphor, symbol, personification, hyperbole, type-scenes, archetypes, fables, miracle stories, pronouncement stories, riddles, speeches, and prophetic utterances.

By creatively blending and arranging these sub-genres through the medium of the natural language, the author superimposes a literary language (or languages) upon the natural one. Consequently, literary meaning surpasses that conveyed by the codes of the natural language. Literary meaning results from an interaction of the codes of the natural language and the literary ones. I will have more to say about this in unit III, where we consider the dynamics of reading.

In the remainder of this chapter I examine literary sub-genres that are present in virtually all literary traditions. While some of the sub-genres in the Hebrew Bible are quite strange to those who have been nurtured in the Western literary traditions, the reader should find the following common forms familiar. The final two chapters of this unit concentrate on the major genres and sub-genres of the Hebrew Bible and New Testament respectively.

Common Literary Sub-Genres

Hyperbole

Briefly defined, **hyperbole** is deliberate exaggeration for effect. An example is 1 Kings 1:40: "And all the people went up after him, playing flutes and rejoicing greatly, so that the ground shook with the sound" (NIV). Did the ground actually shake? That's not the point! The point is that the

---

[5] McKnight, *Post-Modern Use of the Bible*, p. 135.

rejoicing was extremely great. Another well-known example is Yahweh's promise to Abraham that his descendants would be "as numerous as the stars of heaven and as the sand that is on the seashore" (Gen. 22:17). The New Testament also contains many examples. For instance: "If your right eye causes you to sin, tear it out and throw it away" (Matt. 5:29a).

Euphemism

When authors make use of **euphemism**, they substitute a less direct or less distasteful word or phrase for a more direct or shocking one. A euphemism is in one sense the opposite of hyperbole; i.e., euphemism is intentional understatement.[6] Modern translators of the Bible usually supply equivalent euphemisms for the target language. In the third chapter of Judges, Eglon's guards hesitate to enter the king's chambers because they think that he "covereth his feet" (KJV). This euphemistically refers to a bowel movement. The translators of the NIV supply an equivalent euphemism with "He must be relieving himself." In Leviticus, the phrase "uncover the nakedness" (Lev. 18:6–8, etc.) is a euphemism for sexual relations, including incest. Mickelsen suggests that there is an intrinsic delicacy involved in the use of euphemism which modern translators should imitate.[7]

Metaphor

John Gabel defines **metaphor** simply as "a word that is literal in the contexts within which it is usually found and is taken out of those contexts and used in a context of some other kind."[8] In Psalm 119:105 the psalmist says that God's word is "a lamp to my feet." Taken at face value, this statement is false; i.e., obviously a word cannot really be a lamp. Nevertheless, in another sense it is true, for God's word and a lamp to light one's path are similar. These two concepts share an area of commonality or intersection: They both give guidance, keep one from stumbling, and dispel darkness. Ordinarily a metaphor illuminates, clarifies, or completes an abstract idea by replacing it with something observable, familiar, concrete; and the effect of the metaphor may vary according to how much commonality there is between the abstract idea and the object.

---

[6] See Mickelsen, *Interpreting the Bible*, p. 192.
[7] Ibid.
[8] John Gabel and Charles Wheeler, *The Bible as Literature: An Introduction* (New York: Oxford University, 1986), p. 47.

Simile

A **simile** compares two objects, actions, or ideas by using words such as "like" and "as." The meaning of a simile is the comparison itself. In most instances, the two objects of the simile are familiar within the experiences of the audience. Some property of the second half of the simile serves to illuminate an aspect of the first half. When Job says, "A mortal . . . comes up like a flower and withers" (14:1–2a), he is comparing the brevity of a person's earthly existence to that of the field flower. The author is obviously not concerned with other properties of the flower such as color, fragrance, or shape. The comparison is direct and clear within the context. When the suitor in the Song of Solomon says that his beloved's "hair is like a flock of goats moving down the slopes of Mount Gilead," he is not hinting that she should wash her hair. Apparently there is something about the scene of a flock of goats descending down a mountain that recalled the texture or flowing smoothness of his beloved's hair. The reader obviously should not attempt to burden the comparison with other elements such as the smell of a flock of goats or the height of the mountain. When a simile occurs, the reader should question why the author employs the particular simile at this place and how the simile elucidates the concept being presented.

Symbolism

When a concrete object which is found as the referent in a metaphor is displaced and used independently of the metaphorical context while retaining its metaphorical meaning or significance, it is a symbol. We are all familiar with the way in which objects such as the "cross" and the "blood" of the Christ have become **symbols** in Christian soteriology. In the Bible, objects (e.g., sheep, goat, lamb, lion, certain numbers, a race, or a fight) often stand alone to symbolize a more abstract idea or person.

Allegory

When a metaphor or symbol is extended in order to establish a relationship between the two objects in a systematic manner, the result is **allegory.** The metaphor or symbol splits several times into its component parts, and these parts then assume a one-to-one correspondence. For example, the story of Hosea's marriage in Hosea 2 is an allegory of God's relationship to Israel as a nation. Hosea is commanded by Yahweh to take a wife, who is then unfaithful. This becomes an allegory of the family. Gabel describes it as follows: "Speaking to Hosea as his son, Yahweh, the husband, accuses Israel, the wife, of infidelity because she has deserted him and lavished her care on the pagan gods, her lovers."[9] A rather good example is Matthew 22:1–14, the allegory of the wedding feast.

Formal Level (Referent)	Actual Level (Meaning)
King	God
Son	Jesus
Feast	Banquet
Servants	Apostles
Invited guests	The nation of Israel
Those accepting invitation	Church (converts)
Wedding garments	Righteousness
Excluded guests	Those found unworthy

DIAGRAM 4-2

Obviously the meaning of the allegory lies on the actual level and not on the formal. A note of warning is appropriate at this point: The act of writing allegory is not synonymous with the act of reading allegorically. To interpret a biblical passage allegorically when it is not allegory is simply to misinterpret. A sterling example of this error is an allegorical interpretation of the Song of Solomon (a series of love poems describing a relationship between lovers) as a representative of the relationship between Christ and the church.

Personification

In this device an inanimate object or group of persons assume the properties of a single human being. Examples include the **personification** of wisdom, evil, death, and the nation Israel: "Wisdom cries out in the street; in the squares she raises her voice" (Prov. 1:20); "Abaddon and Death say, 'We have heard a rumor of it with our ears' " (Job 28:22); "when Israel was a child, I loved him" (Hos. 11:1a). In each of these examples, a concept (wisdom, destruction and death) or a nation (Israel) assumes some property of a human being.

---

[9] Ibid., p. 29.

Apostrophe

An **apostrophe** is an address (usually of the exclamatory type) to an object or person. The object or person addressed is normally absent. As if thinking out loud, the speaker is addressing someone or something present in thought only.[10] Jesus' lament over Jerusalem is an apostrophe: "Jerusalem, Jerusalem, the city that kills the prophets and stones those who are sent to it! How often have I desired to gather your children together as a hen gathers her brood under her wings, and you were not willing!" (Matt. 23:37). We find a combination of personification and apostrophe in the liturgical Psalm 24: "Lift up your heads, O gates! and be lifted up, O ancient doors! that the King of glory may come in" (v. 7). As the ark of the covenant is brought to the house prepared for it on Mount Zion, the gates are personified and called upon (apostrophe) to open. In verse 8, the personified gates respond with "who is the King of glory?" This type of fine line between personification and apostrophe is commonplace. The two forms are distinct at two points. First, personification always ascribes to an inanimate object some human trait, while apostrophe may refer to a human being; and second, apostrophe will normally involve an exclamatory address, which is not necessarily the case in personification.

Synecdoche

The practice of using a part to refer to a whole or vice-versa is called **synecdoche.** When John says that "God so loved the world" (John 3:16), his reference is not to the created world as a whole but only to human beings. In this synecdoche, the whole stands for the part. An example of the reverse is Matthew 10:38: "And whoever does not take up the cross and follow me is not worthy of me." "Cross" here stands in for a whole range of self-sacrificial acts.

Metonymy

When two objects are so commonly associated with each other that the use of one may imply or even substitute for the other, the result is **metonymy.** For example, in the statement "the pen is mightier than the sword," pen and sword are metonyms for the power of the written word

---

[10] Mickelsen, *Interpreting the Bible*, p. 142.

and military power respectively. This type of substitution is common within most literary traditions. Paul states: "For it is we who are the circumcision" (Phil. 3:3). Most readers know that circumcision was the outward covenantal sign that identified Israel as the chosen people of God. Paul enlists this concept in a new context to suggest that Christians are now the people of God. Paul thus substitutes circumcision for the people of God. Luke informs us that, while walking with the two disciples on the road to Emmaus, Jesus instructed his two companions, "beginning with Moses and all the prophets" (Luke 24:27). Moses here is a reference to the Torah, the first five books of the Hebrew Scriptures, and the Prophets refer to the second division of the Hebrew Scriptures.

Satire

An excellent definition of **satire** is given by Leland Ryken:

Satire is the exposing, through ridicule or rebuke, of human vice or folly. It becomes literary when the controlling purpose of attack is combined with a literary method such as story, description or metaphor. Satire can appear in any literary genre (such as lyric, narrative, or drama) and can be either a minor part of a work or the main point of an entire work. Although satire usually has one main object of attack, satiric works often make a number of jabs in various directions, a feature that can be called "satiric ripples." It is a convention of satire that satirists feel free to exaggerate, overstate, and oversimplify to make their satiric point. Satire is a subversive form. It assaults the deep structures of our thinking and aims to make us uncomfortable. It questions the status quo and unsettles people's tendency to think that their behavior is basically good.[11]

Irony

In dramatic **irony,** the reader, though not the characters, always has a superior vantage point from which all the truth of a situation is known. This contrast between the reader's complete perception and the character's partial one generates irony. An example is the story of Ehud in Judges 3. After returning from the site of the oracle, Ehud informs the Moabite king, Eglon, that he has a word from the Lord for him. The king supposes that the word is the one received from the oracle, but the reader knows that the word is really the double-edged dagger concealed beneath Ehud's coat.

---

[11] Leland Ryken, *Words of Delight: A Literary Introduction to the Bible* (Grand Rapids: Baker, 1987), p. 329.

One of the most gripping instances of irony in the Bible is the book of Job. The reader overhears the conversation and bargain between God and "the adversary," but Job does not. If not given this insight, the reader might assume that Job is being unjustly punished rather than tested. If Job had the same perception as the readers, there would be no irony. Job's ignorance of the situation and the reader's privileged knowledge are both required for the irony.

Irony also exists when a person says one thing and means the opposite or something different. For example, when Paul tells his Corinthian audience that "we [the apostles] are fools for the sake of Christ, but you are wise in Christ" (1 Cor. 4:10), he is not offering a compliment; he means for his statement to be an accusation. Especially sharp irony like this is usually called sarcasm.

Archetypes

Within literature as a whole, characters, symbols, and themes seem to recur with regularity. For instance, the theme "from rags to riches," the character of the sassy servant in comedy, or the symbol of the gathering storm are familiar to most readers. One author suggests that **archetypes** "carry the same or very similar meanings for a large portion of mankind and appeal to what is most elemental in human experience."[12] Since archetypes are symbols or images shared by all, their potential for communication is almost infinite. When we encounter an archetype in literature, we are immediately faced with a whole body of meaning which the author does not need to explain. Archetypes such as the autumn of the year, the valley, the fox, the snake, birth, a smoothly flowing stream, a lamb, a rose, musical harmony, and the vulture communicate meaning without explanation. Phrases such as "Israel has played the harlot" or "tell that fox Herod" employ the archetype. These phrases need no explanation because the archetype immediately suggests and organizes the meaning. Archetypes are master images around which meaning is organized.

The Bible is the great storehouse of master images for literature in the Western world. An appreciation of literature outside the Bible is enhanced by a familiarity with the archetypes within the Bible.

---

[12] Leland Ryken, *The Literature of the Bible* (Grand Rapids: Zondervan, 1974), p. 22.

The primary reason for archetypal studies, however, is that the biblical texts themselves are saturated with these master images. As one author suggests, readers of the Bible can discover as much truth by tracing a master image through the Bible as by tracing some abstract idea.[13]

Summary

The ability to recognize the above sub-genres enhances a reader's appreciation for the literary artistry of literature. The absence of this ability heightens the risk of misrepresentation of the text's message. This is true whether the text is by Chaucer or the author of Job. As stated above, though, these sub-genres form only part of the structure of a text. A concentration on these sub-genres alone results in the neglect of the dynamics of the greater macrostructure as a unified whole. The interpretation of a text is exactly that—the interpretation of the whole and not just the stringing together of the interpretations of disjoined individual units. A narrative, a poem, a gospel, an apocalypse, or an epistle is a single generic whole, and each must be approached with full knowledge of the conventions and dynamics characteristic of it.

REVIEW & STUDY

Key Terms and Concepts

Literary language	Natural language
Referential quality of literature	Mimetic quality of literature
Genre	Hyperbole
Euphemism	Metaphor
Simile	Allegory
Personification	Apostrophe
Synecdoche	Metonymy
Irony	Archetype
Satire	Symbol

---

[13] Ryken, *Words of Delight*, p. 29.

Study Questions

1. Read the prayer of Habakkuk in 3:1–19 and identify at least one occurrence of each of the following:
   Metaphor
   Simile
   Personification
   Irony
   An imaginative reference to an event in Israel's history.

2. Read Luke 24:13–35. Briefly recount the story (what is said *in* the short pericope, i.e., the referential quality of the passage). Now based upon the language and progression of the content of the passage, give an account of what you think the passage is about (what is said *through* the story, i.e., the mimetic quality of the pericope).

3. The Song of Solomon has often been interpreted as an allegory in which the main characters are Christ and the church. Read the first four chapters of the Song and explain why you do or do not agree with such an interpretation.

4. If the authors of the biblical texts employ literary devices common to most secular literary traditions, what do you see as some of the implications of this for the interpretation and truth quality of the Bible?

Suggestions for Further Reading

Alter, Robert and Frank Kermode. *The Literary Guide to the Bible*. Cambridge: Harvard University Press, 1987.

Caird, G. B. *The Language and Imagery of the Bible*. Philadelphia: Westminster, 1980.

Gabel, John and Charles Wheeler. *The Bible as Literature: An Introduction*. New York: Oxford University Press, 1986.

Mickelsen, A. Berkeley. *Interpreting the Bible*. Grand Rapids: Eerdmans, 1987.

Ryken, Leland. *Words of Delight: A Literary Introduction to the Bible*. Grand Rapids: Baker, 1987.

_____. *Words of Life: A Literary Introduction to the New Testament*. Grand Rapids: Baker, 1986.

How the Hebrew Bible
Communicates as Literature

The Hebrew Bible is generally thought to contain two major genres—narrative and poetry—and a variety of sub-genres. Since Hebrew prophecy contains both narrative and poetic sections, we will treat prophecy in this chapter as a distinct genre having its own characteristic sub-genres. The Psalms and wisdom literature may also be treated as major genres. Since they employ the dynamics of Hebrew verse, however, I will approach them here as unique sub-genres of Hebrew verse.

Hebrew Narrative

Anyone familiar with the literary category of narrative recalls the typical features of **narrative**: narrative voice and time, plot, setting, characterization, point of view, and style. The suggestion that parts of the Hebrew Bible can be read in much the same way as other narratives (e.g., a novel or short story) may strike many modern readers as strange or at least surprising. A summary of the features of narrative plus examples from both biblical and secular sources will introduce those unfamiliar with narrative to its basic concepts. Then we can study how these basic concepts are actualized in Hebrew narrative. And finally, no discussion of Hebrew narrative is complete without at least a cursory glance at some of the unique sub-genres and their distinct characteristics.

Narrative Voice and Time

Before the actual poetics (the method of writing) of biblical narrative are discussed, a brief explanation of narratology (the principles of the study of narrative) will set a solid footing. Although there are several theories of narrative, they all have in common a basic structure. An individual living in and conditioned by a real-life situation sets about writing a story (see diagram 5-1). Once this decision is made, the individual becomes someone different; as author, the individual assumes a different identity from his or her real identity, because the purpose and perspective are focused in a particular direction, toward a single literary objective—to convey a message to an audience or reader. The result is that in the process of writing, the **real author** becomes an implied author. The self who writes is somehow different from the self who thinks. For all practical purposes the **implied author** is the one whom the reader constructs from the text itself. For example, the only things we know about the author of Job are what we know from the text—his view of God and humanity; what, for him, constitutes true integrity; and his opinion of death. We know nothing of his everyday life, except what the writer chooses to reveal through the text. The author allows the reader access to only a limited area of his or her intellectual world.

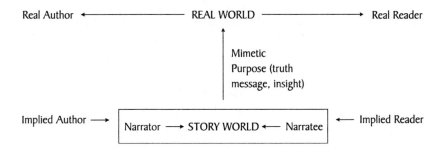

DIAGRAM 5-1

Corresponding to the real author is the **real reader** (to be discussed at length in unit III), who is likewise conditioned by a range of variables—social, economical, political, ecclesiastical, doctrinal, methodological, and philosophical. This real reader or audience of the text may have been the original readers, readers during the Protestant Reformation, or those in an introductory literature class last week. There is also an **implied reader** who is the counterpart to the "implied author." The implied reader is the reader or audience presupposed by the narrative, the reader (or type of reader) whom the author has in mind during the process of composition. What type of readers did the author of the Joseph narrative (Gen. 37–48) have in mind? What assumptions did the author make concerning the readers' background, level of knowledge about Joseph, or relationship to the author? Obviously, the answers to such questions lie within the text itself (although a knowledge of the cultural, ideological, historical world of the author can be extremely helpful here). The extent to which the real reader identifies with this "implied reader" usually determines the plausibility of a particular reading of the text. Some theories also postulate an "ideal reader" who is the persona the author actually creates or formulates during composition. The ideal reader is the hypothetical person with whom the author is in dialogue.

The next complementary duet consists of narrator and narratee. The **narrator** is the voice through which the author tells the story. The **narratee** is the person to whom the narrator is telling the story. The narratee may or may not be a character in the narrative. For example, the narratee in the Gospel of Luke is Theophilus, while in the book of Revelation, the narratee is actually made up of seven churches. I will have more to say about the narrator in the discussion on perspective.

The final pair of concepts consists of the real world and the story world. First, we need to distinguish between historical narrative and mimetic narrative. **Historical narrative** as understood in the modern sense endeavors to present an account of real historical events, persons, and places in their chronological order. Some events, persons, and places will be excluded, but those that are included must be presented in their proper sequence. The historian's ideological bias may dictate what information is included in the narrative and the amount of attention an event may warrant. Nonetheless, the modern understanding of historical narrative is characterized by a sense of "history for history's sake." It is not the modern historian's primary function to present the audience with a universal truth. Historians generally do not utilize formal narrative strategies such as plot, characterization, setting, conflict, complication, and resolution or artistic forms (e.g., personification, metaphor, allegory, archetypes). Modern historical narrative is expected to be as scientifically objective as possible. Its language is intended to be denotative with the historian avoiding the connotative language characteristic of mimetic narrative. Generally, historical narrative seeks to present things as they were, unlike mimetic narrative that seeks to present things as they might possibly be.

Based upon the recognition that art is more similar to philosophy because it addresses universals (i.e., art illuminates some universal human condition), Aristotle claims that art (including literary art) is superior to history. The same (at least in Aristotle's mind) cannot be said of history, for it deals with what happened, as opposed to what happens.

Mimetic narrative is story. It may be historical without being history in the modern sense. I call it "storicized" history. Mimetic narrative transcends history, for what is found in narrative is a redescription of reality, the creation of a literary world or a textual world that reaches beyond itself and beyond its historical milieu. Through a definable and well-structured artistry, it offers to guide the reader into the discovery of some universal truth. The book of Judges is an example. Anyone who reads Judges more than once recognizes a recurring pattern: Israel sins against Yahweh; Yahweh causes Israel to suffer oppression at the hands of one of its enemies; Israel cries out to God for help; God raises up an individual to deliver and judge Israel; and Israel enjoys a time of peace. The cycle then begins all over again. All the action in Judges revolves around this structural paradigm. The reader soon recognizes that Yahweh chooses the most unlikely candidates to be judges: Ehud is a southpaw, which in Hebrew culture was considered abnormal; Deborah is a woman; Barak is a procrastinator; Gideon is the youngest son of a poor farmer; Jephthah is a social outcast and a bandit; and Samson is what Kenneth Gros Louis calls the "county fair strong man." Yet through these most unlikely candidates (or perhaps in spite of them) Yahweh constantly demonstrates his patient love towards Israel. The author has actually taken independent, autonomous stories from Israel's past, paradigmatically woven them together, and successfully communicated a truth through the whole. Some scholars argue that by weaving these separate narratives together in this fashion, the author demonstrates the ineffectiveness of a theocracy and thus intends the work to serve as an apology for the monarchy. Whatever the case, the author has taken events from the life of Israel (i.e., events perceived to be from the real historical world of the nation), arranged them according to a particular order predetermined by a particular political or theological interest, and thereby created a world within the text. This is history at the service of mimesis, and it demonstrates the difference between historical and mimetic narrative. The author of a narrative (or of history for that matter) cannot include every minute detail of the real world in the narrative. Authors must be selective, including some things and excluding others. When we consider that the material included is itself represented in terms of generic conventions, the result is reality reshaped, tailored, redefined from the author's perspective.

The **real world** is the actual world in which the author lived when the text was written. The real world refers to the author's world with its patterns of behavior, social institutions, and ideological, economic, religious, and ethical structures. The **story world** is the world found only in the text. Framed by the beginning and ending of the text, it is a creation of an author who selects and arranges events in a complex structure. The arrangement of events and the characterization of individuals within the story do not correlate exactly with historical chronology or with the real world persona. Events, characters, and places in the story world acquire their meaning and significance from the world created by the author. For example, in the Gospel of Matthew Jesus is defined and given significance only within the world of Matthew's text. The meaning of what Jesus says or does in Matthew must be ascertained from the story world of Matthew, not by recourse to the author's real world. The story world is not a mirror of the real world with the author as the quicksilver behind the glass. Through artistic forms and strategies, the story world assumes its own reality, a reality that is capable of communicating its own truths.

This is something similar to a painter capturing only a moment of a landscape in his or her memory and then subsequently presenting that moment on canvas through the mediums of line, perspective, vanishing point, color, tone, geometrical shapes, and so on. The painting is not the material reality of the landscape, but an interpretation. The painting assumes its own identity. Where should we look for the meaning of the painting? Is it in the natural landscape which served as the pre-image? Does it lie in the viewer of the painting? Or is it in the painting itself? Actually the answer is "in all three." If we could view the landscape or some portion of it again, this might shed light upon the painter's interpretation, but can we ever recapture the identical landscape, the same cloud patterns, air currents, and singing birds? Obviously not! Consequently, to some extent the painting becomes its own source of meaning. At least the potential meaning is in the painting waiting for a viewer to actualize it. A similar case exists for narrative. An author structures a world in the text (story world). This story world is not synonymous with the real worlds of the author or reader. Meaning resides in the mimetic relationship between the story world and the real world. What is said *in* the story world is different from what is said *through* the story world. An example from Judges again illustrates this difference. What is said *in* the story of Jephthah is quite distinct from what is said *through* it. In this narrative, we find (among other things) that Jephthah, whose mother was a prostitute, has been exiled from his people. But because of Jephthah's reputation as an able fighter, the men of Gilead seek his help when they find themselves in trouble with the Ammonites. Jephthah agrees (after some negotiation) to become Gilead's leader. After some interesting diplomacy, Jephthah requests help from Yahweh, vowing to sacrifice the first thing which comes out the door of his house if Yahweh will ensure victory. As we might expect, Jephthah is victorious, but upon his return home, the first to greet him from the door of his house is his daughter. Jephthah does fulfill his vow after his daughter bewails her virginity for two months. Basically, this is what is said *in* the story. But as interesting as the narrative is, what lesson or moral is the author offering the reader *through* the story? What application does the author expect from the reader? What truth about God, life, or humanity does the author suggest by the narrative? Perhaps in combination with the story of Samson (who also has taken a vow but broken it) our author is offering some instruction on the appropriateness or inappropriateness of making vows. As this example shows, meaning resides in the extra-textual reality to which the story world points.

One of the most insightful descriptions of the basic concepts in **narratology** is that by Gérard Genette in his work *Narrative Discourse*. Genette names three main elements in narrative: *récit*, which is the actual order of events presented in the text (the plot); *histoire*, which is the sequence in which those events actually occurred as ascertained from the text (the story); and *narration*, which is the actual act of narrating itself. This means that the chronology of the actual events within the story may differ from the sequence of their presentation. One need think only of the effective use of flashback to see the distinction. For example, in Jonah 4:2a we discover that Jonah prayed to Yahweh, "O LORD! Is not this what I said while I was still in my own country? That is why I fled to Tarshish at the beginning." Here is the narration of an event which occurred *after* God's initial commission in 1:2 and *before* Jonah's flight in 1:3. It is an account of a conversation which Jonah had with Yahweh several episodes back. In other words, the *récit* does not correspond to the *histoire*. Another example is the story of Micaiah and Ahab in 1 Kings 22. After Micaiah is led before Ahab and Jehoshaphat, he relates an event (a vision) which had occurred prior to this meeting: "I saw the LORD sitting on his throne, with all the host of heaven standing beside him to the right and to the left of him. And the LORD said, 'Who will entice Ahab, so that he may go up and fall at Ramoth-gilead?' " (1 Kings 22:19–20).

Again *récit* and *histoire* differ. Genette also offers five analytical categories for narrative. (1) *Order* describes the time-order of the story. It may operate by anticipation, flashback, or discordances between story and plot. The two examples above illustrate flashback. Anticipation is also found in the Micaiah episode. Micaiah, in flashback, anticipates in 1 Kings 22:17 (the defeat of Ahab's army and Ahab's death) that which actually happens in 22:29–38. Here we have a combination of flashback and anticipation. (2) *Duration* concerns the way in which the narrative handles episodes. Episodes may be expanded, summarized, or elided. In Genesis 37:36, the author describes Joseph being sold into slavery: "Meanwhile the Midianites had sold him in Egypt to Potiphar, one of Pharaoh's officials, the captain of the guard." This is summary; the author offers no details of the transaction. Two summaries of episodes flank an expanded episode in Genesis 39:10–23. Preceding the seduction episode (vv. 11–20), we read: "and although she [Potiphar's wife] spoke to Joseph *day after day,* he would not consent to lie beside her or to be with her" (v. 10); and after the seduction episode, the author presents an equally brief account of Joseph's tenure in prison: "he remained there in prison. But the LORD was with Joseph and showed him steadfast love; he gave him favor in the sight of the chief jailer" (vv. 20b–21). The way in which God actually blesses Joseph in prison is described in great detail for 63 verses! (3) *Frequency* is concerned with the relationship between an episode and its narration. An event may happen once in the story and be narrated once, happen once and be narrated more than once (that Joseph was sold to the Midianites and taken to Egypt and sold there is told three times [Gen. 37:28; 37:36; and 39:1]); happen more than once and be narrated more than once (two obvious examples are Abraham's attempt to pass Sarah off as his sister [Gen. 12:10–20 and 20:1–17] and the dual account of creation in Genesis 1 and 2); or happen more than once and be narrated only once. (In Jer. 44, the Jews in Egypt tell Jeremiah that they have been burning incense to the "queen of heaven" and that their fathers, kings, and officials in the towns of Judah had been doing so *repeatedly;* yet the practice is narrated only here in the Old Testament.)

Genette's last two categories are *mood* and *voice.* I briefly mention them here because I address these issues at some length in the discussion of characterization, point of view, plot, and setting in Hebrew narrative. (4) *Mood* divides into the sub-categories of distance and perspective. Distance is the relationship between the narration and its own materials. Is the story told or represented, and is it narrated in direct, indirect, or free direct speech? Perspective is what is usually referred to as point of view. The narrator may be elevated above the characters in the story by being privy to more knowledge than the characters, the characters may be elevated above the narrator in a similar fashion, or the narrator and character(s) may be even-handed in their knowledge. The narrator may be "omniscient" outside the action of the story or within the action of the story. One example of the former is the narrator of the book of Job, while an instance of the latter is the narrator in Joseph Conrad's *Heart of Darkness*, where the narrator is actually a character in the action. Narration may proceed from the author's perspective, from a character's perspective, or from the perspective of various characters. (5) *Voice* concerns the act of narrating itself. What kind of narrator and narratee are implied? A narrator may recount the action as it actually unfolds, before it happens, or after the fact. The narrator may be absent from the narrative, inside the narrative in the first person, the principal character in the narrative, or a combination of these. For example, in Ford Madox Ford's *The Good Soldier*, the narrator is recounting a series of experiences of which he himself was one of the principal characters, while at the same time attempting to make sense of the events in the present. The distinctions in Genette's work highlight the difference between narration (the act of narrating) and narrative (what is actually narrated).[1]

On the one hand, Hebrew narrative is similar in many respects to narrative in general. On the other hand, it has some interesting and unique differences. Meir Sternberg has offered a compelling argument for one of the key characteristics of Hebrew narrative.[2] According to Sternberg the author of Hebrew narrative translated certain doctrinal views into literary correlatives. The doctrinal view of the omniscience of God is reflected in the standard literary use of the omniscient narrator (although there are exceptions, e.g., the books of Ezra and Nehemiah). Just as Yahweh knows all truth, but does not reveal its totality to humanity, so the omniscient narrator does not make the reader privy to all the truth of a narrative world. Human beings stumble and grope their way through life, learning through trial and error, reflection, and retrial. In a similar fashion, readers make their way through a text. The narrator tells the truth, but not the whole truth. As a result, "gaps of indeterminacy" (places in the narrative where some pertinent information is missing) are created in the text which the reader must fill. As the reader moves through the text, information is encountered which generates inferences. As the reading progresses, however, the text offers additional information (e.g., information concerning time, motive, cause, effect)

---

[1] Gérard Genette, *Narrative Discourse* (Oxford: Oxford University, 1980).

[2] Meir Sternberg, *The Poetics of Biblical Narrative* (Bloomington: Indiana University, 1985), pp. 157–58.

which requires the reader to reread the text, adjusting the previous inferences. Another product of these intentional gaps is the raising of "narrative interest": suspense, surprise, and curiosity. This idea is discussed in more detail in unit III. Other translations of doctrinal views into literary correlates include:

> the doctrine of free will into complex characterization, . . . human restrictedness into studies in ambiguity, omnipotence and providence into well-made plots, control of history into cyclical and analogical design imposed upon recalcitrant matter, and the demand to infer from past to present into ordeal by interpretation.[3]

With this background to narratology, we are in a better position to examine the poetics of Hebrew narrative. We proceed by discussing in turn the concepts of plot, setting, characterization, point of view, and repetition.

Plot

Aristotle describes **plot** as action having a beginning, middle, and end. Some type of conflict occurs at the beginning of the narrative, is complicated in various ways through the middle, and is finally resolved at the end. The basic plot, therefore has a three-part structure: conflict, complication, and resolution (*dénouement*). In the Joseph narrative, the conflict arises between Joseph and his brothers when the brothers perceive that their father Jacob loves Joseph more than them (Gen. 37:1-4). This conflict is complicated by Joseph's dreams, by the brothers' plot to kill Joseph, and by the brothers' selling Joseph into slavery. There is no resolution until Joseph's final revelation to his brothers in Egypt. The Joseph narrative, however, actually has multiple conflicts (Joseph/brothers, Jacob/sons, Joseph's dreams/the fulfillment of the dreams). Each of these conflicts is complicated throughout the story and is finally resolved at the end.

In the tragic plot, the protagonist makes a miscalculation due to a bit of missing information. At some point in the action, the protagonist discovers this missing bit of information, a discovery which propels the protagonist into a state of misery. Again, the Jephthah story offers a prime example. Jephthah promises to offer as a burnt offering to God the first thing coming out of his house if God will grant victory. Due to the layout of the common home (it would have a type of fenced yard

---

[3] Ibid., p. 157.

around it where the animals were kept) Jephthah assumed that he would be greeted by livestock. It was a perfectly logical assumption. Little did he know that he would be greeted by his only child, a daughter. The discovery of the missing information propels Jephthah from a state of happiness to a state of misery ("When he saw her, he tore his clothes, and said, 'Alas, my daughter! You have brought me very low; you have become the cause of great trouble to me. For I have opened my mouth to the LORD, and I cannot take back my vow' " [Judg. 11:35]).

Setting

Setting is also a vital aspect of narrative. The setting provides the physical background for the action in the narrative. The setting of an event is usually crucial for interpreting a narrative unit. For example, David's encounter with Bathsheba takes place in the capital city of Jerusalem, a place where the king would not normally be during time of war. The Matthean account of Jesus' discourse on the law takes place on a mountain. This setting is not incidental when the reader discovers that Matthew is identifying Jesus (who reinterprets Torah) with Moses who received Torah on Mount Sinai.

Biblical narrative usually exhibits a special relationship between the action, the characters involved in the action, and the setting.[4] The setting in Hebrew narrative serves an aesthetic purpose, creating a distinct atmosphere. The setting may accomplish this through symbolic significance, such as the pit and prison scenes in the Joseph narrative and the pastoral scene in Genesis 18:1-8. In this latter example, Abraham spots three travelers while he is sitting at the entrance of his tent in the heat of the day. In accordance with proper Mediterranean hospitality, Abraham goes out of his way to persuade the strangers to visit: "Do not pass by your servant. Let a *little* water be brought, and wash your feet, and rest yourselves under the *tree*. Let me bring a little bread, that you may refresh yourselves, and after that you may pass on" (Gen. 18:3-5). At this point, Abraham seems to behave quite nonchalantly. But his actions when he leaves to get a *little* water and some food testify to the contrary: "And Abraham *hastened* into the tent to Sarah, and said, 'Make ready quickly *three measures* of choice flour, *knead* it, and *make* cakes.' Abraham ran to the herd, and took a calf, *tender and good*, and gave it to the servant, who *hastened* to prepare it. Then he took *curds and*

---

[4] See Ryken, *Words of Delight*, pp. 54-62.

milk and the calf that he had *prepared, and set it before them;* and he stood by them *under the tree* while they ate." Two features about this setting are important: its pastoral tranquility (trees, shade, tent) and its accompanying hospitality. Abraham's hospitality complements the pastoral tranquility. The result of the action is a blessing pronounced upon Sarah.

This example illustrates a conflict in Hebrew narrative—the conflict between the historical, aesthetic, and ideological purposes.[5] In some instances of setting, the historical purpose predominates and gives a verity and vividness to the narrative. For example, notice the physical precision of Genesis 12:4–9:

> So Abram went, as the LORD had told him; and Lot went with him. Abram was *seventy-five* years old when he departed from Haran. . . . When they had come to the land of Canaan, Abram passed through the land to the *place at Shechem, to the oak of Moreh.* . . . From there he moved on to *the hill country on the east of Bethel,* and pitched his tent, with Bethel on the west and Ai on the east; and there he built an altar to the LORD and invoked the name of the LORD. And Abram journeyed on by stages toward *the Negeb.*

At other times the ideological purpose will predominate in settings, like in the pastoral scene above. The aesthetic purpose can also be seen in this pastoral setting, in the contrast between the country and city life. In reality, however, these three purposes usually occur in combination within an elaborate interconnectedness resulting in an enjoyable reading experience.

Characterization

Adele Berlin identifies three kinds of characters in Hebrew narrative: Full-fledged, the type, and the agent.[6] The *full-fledged* character is multi-dimensional and complex, manifesting a range of character traits. This character confronts the reader with psychological, emotional, and spiritual complexities. David's wife Michal is a full-fledged character. The author goes to great lengths in presenting her as a woman with her own emotions and opinions.

A single character trait distinguishes the *type.* Such a type is Laban. From the first time we meet him in Genesis 24, we are struck by his distinguishing trait of materialism. In Genesis 24:28–31, the author hints at this trait:

---

[5] See Sternberg, *Poetics of Biblical Narrative,* pp. 44–56.

[6] Adele Berlin, *Poetics and Interpretation of Biblical Narrative* (Sheffield: Almond, 1983), pp. 23–32.

Then the girl ran and told her mother's household about these things. Rebekah had a brother whose name was Laban; and Laban ran out to the man, to the spring. *As soon as he had seen the nose-ring, and the bracelets on his sister's arms, and when he heard the words of his sister Rebekah, "Thus the man spoke to me,"* he went to the man; and there he was, standing by the camels at the spring. He said, "Come in, O blessed of the LORD. Why do you stand outside when I have prepared the house and a place for the camels?"

Laban's materialistic motivation is sustained in 24:47–51 and in his dealings with Jacob in Genesis 29.

The *agent* type of character is nothing more than a functionary which the author uses to fill out the narrative. This character is usually not characterized at all, but simply serves the purpose of providing the necessary characters for a story. Depending upon the narrative and the purpose of the narrative, however, a single character's role may change. A full-fledged character may thus become an agent or a type in another narrative. What are the techniques of **characterization** in Hebrew narrative? To this repertoire of poetics we now turn.

Description. Hebrew narrative is rather sparse in its descriptive details. Some descriptive details are present, but only in the service of the plot. For example, the information that Eglon in Judges is fat leads the reader to see Eglon as the fatted calf for the slaughter. The uprightness and blamelessness of Job heightens Job's tragic loss. Bathsheba's beauty partly anticipates David's actions. But beyond general descriptions (e.g., the ruddiness of David, the height of Saul, the handsomeness of Absalom, the beauty of Sarah), Hebrew narrative gives precious little specific detail. Physical concretization of characters is simply not present in Hebrew narrative. The reader must gain insight into character differently than one would in most modern novels. It seems, therefore, that Hebrew narrative is less interested in presenting the appearance of a character than in guiding the reader into a discovery of what kind of a person the character is. This observation leads us to look at the other methods in the author's repertoire.

Interiorization. When the narrator supplies the reader with windows into the mental or emotional state of a character, the reader views the action (or a portion of it) through the eyes of the character. The author effects this interiorization in two ways. First, the *narrator* may comment on a character's thought or opinion. We become privy to the thoughts of a character, but the thoughts are expressed in the words of the narrator: "So Noah *knew* that the waters had subsided from the earth" (Gen. 8:11b). Even God himself is not exempt: "God heard their groaning, and God *remembered* his covenant with Abraham, Isaac, and Jacob. God looked upon the Israelites, and God *took notice* of them" (Exod. 2:24, 25). This type of interiorization is called external interiorization. Second, the narrator makes extensive use of direct quotes of a character's thoughts. This is **interior monologue:** "Then Moses was afraid and thought, 'Surely the thing is known' " (Exod. 2:14); "Then Moses said, 'I must turn aside and look at this great sight, and see why the bush is not burned up' " (Exod. 3:3). These windows into a character's thoughts enable the reader to make judgments about a character's emotion and motivation. These judgments in turn help the reader fill out the character, to know what *kind* of a person he or she might be.

Direct Dialogue.   Direct speech is the preferred method in Hebrew narrative for sustaining the action within the plot. **Direct dialogue** conveys the internal psychological and ideological dimensions of a character and is much more dramatic than exterior narration. The direct speech of Samson in Judges 14–16 illustrates the point. After returning from Timnah, Samson says to his parents, "I saw a Philistine woman at Timnah; now *get her for me* as my wife" (14:2). Although he is discouraged from taking a foreign wife, Samson replies, "*Get her for me,* because she pleases me" (14:3b). The sharp, demanding tone of this speech reveals Samson's character, a character marked by a sense of immediate, thoughtless gratification. Even in his remarks to God, Samson exhibits this same tone of ingratitude: "By then he was very thirsty, and he called on the LORD, saying, 'You have granted this great victory by the hand of your servant. Am I now to die of thirst, and fall into the hands of the uncircumcised?' " (Judg. 15:18). Gratification and revenge mark Samson's character as seen through his direct speeches. Nothing changes at his death, for even here revenge is his motivation: "Lord GOD, remember me and strengthen me only this once, O God, so that with this one act of *revenge I may pay back the Philistines for my two eyes*" (Judg. 16:28).

Actions.   While in Hebrew narrative direct speech and actions are usually combined, actions can be narrated without speech. These speechless accounts of actions highlight character. They tend to serve as unannounced commentary on a character's speech. We already know from Laban's past record that he is adept at deception. Therefore, when we hear Jacob's proposal to Laban in Genesis 30:30–33 and Laban's response in 30:34, we suspect that we are in store for yet another ruse:

> For you had little before I came, and it has increased abundantly; and the LORD has blessed you wherever I turned. But now when shall I provide for my own household also?" He said, "What shall I give you?" Jacob said,

"You shall not give me anything; if you will do this for me, I will again feed your flock and keep it: let me pass through all your flock today, removing from it every speckled and spotted sheep and every black lamb, and the spotted and speckled among the goats; and such shall be my wages. So my honesty will answer for me later, when you come to look into my wages with you. Every one that is not speckled and spotted among the goats and black among the lambs, if found with me, shall be counted stolen." Laban said, "Good! Let it be as you have said."

Sure enough, Laban does not disappoint us. His action is exactly opposite of his speech:

But that day Laban removed the male goats that were striped and spotted, and all the female goats that were speckled and spotted, every one that had white on it, and every lamb that was black, and put them in charge of his sons; and he set a distance of three days' journey between himself and Jacob, while Jacob was pasturing the rest of Laban's flock (Gen. 30:35–36).

But we also know that Jacob will not take a back seat to Laban when it comes to ingenuity and originality in trickery. So we are not entirely surprised at Jacob's response to Laban's ploy, but we are at least entertained by his creativity!

Then Jacob took fresh rods of poplar and almond and plane, and peeled white streaks in them, exposing the white of the rods. He set the rods that he had peeled in front of the flocks in the troughs, that is, the watering places, where the flocks came to drink. And since they bred when they came to drink, the flocks bred in front of the rods, and so the flocks produced young that were striped, speckled, and spotted. Jacob separated the lambs, and set the faces of the flocks toward the striped and the completely black animals in the flock of Laban; and he put his own droves apart, and did not put them with Laban's flock. Whenever the stronger of the flock were breeding, Jacob laid the rods in the troughs before the eyes of the flock, that they might breed among the rods, but for the feebler of the flock he did not lay them there; so the feebler were Laban's, and the stronger Jacob's. Thus the man grew exceedingly rich, and had large flocks, and male and female slaves, and camels and donkeys (Gen. 30:37–43).

Contrast. By placing characters in juxtaposition, an author highlights character traits, especially those traits which appear to be incongruent to a character's social status. For instance, Adele Berlin describes how the author in 1 Samuel 18–20 successfully, yet subtly, contrasts character traits in Michal and Jonathan.[7] The reader is struck with the incongruity. Jonathan displays characteristics usually identified as

---

[7] Ibid., pp. 24–25.

feminine, while Michal exhibits definite masculine traits. The relationship between Michal and David is marked by purely pragmatic considerations and "the feelings of love and tenderness that David might have been expected to have for Michal are all reserved for Jonathan."[8]

Even at their final parting, David cries, "I am distressed for you, my brother Jonathan; greatly beloved were you to me; your love to me was wonderful, passing the love of women" (2 Sam. 1:26). I am not suggesting any sexual orientation here, but only that this contrast underscores elements in the personalities of Michal and Jonathan (and certainly David also). Michal is consistently portrayed as physical and aggressive, while Jonathan is usually depicted as accomplishing his deeds through carefully placed words. Also, Michal never gave birth to a child, the ultimate Hebraic sign of femininity.[9]

The story of Deborah and Barak is another example of character contrast (Judg. 4–5). Deborah is always decisive. She sizes up a situation and then without delay acts. She says to Barak, "The LORD, the God of Israel, commands you: 'Go, take position at Mount Tabor, bringing ten thousand from the tribe of Naphtali and the tribe of Zebulun'" (Judg. 4:6). But Barak hesitates: "If you will go with me, I will go; but if you will not go with me, I will not go" (Judg. 4:8). At once Deborah recognizes his hesitation, rebukes him, and then goes with him. Later, once again Barak does not move until Deborah commands him: "Up! For this is the day on which the LORD has given Sisera into your hand. The LORD is indeed going out before you" (Judg. 4:14a). Without a doubt, each character's personality is heightened by contrast.

Characterization by contrast is a creative and intriguing literary device, highly developed in Hebrew narrative. The reader is encouraged to watch for this device and to allow it to enhance the reading of Hebrew narrative.

Point of View

Point of view or perspective is actually inseparable from characterization. But because of its complexity and centrality in Hebrew narrative, we need to examine it independently of characterization.

Like narrative in general, Hebrew narrative discloses only what the author desires. The author can elaborate or condense. Also, like most

---

[8] Ibid., p. 25.
[9] Ibid.

narrative, Hebrew narrative employs several voices or vehicles for narration; the author may present information through the voice and eyes of the omniscient narrator or any one of several characters within the narrative. The consequence of multiple narrative voices is multiple points of view. The multi-perspectival quality of Hebrew narrative affords a depth and fullness, for the narrative is presented from alternating perspectives, shifting from narrator to character to character.

The David and Bathsheba passage in 2 Samuel 11 is a case in point. The passage begins with background information by the narrator: "In the spring of the year, the time when kings go out to battle, David sent Joab with his officers and all Israel with him. . . . But David remained at Jerusalem" (v. 1). In the next verse, readers are given the opportunity to see what David sees: "he saw from the roof a woman bathing; the woman was very beautiful." The third perspective is that of a messenger: "This is Bathsheba daughter of Eliam, the wife of Uriah the Hittite" (v. 3). In the remaining verses of the chapter, the author shuttles the reader from one character's perspective to another's—David's, Uriah's, Joab's, the messenger's, and Bathsheba's. The author even gives us Joab's perception of David's perspective. The last statement in the passage ("But the thing that David had done displeased the LORD" [v. 27b]) is the voice of the narrator. This statement is an example of what is called "breaking frame." The narrator turns away from the action and directly addresses the audience. In so doing, the narrator offers an evaluation of the story. Thus, the narrator gives the reader his or her conceptual point of view.

This shift from one point of view to another may result not only in different perspectives, but also in disparate ones. The result may be either irony or ambiguity. We have already seen in the story of Job that the reader may possess knowledge that the characters do not. We as readers know why Job is suffering, while the characters have other perspectives. The result is irony. The reader finds two disparate perspectives in the Joseph narrative. When Joseph's brothers return to their father with the blood-drenched coat, Jacob cries out, "Joseph is without doubt torn to pieces." But the readers and the brothers know differently. There is also an ambiguity in this narrative centering around Reuben. In chapter 37, as the narrator shuttles back and forth between the perspectives of the brothers in general and Reuben in particular, some unresolved questions arise. We are told in verses 21–22 that Reuben suggests that the brothers throw Joseph into a cistern with the clear intention of later returning to rescue him: "Reuben said (this to) rescue him out of their hand *and restore him to his father*" (v. 22). The "brothers" later pull

Joseph from the cistern and sell him to the Ishmaelites (vv. 25–28). But then we discover that Reuben must not have been with the brothers when this occurred: "When Reuben returned to the pit and saw that Joseph was not in the pit, he tore his clothes. He returned to his brothers, and said, 'The boy is gone; and I, where can I turn?'" (vv. 29–30). Where was Reuben when the brothers sold Joseph? Do the brothers tell him of their actions? We do not know. The narrator has left us with some unanswered questions. When later we discover that Joseph had pleaded with his brothers for his life (42:21), Reuben replies, "Did I not tell you not to wrong the boy? But you would not listen" (v. 22). Is this Reuben's first knowledge of their crime? The narrator sustains this ambiguity which centers around Reuben.

Generally in Hebrew narrative, the reader and characters are even-handed in their knowledge. There are also instances, however, when the reader is privy to knowledge not available to characters. Such is the case with the story of Jacob mentioned above. This type of perspective is called *reader-elevated*. At the same time, although rare in Hebrew narrative, there are instances where a character may know more than the reader. An instance of this is in the Joseph narrative where the reader finds out about Joseph's reaction to being thrown into the cistern, a knowledge which the brothers had all along. This type of perspective is called *character-elevated*.

Style

Many scholars feel that if the stylistic uniqueness of Hebrew narrative could be captured in one word, it would be repetition. This is true for both the number of occurrences of repetition and the number of different types of repetitive devices. The majority of the sub-genres of Hebrew narrative are actually no more than forms of repetition. This proclivity toward repetition takes on vital importance for literary considerations in light of the Hebrew Bible's further tendency to suspend or limit description. The different types of repetition are deliberate narrative techniques. An ability to recognize these sub-genres of repetition enhances our understanding and appreciation of the art of Hebrew narrative. Below is a brief discussion of some of the more common repetitive sub-genres.

Leitwort.   Sometimes an author may exploit the range of meaning of a word-root by repeating different forms of the root within a pericope or across several units. This technique, called **Leitwort,** may provide thematic cohesion or thematic emphasis within a unit of Scripture. Actually the individual context of a passage dictates the function of a *Leitwort*. An example is the twenty-one repetitions of the root for "to bless" in Genesis 27:1–45. The first eleven chapters of Genesis contain a theme that is traceable throughout the remainder of the Hebrew Bible. This theme is the separation between humankind and God. This theme of separation is reflected at the level of the family, especially in the patriarchal (Gen. 12–50) and monarchial (1 and 2 Sam., 1 and 2 Kings) narratives. The Hebrews, like other social groups, established social conventions to safeguard family cohesion. One of these conventions was the father's practice of passing on to the eldest son the family inheritance and paternal blessing. When Jacob steals Esau's blessing in the Genesis 27 story, the established social convention has the opposite effect. Instead of safeguarding the family cohesion, it is actually the source of family division and separation. Through the repetitive use of the word "to bless," the author draws the reader's attention to the convention and its reverse effect.

Key Phrases or Sentences. Hebrew authors repeat certain phrases or sentences in order to establish thematic unity in larger sections. These repeated phrases or sentences have a formulaic air about them. An example is the sentence "In those days there was no king in Israel; all the people did what was right in their own eyes." This occurs in full or part in Judges 17:6; 18:1; 19:1; and 21:25. The author emphasizes the theme of social anarchy by this repetition.

Motif. A motif is the recurrence within a narrative of some object, image, or action. Examples are stones in the Jacob narrative, water in the Moses story, or fire in the Samson story. Motifs may give thematic unity or coherence to a narrative, or they may carry symbolic significance (e.g., the stones in the Jacob story symbolize the hard realities of life with which he constantly wrestles, as opposed to the dream world of his son Joseph).

Themes. Certain themes occur with regularity in Hebrew narrative. Three such themes are the barren wife (Gen. 11; 16; 20; 25; and 30), obedience and rebellion in the wilderness stories, and the reversal of primogeniture (Gen. 21; 25; 27; 37; 42; and 48). Themes tend to organize meaning according to patterns that the author invites the reader to discover. These themes also indicate elements of the author's world-view. For example, by repeatedly using the reversal of the rule of primogeniture, an author may be suggesting that God is not bound by human social conventions, but is free to circumvent these when the occasion calls for it.

Repetition of Sequences. This is a repetition of an activity, usually three times or three times plus a fourth with an intensification from one to the next occurrence. Examples include the three actions of Saul's messengers, Balaam's three failures to give directions to the ass, and the catastrophes in Job's story.

Chiastic Patterns. Words or events inversely repeated in order to shape episodes, speeches, or entire cycles of stories are termed **chiastic patterns** (chiasm). An example is Numbers 11:11–15:

A First question: Why has God mistreated Moses? ("Why have you treated your servant so badly?")
   B Second question: What has Moses done to deserve an undue *burden*? ("Why have I not found favor in your sight, that you lay the burden of all this people on me?")
      C Third question: Why should Moses *carry* these people as a nurse carries a baby? ("Did I give birth to them, that you should say to me, 'Carry them in your bosom, as a nurse carries a suckling child,' to the land that you promised on oath to their ancestors?")
         D Fourth question: How can Moses supply food? ("Where am I to get meat to give to all this people?")
         D′ Response to fourth question: ("For they come weeping to me and say, 'Give us meat to eat!' ")
      C′ Response to third question: ("I am not able to *carry* all this people alone")
   B′ Response to second question: ("for they are too heavy for me")
A′ Response to first question: ("If this is the way you are going to *treat* me, put me to death at once")

Type scenes. This literary device is similar to themes, but differs slightly. George W. Savran defines **type scenes** as the repetition of "conventions of speech and behavior in analogous situations, such as betrothal scenes (Genesis 24:10–61; 29:1–20; Exodus 2:15b–21) and annunciation stories (Genesis 18:1–15; Judges 13; 1 Samuel 1; 2 Kings 4:8–37)."[10] To this list of type scenes, one might add the trial in the wilderness, revival of the dead child, and the hero's journey from his homeland to a foreign country.

Each of these type scenes has its own basic literary structure. The betrothal and annunciation scenes are two helpful illustrations. In the

---

[10] George W. Savran, *Telling and Retelling: Quotation in Biblical Narrative* (Bloomington: Indiana University, 1988), p. 7.

betrothal type scene, a prospective bridegroom or his representative journeys to a foreign land where he encounters a young woman or women at a well. Either the man or the woman draws water from the well. After this initial meeting, the woman (or women) hurries home to share the news of the stranger's arrival. A betrothal is then finalized, often after the stranger has shared a meal with the woman's family. This is the pattern followed in the servant's search for a wife for Isaac in Genesis 24.

The betrothal scene—all others as well—may be innovatively re-fashioned depending upon the author's purpose. For instance, in the Jacob narrative, the hero first meets shepherds at the well (Gen. 29:1–8), and only later does Rachel approach the well (Gen. 29:9). Not only does Jacob draw the water, but he must remove an obstacle (a stone) from the mouth of the well. This obstacle adumbrates the obstacle (fourteen years of labor) which he must overcome before he is given Rachel as his wife.

In the Samson story, the hero journeys to a foreign country, leading the reader to expect a betrothal scene. But neither drawing of water from a well nor a meal of hospitality follows. This foreshadows Samson's characteristic penchant for disregarding accepted protocol.

An interesting New Testament application of this type scene occurs in the Gospel of John (4:1–42). Jesus travels from Judea to Sychar in Samaria. While Jesus is resting at Jacob's well, a woman comes to draw water. A conversation ensues and the woman subsequently runs into the town and announces what the stranger at the well has told her. This prompts the whole town's exodus to the well, which finally results in the conversion of many of the Samaritans. Because of John the Baptist's remark in 3:29 ("He who has the bride is the bridegroom. The friend of the bridegroom, who stands and hears him, rejoices greatly at the bridegroom's voice"), the reader must inquire about John's purpose in using this type scene, especially since there is no mention of a hospitality meal.

The annunciation type scene also follows a well-established pattern. Usually a barren or aged woman receives a promise (normally from a messenger of Yahweh or a prophet) of a miraculous birth of a child. Ordinarily this child of miraculous birth is to be used by God in some significant way. Sometimes the story is complicated by the presence of another wife or concubine who is quite fertile. The births of Isaac, Samson, Samuel, the Shunammite woman's son, and Jesus are examples. As stated earlier, each type scene may have its own innovative refashioning. The scene involving the Shunammite woman in 2 Kings 4 is

complicated by the death of the child of miraculous birth. To
further complicate and add suspense to the scene, the author has Elisha
attempt to revive the child four times before he is successful. By report-
ing an event through a well-known sub-genre, an author immediately
attracts the interest of the readers. Readers familiar with the sub-genre
expect standard elements within it. When the author modifies these
elements or simply omits them, the readers are supposed to ask why.

Quotations. The Old Testament authors show a distinct fondness
for direct speech instead of third-person "telling." Through this technique the author establishes attitudes, motivations, and personalities;
the writer thus forms a character by using the character's own words
instead of simply describing the character in detail. Within this technique of direct speech, the author records instances where one character
quotes another. A quote is said to be verifiable if the original speech is
retrievable. In this case the original speech and its subsequent quotation
can be compared. If the original speech is not available, then the
quotation is unverifiable. When the reader is able to verify a quotation,
some variations on the original may be observed: abbreviating, expand-
ing, or paraphrasing. The differences between the original and the quote
establish a character's motive or personality. An insightful illustration of
this is found in Genesis 42. Verses 18–20 contain Joseph's ultimatum to
his brothers:

> Do this and you will live, for I fear God: if you are honest men, let one of
> your brothers stay here where you are imprisoned. The rest of you shall
> go and carry grain for the famine of your households, and bring your
> youngest brother to me. Thus your words will be verified, and you shall
> not die.

When the brothers report this to Jacob, the message changes:

> By this I shall know that you are honest men: leave one of your brothers
> with me, take grain for the famine of your households, and go your way.
> Bring your youngest brother to me, and I shall know that you are not spies
> but honest men. Then I will release your brother to you, and you may
> trade in the land (vv. 33–34).

The quotation of Joseph's speech is significantly different in several ways
from its original. First, the brothers twice refer to their being honest
men. Second, Joseph does not promise that he will give the brother
back, but only that they will not die. Third, the brothers' addition of
"then I will release your brother to you" is ambiguous; which brother do
they want Jacob to assume is to be returned; the hostage or their

youngest brother? Or does the reader know that "the brother" is none other than Joseph himself? Either this is a ploy by the brothers to soften the effect on Jacob or another attempt to deceive him. Judging from their behavior after they return to Egypt, the former is more likely the case. And last, the brothers put yet another promise in the mouth of Joseph—the promise that they will be allowed to move freely about the land. This misquote by the brothers reveals something about their character. They reformulate Joseph's ultimatum in a more positive light for the benefit of their aging father. This reformulation is additional evidence for the reader (not Joseph, since he is out of the picture here) that the brothers have indeed changed in their attitudes concerning their father.

It is interesting that when Yahweh himself quotes someone, each instance is a verbatim repetition of the verifiable original. This circumstance is determined by the author's view of the absolute consistency and truthfulness of Yahweh's character.

Since these repetitive techniques rarely occur in isolation, but are interwoven in a variety of ways, Hebrew narrative is rich in aesthetic quality. Plausible interpretations are virtually unobtainable if the interpreter is unwilling or unable to give appropriate attention to the details of these literary forms and sub-genres. To plumb the depths of meaning in Hebrew narrative, the reader should be willing to "first gain a better understanding of each of these individual genres in their distinctiveness and interrelationships in the narrative."[11]

Intratextual Dynamics

The reader may be asking at this juncture if there is really a homogeneity of literary practice within such a heterogeneous work as the Hebrew Bible. Can the reader really expect so much commonality or agreement in form within a volume of literary works that span over nine centuries? Yes and no. There is both continuity and discontinuity. There is continuity due to the constant dialogue which later literary compositions hold with earlier ones. This dialogue is present at a variety of levels. First, there is the practice of recasting and reapplying earlier texts to later situations. This is especially true of the prophetic texts. Second, there are numerous instances of one author consciously offering a critique or even a parody of an earlier text or literary type. For example,

---

[11] Ibid.

the author of Ecclesiastes seems to challenge the idea of linear, progressive history found in earlier works like Genesis. This same author also questions the conventional view of wisdom. LaSor states it well:

> In a word, he sought to use traditional tools of wisdom to refute and revise its traditional conclusions. Like Job, he protested the easy generalizations with which his fellow teachers taught their pupils to be successful. They had oversimplified life and its rules so as to mislead and frustrate their followers. Their observations seemed superficial and their counsel thin in a world beset by injustice, toil, and death.[12]

Finally, there is the common practice of **allusion,** where one author (perhaps sometimes unconsciously) frames a story or an episode like one written much earlier. For example, by constructing an analogy between the stories of Ruth and Abraham, the author of Ruth portrays Ruth as a matriarch of the Davidic line. Without going into great detail here, suffice it say that the reader needs only to compare a couple of texts (one concerning Ruth and the other Abraham) to see the beginning of the analogy: Boaz says to Ruth: "All that you have done for your mother-in-law since the death of your husband has been fully told me, and how you *left your father and mother and your native land and came to a people that you did not know before*" (Ruth 2:11). Compare God's word to Abraham: "Go from your country and your kindred and *your father's house to the land that I will show you*" (Gen. 12:1). The regularity of allusions like this is persuasive evidence that the writers were at home in texts written hundreds of years earlier. This is possible because the texts are all part of the same religious tradition, sharing common literary as well as world-view elements.

The "no" part of the answer to the above question derives from the evolutionary nature of the Hebrew Bible. The so-called golden age of Hebrew narrative is pre-exilic. This period includes the books from Genesis through Kings. By the time of the post-exilic period, new patterns of narrative expression emerge. The "classical" period of Hebrew narrative exhibits the narrative structure outlined above. Throughout the post-exilic period, however, there is a range of narrative styles (though still similar in many ways, especially in the use of common sub-genres). For example, the more historical texts of Ezra, Nehemiah, and Chronicles do not employ the omniscient narrator, but personal, first-person accounts. Further, if one moves from a text like Genesis into Jonah or

---

[12] William LaSor, David Hubbard, and Frederic Bush, *Old Testament Survey* (Grand Rapids: Eerdmans, 1982), p. 589.

Esther, the differences are striking. Many of the familiar characteristics of Hebrew narrative are replaced in Jonah and Esther by elements of farce, comedy, and detail. Examples of comic farce include the dimensions of Nineveh in Jonah and the one-year perfumed bath of the virgins in the story of Esther.

Obviously there is a dialectic of a sort in the narrative literature of the Hebrew Bible between the generic structure and the evolution of time. But it is a safe wager to concentrate on the explication of Hebrew narratology. These are texts in which the narrative worlds were formulated by authors with different purposes and perspectives. But they are also texts whose narrative worlds were created in an active, dynamic, and conscious dialogue with earlier texts. So, while there is discontinuity within the corpus of the Hebrew writings, the literary continuity is weighty enough to justify similar narrative analysis of the canon.[13]

As one part of the sacred canon of Christianity, the Hebrew Bible holds for many people a special place in revealed truth. For this reason, many well-meaning Christians wave red flags when descriptive terms such as "story world," "narrative world," "artistic creativity," or "literary archetypes" are mentioned. In more Fundamentalistic circles, there has been a persistent, unconscious misperception in the "correlation of the truth-falsity distinction with the history-fiction distinction."[14] Elements regarded as historically verifiable are understood as truth, and mimetic or imaginative elements as false. The basic problem concerns the confusion between truth and **truth value.** Is it possible for a mimetic text whose content was never intended to be historically accurate to communicate truth? If the answer is *yes*, then the text has truth value. An author communicates truth by creating a mimetic relationship between the world of the text and the real world, even though the state of affairs depicted in the text is not historically verifiable. So a mimetic text asserts some truth by telling a story; it conveys truth about the real world. Authors of mimetic texts generally are not interested in communicating propositional truth, but literary truth. Mimetic narrative is not instructional in the same way as a lecture in history. Hebrew narrative contains history, but it is not historical narrative; it is mimetic narrative. It uses gaps, perspective, characterization, patterned repetition, setting, plot, and a host of other literary devices to communicate its message. All this

---

[13] See Robert Alter and Frank Kermode, "Introduction to the Old Testament," in *Literary Guide to the Bible.*

[14] Walhout, *Responsibility of Hermeneutics,* p. 74.

engages the reader. The reader cannot stand outside the text, but becomes a participant, filling out the work, making connections between textual segments, evaluating new perspectives, and reevaluating previous ones in light of new information. The reader of modern history may remain outside, simply absorbing the facts. But in mimetic narrative, the author challenges (indeed requires) the reader to actualize the meaning latent in the text.

A rather extended example illustrates that claim. After David carries through his plans to have Uriah killed in battle and to marry Bathsheba, Nathan, the prophet, confronts him with a story in 2 Samuel 12:1–4. David is appalled by what he perceives to be a real (historical) life event and proclaims, "As the LORD lives, the man who has done this deserves to die; he shall restore the lamb fourfold, because he did this thing, and because he had no pity" (vv. 5–6). Having taken the story as a description of an actual theft of a lamb, David passes sentence upon the perpetrator of such a despicable act, making reference to the laws of property protection in Exodus 22:1: "When someone steals an ox or a sheep, and slaughters it or sells it, the thief shall pay five oxen for an ox, and *four sheep for a sheep.*" What David does not realize is that he is passing sentence upon himself. What the reader must determine is whether the sentence was carried out or not. Did David pay back with four lambs? The child born to Bathsheba dies on the seventh day after birth. That this child is the firstborn male, coupled with the significance of the seventh day in the sacrificial system (cf. Num. 29), hints that for the narrator the first of the four required payments has been made.

If there is any doubt that the narrator is carefully and creatively presenting the fulfillment of David's announced sentence, one need only read further of the account of Amnon's death. Two years after Amnon's rape of his sister, Absalom has Amnon killed at Baal Hazor, where the *sheepshearers* are gathered: "Then Absalom commanded his servants, 'Watch when Amnon's heart is merry with wine, and when I say to you, "Strike Amnon," then kill him' " (2 Sam. 13:28). The word used here for "strike" (*nakah*) is the same one Nathan uses in reference to Uriah's death. The hiphil form of the verb here and the reference to the sheepshearers have strong lamb and sacrificial overtones. This knowledge should be enough to spur the reader to anticipate the sacrifice of a third son (lamb). This expectancy is fulfilled in the person of Absalom. The author prepares the reader in 14:25–26 with a bit of information which seems to interrupt the flow of the narrative:

Now in all Israel there was no one to be praised so much for his beauty as Absalom; from the sole of his foot to the crown of his head there was no blemish in him. When he cut the hair of his head (for at the end of every year he used to cut it; when it was heavy on him, he cut it), he weighed the hair of his head, two hundred shekels by the king's weight.

The lamb imagery here is unmistakable. Like the sacrificial lamb, Absalom is perfect, without blemish. He also "sheared" his head when his hair became too long (like a lamb would be sheared when the wool became too long) and would weigh the hair. We are then told that the weight of the hair was about 200 shekels (five pounds). So just as a lamb was sheared and its wool weighed for sale, Absalom (the perfect lamb) sheared his hair and then weighed it. If the reader has picked up the pattern thus far, there should now be an expectation that the narrator will shortly offer an account of Absalom's death, and that the death will be clothed in lamb and/or sacrificial imagery. The account takes place in 2 Samuel 18:9–15. A couple of significant references almost leap out at the reader here. First, Absalom's mule runs under the "thick branches" of a large oak, and Absalom is left hanging in the tree by his hair (v. 9). And second, after Joab upbraids a soldier for not killing Absalom, the soldier replies, "I would not raise my hand against the king's son" (v. 12a). Both references are distinctly reminiscent of the language concerning Abraham's sacrifice of Isaac and the intervention of Yahweh's messenger in Genesis 22. In verse 10, Abraham "reached out his hand and took the knife to kill his son." Verse 13 tells us that "Abraham looked up and saw a ram, caught in a thicket by its horns. Abraham went and took the ram and offered it up as a burnt offering instead of his son." The first reference (Gen. 22:10) is strikingly similar to the language of 2 Samuel 18:12a. The second (Gen. 22:13) uses the same word, *s^ebak* ("thicket"), while 2 Samuel 18:9 uses *sobek* ("thick branches"). The words are quite similar in sound and construction. The third lamb has been slain in payment.

The fourth and final payment is David's son, Adonijah. Fearing Solomon, Adonijah fled into the tabernacle and "went to grasp the horns of the altar" (1 Kings 1:50). This description has obvious sacrificial imagery (cf. Lev. 4:7, 18; 8:15; Ps. 118:27). As the reader should expect by now, after a short reprieve, Adonijah is slain (1 Kings 2:25).

Now the author of this extended narrative could have simply informed the readers that David sinned and that he paid with the death of four sons. This would have taken about two sentences. But that would have made for dull reading. The author desired to construct a narrative in such a way that, given just enough hints, foreshadowings, and gaps, the readers might discover these facts on their own. The author has created the possibility that a reader can discover a mimetic relationship between the narrative and a truth in the real world. That truth may be that Yahweh is faithful to his law in judgment as well as in blessing. The author does not offer this truth propositionally, but mimetically. So what we have here is history in the service of mimesis. If we accept this distinction between history and mimesis and do not impose demands of historical verisimilitude upon texts that were never intended to be objective history in the modern sense, most troublesome issues, such as chronological and logical contradictions, simply evaporate. As modern readers of the Hebrew narratives, we should allow the narratives to speak truth as narratives.

Hebrew Poetry

Poetry in general is highly structured and compact, and Hebrew poetry is no exception. **Hebrew poetry** utilizes figurative, metaphorical language and is especially characterized by thought parallelism. The following examples illustrate the way thought is paralleled in Hebrew poetry.

> As the deer longs for flowing streams, so my soul longs for you, O God (Ps. 42:1).

> Oh that my vexation were weighed, and all my calamity laid in the balances! (Job 6:2).

> Your cheeks are like halves of a pomegranate behind your veil (Song of Sol. 4:3b).

Besides sharing figurative language, these texts evidence other noteworthy traits. Each example contains two parts, which Alter calls "versets."[15] Furthermore, the second verset seems to be related in some way to the first verset. In the second example, "vexation" and "calamity" are related as are "weighed" and "laid in the balances." Scholars have traditionally referred to this relationship between the versets of a line in Hebrew poetry as parallelism of thought. **Parallelism of thought** generally consists of three types: synonymy, antithesis, and synthesis. In synonymous parallelism the second verset restates in a different way the thought of the first verset:

---

[15] See Alter, *The Art of Biblical Poetry*.

> he washes his garments in wine
> and his robe in the blood of grapes (Gen. 49:11b).

Antithetical parallelism expresses in the second verset the same idea as in the first but in a negative manner:

> A wise child makes a glad father,
> but a foolish child is a mother's grief (Prov. 10:1).

In synthetic parallelism, the second verset complements the first by clarification or explanation:

> So I will send a fire on the wall of Gaza,
> fire that shall devour its strongholds (Amos 1:7).

The consuming of the fortresses is the result of the fire upon the walls.

But there is something more going on in most Hebrew poetic parallelism than simply static synonymy, antithesis, or synthesis. There is movement from verset to verset. For example:

> Wine is a mocker,
> Strong drink a brawler (Prov. 20:1).

"Wine" has been intensified in the second verset with "strong drink," and "mocker" has been heightened to "brawler." Clearly, words spoken in mockery are not as strong as the physical actions of the "brawler." There has been a focusing through *intensification*.[16] It should be added that this focusing or intensification is quite common in the occurrences of graded numbers which follow the pattern of x, x + 1:

> Once God has spoken; twice have I heard this (Ps. 62:11).

> We will raise against them seven shepherds,
> and eight installed as rulers (Mic. 5:5b).

Another type of movement between versets occurs in Amos 8:10:

> I will turn your feasts into mourning,
> and all your songs into lamentation.

In this line, "all your songs" is a specific element within the larger event of "feasts" as is "lamentation" of "mourning." This type of focusing is what Alter calls focusing through *specification*.[17] Most instances of antithetical and synthetic parallelism are actually variations on the above

---

[16] Ibid., pp. 27–61.
[17] Ibid., p. 35.

types of focusing. Alter offers yet another type of movement within a line of verse—movement from *cause to effect*:

> I call upon the LORD, who is worthy to be praised,
> so I shall be saved from my enemies (Ps. 18:3).

The relation between these two versets is obviously one of cause ("call") and effect ("saved").[18] On the one hand, the importance of at least an elementary acquaintance with the structures and dynamics of Hebrew verse cannot be overemphasized. This emphasis becomes at once justified when the reader recognizes how much of the Hebrew Bible (Wisdom literature, prophecy, Psalms, and poetic sections within narrative books) is Hebrew verse.

On the other hand, as intriguing and essential as the dynamics of parallelism are, to concentrate attention only here will result in neglecting another essential quality of Hebrew poetry. Above I described poetry as heightened language. By this I mean that poetry (especially Hebrew poetry) is the language of imagery and the picturesque. It confronts the reader with word pictures, concrete images. Narrative examines a concept by telling a story through the instruments of plot, characters in action, and setting, having as its basic unit the scene; but the poet examines the same concept by drawing a verbal picture and asking the reader to pause long enough to form a mental picture.

The warp and woof of the poet's art are metaphor and simile. These are similar in form and operation. Whereas a simile says that one object or concept is "like" another ("your teeth are like a flock of shorn ewes," Song of Sol. 4:2a), the metaphor claims that one object "is" another ("A garden locked up is my sister, my bride," Song of Sol. 4:12a).

Through this use of metaphor and simile (along with other forms such as personification, hyperbole, apostrophe), the poet pictures reality and challenges the reader's imagination. Leland Ryken offers the following advice:

> The prevalence of images in poetry requires us to read poetry with what psychologists call the right side of the brain. This is our mental capacity to think in pictures. We first need to experience poetry with our senses and then become analytic in determining the connotations and logic of the images in their context in a poem.[19]

---

[18] Ibid., p. 33
[19] Ryken, *Words of Delight*, p. 162.

This brings us to a crucial point: The metaphorical nature of most Hebrew poetry requires the reader to experience an effect on one level (the literal level of the metaphor) and then to transfer that experience to another level. The reader must first pause long enough to allow the metaphor or simile to construct the literal picture before too quickly rushing on to the second level of meaning where logical associations are made between the bifocaled levels of the metaphor or simile.[20] Simply put, two things must occur when reading poetry—a seeing and a thinking.[21]

The seeing occurs on the literal level of the image, while the thinking takes place when we trace the associations and meanings between the literal and interpretive levels. How does the hermeneut actualize this movement between the literal level of imaging and the level of interpretation? One of the best articulations of this process (which I summarize below) is by Ryken.[22]

The explication of Hebrew poetry requires above all else a discernible strategy marked by a systematic, complete, and logical progression. This strategy consists of six steps. The first is to identify the sub-genre. For example, is the poem a psalm, and if so, what type (e.g., a psalm of praise, a psalm of worship, or a psalm of lament)? We may ask the same question of prophecy in poetic form or of wisdom literature. Knowing the sub-genre of the poem helps explain the poem's organization, for each type carries its own structure.

Second, try to determine the situation of the poem. This allows its dynamics to become more understandable. The setting of the poem may become apparent as the poem unfolds. If the author is assumed to be in exile, or in a life-threatening situation, the dynamics of the poem make more sense.

Third, determine the topic and theme of the poem to be able to recognize the message of the poem. The topic is what the poem is all about, while the theme is the poet's assertion concerning the topic. The poet's topic in Psalm 23 is God's providential care. The theme, however, is the satisfaction and contentment that come from trusting in that providence.

Fourth come structure and unity. The structure develops the theme and assumes a unified whole. Most poems have their particular units

---

[20] Ibid., p. 207.
[21] Ibid.
[22] Ibid., pp. 207–11.

bracketed by ideas or images. Moving from one unit to another assures a systematic flow of thought in explication. Four types of material can account for structure. (a) If the poem describes a person, a scene, or an event, it has a descriptive structure. (b) The poem has an expository structure if it presents a series of emotions or ideas. (c) If the units present occurrences of events in succession, the poem has a narrative structure. (d) The poem is dramatic in structure if it is an address by a speaker. The reader should be cautioned, however, that although one of these structures may dominate, an overlapping or a combining of structural elements usually occurs. While these four are the main structural forms that guarantee unity, Ryken does offer others, two of which need mention here. A poem has a catalogue structure when it primarily lists aspects of a single topic. The other structural element is best described as psychological. A poem will have this structure when the poem evidences that it was composed during great emotional moments, with the speaker's or writer's consciousness jumping from one topic to another. The only point of unity is the writer's consciousness.

Fifth, isolate the details of a poem—the literary devices and figures of speech (e.g., metaphors, hyperboles, similes, and personification). These devices are bearers of the message. These details make up what is usually referred to as *poetic texture*. The exploration of their meanings is not an option, but a necessity, and may occupy most of the reader's time. When analyzing the poem, the reader must ask why a particular literary device occurs in a particular context. An examination of the figures within a poem should follow the structure of the poem itself.

Finally, the reader should not ignore the sheer artistic excellence and beauty of the poetic parallelism and imagery. Any explication that neglects the aesthetic dimension of the poem is incomplete.

Hebrew Prophecy

Since we have already discussed both narrative and poetry, we confine our remarks here to the arrangement of the prophetic texts and to some of the forms through which the prophetic messages are communicated. Generally, the prophetic texts of the Hebrew Bible are not chronological but are collections of materials. These materials were initially preserved together in larger or smaller collections and only at a later time became the groundwork for the prophetic texts. Collectors had a wide variety of material at their disposal. Primarily oracles, other sayings, larger prophetic compositions, and short narratives about episodes in the life of the prophet were collected. In many cases, the utterances were not preserved in their original form, but are in the form of free summaries or abstracts.

The principles that guided the collectors vary. The most dominating factor was similarity in subject matter. Antithetical ideas such as righteousness and unrighteousness or judgment and salvation also governed the association of passages. Passages consisting of the same structure often occur in a series, like woe-speeches and sermons beginning with "hear." Catch-words were also used in grouping different passages; and often, but not always, passages were grouped chronologically.

As a rule, the collectors did their work after the death of the prophet whose teachings and utterances they recorded. They frequently recorded in writing, but smaller collections may have circulated in oral form. The main intention was to preserve the prophecies for posterity and to adapt them for practical use.

Redactional (editorial) work occurred after the work of the collectors. Our present prophetic books are not identical with the original collections, for these have undergone changes and transformations of different kinds. There are numerous examples of additions, enlargements, and comments showing that the texts were subjected to alterations in accordance with the tastes and needs of later times. The texts remained fluid for many centuries.

The redactors of the prophetic books (collections) developed the prophets' original words in order to bring out their significance for a later age. This accounts for the presence of unfulfilled prophecies. For example, Micah's prediction in the eighth century of the fall of Jerusalem, which appears to conflict with the prophecies of Isaiah that the city would be protected by God, was regarded as unfulfilled as late as Jeremiah's time (Jer. 26:17–19). Yet, Micah's prophecies were preserved. Clements comments that "very significantly an important aspect of the redactional work on the prophetic books was to adapt and reinterpret prophecies in the light of later historical circumstances."[23] This indicates that the question of the truth of prophecy was seen to be a larger truth than could be contained within a simple prediction-fulfillment formula. Hosea, whose message was originally directed to the northern kingdom, is an example. Sometime later, however, slight editing—the insertion of the name "Judah" at several places—gave Hosea's message a new address to the southern kingdom. Von Rad offers the following explanation:

---

[23] R. E. Clements, *Prophecy and Tradition* (Atlanta: John Knox, 1975), p. 53.

It was never presumed that the prophet's oracles were addressed to one set of people and one only, and were thereafter to be wrapped up in their rolls and deposited among the records. There must have been people who never forgot that a prophet's teaching always remained relevant for a coming day and generation, and who themselves played their part in making it appear relevant—in many cases their work can be clearly seen in the various secondary additions which they made.[24]

Several rhetorical and literary forms are present in the prophetic texts, and like other texts, the message of the prophetic texts or singular oracles within them is inseparable from the form. Probably the most common form used to convey the prophetic message was the **messenger formula.** The Mari texts have revealed a type of prophet-messenger similar to the one in the Old Testament. The god Dagon sends prophets to convey messages to the king, and as in Israel, the messages were delivered by means of prophetic rhetoric. In the revelation of Dagon to Malikdagon, his prophet, we see a messenger formula similar to the one in Exodus 3:10—the vision of the burning bush. We read there, "So come, I will send you to Pharaoh," and in the revelation of Malikdagon, "now go, I send you, thus say. . . . " We read in Isaiah 6:8, "Whom shall I send? And who will go for us?" This convention appears also in the Akkadian Maqlu text and also in the assigning of a mission to a man by the supreme gods Anu and Antu ("whom shall I send?"). These examples demonstrate that the type of the divine messenger and messenger formula was known for a long time in Mesopotamia.

Yet the Hebrew prophets usually prefaced this formula with another form designed to draw the recipient's attention to the message. This preface to the message was a designation of those for whom it was intended. Von Rad comments: "In the case of a divine threat, what was prefixed was a diatribe; in the case of a promise, an exhortation. These two, the messenger formula and prefixed clause, must both be present before we have the literary category of prophetic oracle."[25] As a rule, the prophets (until the time of Jeremiah) drew a clear distinction between the messenger formula and the diatribe or exhortation which introduced it. The messenger formula was the Word of God, while the prefaced form was an editorial addition by the prophet. This prefaced form had the purpose of leading up to and preparing the way for God's Word and gave it its reference.

---

[24] Gerhard von Rad, *Old Testament Theology*, 2 vols. (New York: Harper & Row, 1965), vol. 2, p. 43.

[25] Ibid., p. 37.

But the messenger formula is only one among many forms in the prophetic texts. There was no hesitation in using multiple forms to clothe the messages. There are exhortations to repent, reproaches, woe and satire, lamentations, hymns, prayers, judicial debating, and ritual utterances. There are short messages and extended sermons, historical retrospects, parables and allegories, similes, and wisdom sayings.

By choosing a particular form, these prophets intended to attract attention. For example, when a prophet drafted into service a time-hallowed sacral form, his purpose was to shock the audience. In Isaiah 40–55, the author drew from the priestly oracle of weal and, by reshaping it into something more sweeping, made it the form of his preaching. Other messages were clothed in the form favored by wisdom teachers (Amos 3:3ff.) or popular songs (Isa. 5:1ff.). A vivid example of the way a prophet would take a well-known form or a literary device and drastically change it to the point of almost non-recognition is the dirge. The later prophets actually turned it upside down and parodied it (Amos 5:1; Isa. 23:1ff.; Ezek. 19:1ff.; 27:2ff.; Isa. 14:4ff.).

The prophets thus attired their prophetic messages and oracles in non-prophetic, secular garb. However, the reverse is also true: The prophets also tailored their messages to the forms. Ezekiel derives a number of subjects from folk tales and songs (cf. Ezek. 14:12–23; 16:1–43; 17:1–10; 19:1–14; 21:13–23; 23:1–27; 26:19–21; 28:1–10; 31:1–18; 32:17–32). Isaiah utilizes the type of the love song (5:1–7) and a wisdom instruction (28:23–29).

All of this means, of course, that interpretation must address the *texts* of the prophets with their multiple forms and sub-genres. While the prophetic texts differ from the narrative texts we discussed earlier (there is really no narrative or story world in the strict sense), they are replete with forms constitutive of meaning.

Summary

This chapter has described the genres of Hebrew narrative, poetry, and prophecy. Regardless of the genre in which the authors chose to write, communication was the primary goal. But communication proceeds differently through each genre. Each genre combines techniques, sub-genres, and literary devices in characteristic ways in order to convey an ethical, cultic, historical, or social message. Narrative communicates through plot, characterization, and setting; poetry through images and word pictures; and prophecy through arranging collected materials according to subject matter or around some literary device. A knowledge of the sub-genres within these three genres and an appreciation of the manner in which these sub-genres are strategically arranged and presented are prerequisites to successful interpretation. While all three of these genres share some common elements with narrative and poetry in general, they also have their distinctive characteristics. Not only was the world which produced the works of the Hebrew Bible different from ours, but the world within the texts differs from our real world. To impose modern expectations (whether theologically, doctrinally, or ethically generated) upon these texts while neglecting their generic worlds and literary qualities is to treat them irresponsibly.

REVIEW & STUDY

Key Terms and Concepts

Real author	Characterization
Implied author	Interior monologue
Real reader	Direct dialogue
Implied reader	Point of view
Narrator	*Leitwort*
Narratee	Type scene
Real world	Allusion
Story world	Truth value
Historical narrative	Parallelism of thought
Mimetic narrative	Hebrew poetry
Narratology	Plot
Setting	Chiastic patterns
Narrative	Messenger formula

Study Questions

1. The book of Jonah has been described as a series of descents. Read this brief work and see if there might be merit in this description. Should these events be taken literally? If your answer is yes, does this vitiate the mimetic quality of the work? Why or why not?

2. In *The Art of Biblical Narrative*, Robert Alter refers to Hebrew narrative as "fictionalized history" or "historicized fiction." If he is correct, does this mean that the narratives are untrue? Explain.

3. Read the story of Judah and Tamar in Genesis 38 and comment on the following:
   a. difference between *récit* and *histoire*
   b. narrative voice
   c. duration
   d. distance
   e. perspective
   f. voice
   g. setting
   h. characterization
   i. quotation

4. Is there a betrothal type scene in the book of Ruth? If so, how does it differ from the paradigm?

5. Read the book of Numbers. Identify the motif of "water" and offer a brief discussion of its function within the text.

6. Read Isa. 53:8–12. List the parallelisms and identify the type of each. For each parallelism, name the type of focusing and comment on the poet's theological assumptions based upon the poet's identification of terms through the device of focusing.

Suggestions for Further Reading

Alter, Robert. *The Art of Biblical Narrative*. New York: Basic Books, 1981.
_____. *The Art of Biblical Poetry*. New York: Basic Books, 1985.
Bellinger, W. H., *Psalms: Reading and Studying the Book of Praises*. Peabody, Mass.: Hendrickson, 1990.
Berlin, Adele. *Poetics and Interpretation of Biblical Narrative*. Sheffield: Almond Press, 1983.
Fisch, Harold. *Poetry with a Purpose: Biblical Poetics and Interpretation*. Bloomington: Indiana University Press, 1988.
Kort, Wesley A. *Story, Text, and Scripture: Literary Interests in Biblical Narrative*. University Park, Penn.: Pennsylvania State University Press, 1987.
Rosenberg, Joel. *King and Kin: Political Allegory in the Hebrew Bible*. Bloomington: Indiana University Press, 1986.
Sternberg, Meir. *The Poetics of Biblical Narrative*. Bloomington: Indiana University Press, 1985.

How the New Testament Communicates as Literature

When critics talk about the literary artfulness of the Bible, the reference is generally to the Hebrew Bible. From Origen to Dibelius to Sternberg, the New Testament is regarded as less artistic, less literary than the Hebrew Bible. The fact is, however, that while some literary conventions and theological bases differ from those of the Hebrew Bible, the majority of the literary characteristics of the New Testament are also recognizable as Hebraic. More simply put, the literary forms in the New Testament are, to a great degree, modifications of existing literary forms and strategies. The New Testament writers make extensive use of the Hebrew Bible, suggesting a firsthand familiarity with most of its genres and sub-genres. With their plots, characters, conflicts, complications, and resolutions, the Gospels and Acts remind us of the narratives of the Hebrew Bible; Revelation also shares the properties of Old Testament apocalypse.

Throughout the New Testament, we find language that transcends the simple expository and descriptive, a language embellished with literary devices and pregnant with imagery. Any hermeneutical approach that consciously or unconsciously neglects this literary nature of the New Testament is incomplete and unbalanced.

Our examination of the literary context of the New Testament involves two primary considerations: (1) the development of the defining structures of the three major genres—narrative, epistle, and apocalypse; and (2) a discussion of the sub-genres and literary forms within these three genres.

The Gospels and Acts

The New Testament's four Gospels and Acts can be classified as narrative. While they do compare significantly to both hellenistic biography and historiography, the Gospels are not biographies of Jesus in the strictest sense; neither are they history in the modern sense. They are above all else *story*. In order to counter any confusion over this statement, let's review the earlier discussion concerning story and then demonstrate the way in which the Gospels fall into this category.

Every effective story must necessarily have a beginning, middle, and end. A story must have established limits within which the elements such as plot, characterization, setting, conflict, complication, and resolution are employed. This requirement naturally assumes that the author recognizes the utter impossibility (indeed futility) of incorporating every minor detail. So what do authors do? First, authors know what truths they wish to communicate. They then select, arrange, and interpret events, characters, and settings through the literary forms and devices that most effectively and artistically convey those truths.

Understanding this process of selection and arrangement is vital. The author (storyteller) does not flatly state the case, but through the selective process, seeks to guide the reader into the construction of the message. The author invites the reader, therefore, to become involved in and engaged by the story. The author seeks to move the reader from one event or scene to another, leaving sufficient gaps of information so that the reader can make necessary inferences. Story does not allow the reader to remain static.

This suggests that the world in the story points to a reality beyond itself. That is, meaning does not reside just in the events within a story, but in the reality that the story asks the reader to help create. The story is itself really one half of a metaphor, the other half being the interpretation to which the story leads. The story is like a map to a truth outside the world of the story. Story is not story for story's sake, but an invitation to encounter some truth about the real world or perhaps about the world to come. For example, in the book of Job, there is a beginning, middle, and end, with characters involved in dialogues, thought, and events. But is this all the story tells us? Certainly not! It asks the perennial question, "Why do bad things happen to good people?" Whether it offers an answer is debatable. The point is that in interpreting a story, the reader must move beyond what is said *in* the story to what is said *through* the story. Movement from the referential level to the mimetic level must occur.

Again, the Gospels are stories. This statement does not imply that the Gospels are fictional. The historical validity of the events need not be rejected in order to read the Gospels as story; however, as we will demonstrate below, the telling of objective, chronological history was furthermost in the writers' minds. If there is any doubt concerning this assumption, one need only read the Gospels side by side and note the different contexts within which a single event is found. For example, the passage in which Jesus foretells the temple's destruction occurs in Luke at 13:34-35 *before* Jesus' arrival in Jerusalem, while in Matthew 23:37-39, it occurs *during* his final visit to the city.

Ultimately, where should we direct our attention in the interpretation of the Gospels? Should we direct it to Jesus' teaching or to the evangelists' narrative of Jesus' words and actions within a particular context? For instance, both Matthew and Mark record a time when Jesus teaches in parables. Yet, while Mark places it near the beginning of his Gospel (ch. 4), Matthew records it in the middle of his (ch. 13), and John does not even mention that Jesus spoke in parables! Perhaps more illustrative is John's placement of the temple cleansing by Jesus at the beginning of his Gospel (ch. 2), whereas the authors of the Synoptics place it during the passion week, at the end of their narratives. We may conclude, therefore, that the Gospels paint verbal portraits of Jesus and the events surrounding his ministry, giving individual interpretations of his person and mission. The evangelists accomplish this through selection, emphasis, and arrangement. While each Gospel presents the "good news" of Jesus, each does so in a particular way. Consequently, we must allow each Gospel to stand on its own and approach it as a single literary whole. As Gordon Fee rightly observes, "the Gospels in their present form are the word of God to us; our own reconstructions of Jesus' life are not. Many of the Gospel materials owe their present context to the evangelists."[1] Leland Ryken similarly notes: "The individual Gospels have their own characteristic ideas, images, settings, and emphases. Knowing that individual Gospel writers build their own world in this way can go a long way toward unifying our experiences of the Gospels."[2]

Nevertheless, some qualifying discussion is in order. While the Gospels are not strictly biographies of Jesus, but complete and unified literary narratives, they are not entirely unique narratives. The Gospels may be unique in their christological emphasis, but they are not unique

---

[1] Fee and Stuart, *How to Read the Bible*, p. 113.
[2] Leland Ryken, *Words of Life: A Literary Introduction to the New Testament* (Grand Rapids: Baker, 1987), p. 34.

as to their form of presentation. Indeed, it is inconceivable that the evangelists would not capitalize on the modes of literary production current in their day. Charles Talbert has argued brilliantly that Luke–Acts is patterned after the hellenistic **biography**,[3] and in a somewhat neglected work, Elizabeth Haight discusses the parallels between the Gospels/Acts and the hellenistic genre of **romance**.[4]

Since a detailed treatment of the hellenistic biography and romance would take us too far afield, I offer the following summary of elements found within these two genres with brief comments, and encourage the interested reader to pursue the subject further. In the words of Helmut Koester, the hellenistic biography

> grew out of an increasing interest in the lives of famous poets and philosophers. Greek biography was born when one began to inquire into the relationship between the works and the life (*bios*) of such persons, and when one began to search for examples for the right conduct of the wise man. . . . Thus it was the purpose of these biographies to present the principles of philosophical doctrines, conduct of life, and formation of character in the form of a *bios*.[5]

Included in these biographies were biographical anecdotes, legends, panegyric (extravagant praise), aretology (miracle stories), thematic approach, amplification, and comparison. Exploring the Gospel of Matthew alone would reveal countless examples of each of the above, but two will illustrate that Matthew was versed in the genre of the hellenistic biography. Matthew uses the thematic approach. The Sermon on the Mount (chs. 5–7) deals with righteousness. Matthew 10 relates the sending of the Twelve and the cost of discipleship. And the parables in chapter 13 concentrate on the kingdom of God. The emphasis upon the progressive disclosure of Jesus' identity mentioned in Matthew 14:1–16 is one example of amplification. A second, according to Shuler, is the treatment of events surrounding the death of Jesus.[6] Both examples emphasize supernatural phenomena and the additional testimony of eyewitnesses.

---

[3] Charles Talbert, *Literary Patterns, Theological Themes and the Genre of Luke–Acts*, SBLMS 20 (Missoula: Society of Biblical Literature and Scholars Press, 1974).

[4] Elizabeth Haight, *Essays on the Greek Romances* (Port Washington, N.Y.: Kennikat, 1943).

[5] Koester, *Introduction to the New Testament*, vol. 1, p. 133.

[6] See Philip I. Shuler, *A Genre for the Gospels: The Biographical Character of Matthew* (Philadelphia: Fortress, 1982).

Parallels between Hellenistic Romance
and the Gospels and Acts

Romance	Gospels and Acts
Travel Motif	Luke 9:51–19:44; Acts 19:21–21:16, 27:1–28:16
Aretology	Numerous in Gospels and Acts
Prevention of suicide	Acts 16:25–34
Dreams	Matt. 1:20–25; 2:13; 27:19;
Visions	Luke 1:22; 24:23; Acts 9:10, 12; 10:3, 10–19; 11:5; 16:9–10; 18:9
Courtroom scenes	Matt. 26:57–67; 27:11–26; Luke 22–23; Acts 22–26
Letters	Acts 15:23–29; 23:26–30
Crowd motif	Seen surrounding Jesus in all the Gospels and the disciples in Acts (e.g., 2:14 and 19:35)
Speeches	Matt. 5–7; Acts 2:14–36; 7:1–53; 17:22–31
Storms	Matt. 14:22–33; Acts 27:13–26
Shipwreck	Acts 27:27–44
Narrow escapes	Matt. 2:13–20; Acts 12:1–18; 14:19–20; 17:5–10; 21:27–32; 27:42–44
Ethnography	John 4:1–27; Acts 8:26–27; 14:11–13; 17:21; 28:1–6
Origin and birth of hero	Matt. 1–2; Luke 1–3; John 1:1–18
Historical characters	Pilate, Festus, Herod the Great, Felix, Herod Agrippa, etc.
Divine direction	Throughout Gospels and Acts

CHART 6-1

The various generic forms within Hellenism seem to have been concentrated in the genre of romance. The identifying elements of the hellenistic romance are legion. Above is a chart listing some of the elements within the hellenistic romance that have parallels in the Gospels and Acts.[7] These are only a few of parallels that the New Testament shares with hellenistic romances. When the parallels are placed side by side, there is an obvious similarity between the Gospels/Acts and the

[7] Albin Lesky, *History of Greek Literature* (New York: Thomas Y. Crowell Co., 1966), pp. 858–67; and Koester, *Introduction to the New Testament*, vol. 1, p. 137.

hellenistic biography/romance. Thus, we might at least conclude that the evangelists employed several elements common in the biography and romance. Indeed the messages of the Gospels and Acts may be unique, but the form(s) may not be.[8]

If we accept each individual Gospel as a story, as a literary whole, with a distinct purpose determining a particular framework, then the most plausible interpretation of any portion will be that one which seeks to relate the part to the whole. While the individual units (like the Sermon on the Mount in Matthew) may be rhetorically self-contained, in some fashion they must be understood *now* within the context of the Gospel's world. Since some find it difficult to think of the smaller units in light of the whole story, a brief discussion of the Gospel of Matthew as a literary whole should help. This discussion is followed by a look at the different sub-genres that are the tools for constructing the Gospels.

The Gospel of Matthew: A Model

If Mark paints Jesus as the suffering messiah and defines discipleship as following in this path of suffering, Matthew portrays Jesus as the great teacher, fulfiller, and personification of the Torah.[9] Matthew's chronological arrangement is based upon Mark's; however, the additional material and arrangement of all the material is Matthew's.

Concerning Matthew's setting, recent scholarship has suggested that Matthew was consciously composed in dialogue with rabbinic Judaism. It was written during the last quarter of the first century when the church was struggling for its identity as an institution apart from Judaism, yet appropriating the actual symbols of Judaism as a means of definition. The foremost symbol of Judaism was the **Torah.** How does Matthew present Jesus as the fulfillment, interpretation, and personification of the Torah? And how does the resultant definition of discipleship fit within this context?

---

[8] In his book *The New Testament in Its Literary Environment* (Philadelphia: Westminster, 1989), David Aune offers a detailed and coherent discussion of the Greco-Roman biography and historiography. In his excellent discussion, Aune demonstrates that the Gospels of Mark, Matthew, and John share most of the constituent parts of the Greco-Roman biography and some of the *topoi* characteristic of the Hebrew biographical writings. He argues that Luke–Acts is closely akin to Greco-Roman historiography and shares some of the characteristics of Hebrew historiography.

[9] Johnson, *Writings of the New Testament*, p. 185.

Matthew accomplishes his purpose with structural patterns. The first concerns Matthew's polemic against experts in the law and Pharisees. The combining of the piety of the Pharisees with the legal expertise of the scribes defined rabbinic Judaism developing during the period immediately before and after the fall of Jerusalem in A.D. 70. This polemic against rabbinic Judaism surfaces in chapter 23, where Matthew has creatively placed it between the Jerusalem controversies (22:15–46) and Jesus' private eschatological instruction to the disciples (24:1–25:46). The polemic contains seven woes (23:13, 15, 16, 23, 25, 27, 29). Polemical statements are directed against the Pharisees and scribes throughout Matthew, but the polemic here in chapter 23 assumes a formal, more caustic nature. Johnson suggests that chapter 23 brings the polemical elements together here in a kind of crescendo.[10]

Within this polemical emphasis Matthew presents Jesus as the true and perfect teacher or interpreter of the Torah. Matthew accomplishes this is in two ways. First, throughout his narrative, Matthew presents Jesus in strategic settings that reveal him to be the authoritative interpreter Torah. These settings are controversies with the Pharisees and experts in the law in which Jesus consistently challenges his opponents' understanding of the Torah by asking, "have you not read in the law/ Scripture?" On one occasion he challenges his opponent to "go and learn what this means" (9:13).

Second, the section of discourse commonly referred to as the Sermon on the Mount functions paradigmatically as the true interpretation of the Torah. Appealing to the Torah five times (5:21, 27, 31, 33, 38) and to midrash once (5:43), Jesus illustrates how the Torah is to be truly interpreted. The law is not a legalistic code to be observed outwardly, but its true interpretation is an internalization; true obedience to the Torah brings about an inner disposition.

But Jesus is more than the true interpreter of the law; he is also its fulfillment. The third structural element supports this conclusion. Fifty-seven times Matthew refers directly to the Hebrew Scriptures and some thirty times indirectly. Matthew's approach is an interesting one. He identifies particular moments in the life of Jesus with Old Testament texts in such a fashion that the events or moments in Jesus' life interpret the Scriptures. Jesus is the real meaning of the law. But the coin has two sides—the Torah also reveals Jesus, that is, Jesus and Torah are mutually interpretive.

---

[10] Ibid., pp. 189–90.

Besides being the true interpreter and the fulfillment of the Torah, Matthew's Jesus is also the personification of the Torah. Matthew completes the three-dimensional portrait by inviting the reader to make connections between Jesus' words and the Torah in rabbinic Judaism. Some of these connections are illustrated in the chart below.

Parallels Between Jewish Understanding of Torah
and Matthew's Portrait of Jesus

Wisdom or Rabbinic Reference	Matthew's Parallel
1. Wisdom personified (cf. Wis. of Sol. 7:25–27) and Wisdom identified with Torah (cf. Baruch 4:1).	When Jesus was ridiculed for associating with sinners, he responded: "Yet wisdom is vindicated by her deeds" (11:19).
2. Torah is eternal (Baruch 4:1).	In the Sermon on the Mount, Jesus refers to the Torah, "until heaven and earth pass away, not one letter, not one stroke of a letter, will pass from the law until all is accomplished" (5:18). Then later he says, "heaven and earth will pass away, but my words will not pass away" (24:35).
3. Torah is the yoke of the kingdom (Sirach 6:19–31; Pirke Aboth). Also see Acts 15:10.	Jesus describes his "yoke" as "easy" (11:28–30).
4. Torah provides God's rest for those who study it (Wis. of Sol. 8:16; Sirach 6:28; 51:26–27).	As Torah brings one into God's sabbath, so Jesus says, "I will give you rest" (11:28).
5. The Shekinah is found among so few as two or three gathered to study Torah (Pirke Aboth 3:2).	Jesus says, "For where two or three are gathered in my name, I am there among them" (18:20).

CHART 6-2

Indeed, the reader is led to conclude that Jesus is the very personification of the Torah. The reader is left to observe other implicit associations between Jesus and the background material given above.

The final structural device in Matthew pertains to the entire work. Scholars have long noted Matthew's placement of Jesus' teachings into five major groupings, each ending with the formula "When Jesus had finished these sayings, . . . " or something very similar. Preceding each block of discourse is narrative material. Many have suggested skeletal structures similar to the following one.

Prologue:	Birth narrative and the Spirit's activity (chs. 1-2)
Division I:	Narrative material (3:1-4:25)
	Discourse on the Mount (5:1-7:27)
	Formula (7:28-29)
Division II:	Narrative material (8:1-9:35)
	Discourse on mission and discipleship (9:36-10:42)
	Formula (11:1)
Division III:	Narrative material (11:2-12:50)
	Discourse on kingdom (13:1-52)
	Formula (13:53)
Division IV:	Narrative material (13:54-17:21)
	Discourse on church administration (17:22-18:35)
	Formula (19:1)
Division V:	Narrative material (19:2-22:46)
	Discourse on eschatology (23:1-25:46)
	Formula (26:1)
Epilogue:	Last Supper and resurrection (26:3-28:20)

Is it possible that Matthew intended this arrangement to suggest the five books of the Pentateuch along with its primeval prologue and epilogue (the farewell speech by Moses in Deuteronomy)? An affirmative response would see this structure as being consistent with Matthew's portrayal of Jesus as Torah discussed above. If further evidence is needed, I should point out the very subtle Mosaic overtones in Matthew. First, whereas Mark begins his Gospel with "the beginning of the good news of Jesus Christ, Son of God," Matthew begins with "the book of the genesis of Jesus Christ." Second, consistent with Old Testament usage, the genealogy in Matthew suggests the beginning of a new epoch in history. This is further supported by Matthew's record of the Spirit's activity in the birth of Jesus, perhaps recalling the activity of the Spirit of Yahweh at creation. Third, Herod's order to have all male children who were two years old or under killed (2:16) is reminiscent of Pharaoh's order to have all male children killed (Exod. 1:22). Fourth, Moses received the law on Mount Sinai, and Jesus interprets the law on the mountain (5:1-7:27). Fifth, Jesus performs ten miracles in chapters 8-9, as Moses performs ten marvels in Exodus 7-10. Finally, the account of the transfiguration in Matthew 17:1-4, with its reference to the appearance of Jesus' face, immediately recalls the description of Moses' face when he came down from the mountain (Exod. 34:29–34).

Before moving to the sub-genres, a brief glance at the disciples in Matthew will be illuminating. The experts in the law and the Pharisees were the interpreters of Torah. But if Jesus is the personification of the Torah, who will be *his* interpreter? For Matthew, there must be an equivalent to the "experts in the law" who will interpret *the* Torah. The most likely candidates, of course, are the disciples, who after the resurrection (i.e., only after the new Torah is complete) are instructed by Jesus to make disciples of all nations, teaching them to observe all the commandments they have received (28:16–20). The new Torah requires the authoritative interpretation of the disciples. Therefore, the disciples become the new interpreters of the new Torah.

The foregoing discussion of the Gospel of Matthew is in no sense to be taken as comprehensive or definitive. It illustrates, though, the literary nature and creative artistry of the work as a whole. But wholes are constructed by weaving smaller units or parts together. The whole can be meaningful only through the parts, and the parts must be interpreted in light of the whole. This seems to be asking, Which comes first, the chicken or the egg? Welcome to the infamous hermeneutical circle. More will be said concerning this circle (which is actually a spiral) in the next unit. For the present, our purpose is to introduce the reader to the literary forms (the parts) used by the authors of the Gospels to produce coherent, narrative wholes.

Sub-Genres in the Gospels

Sayings and Sayings Stories

Most scholars are convinced that many sayings of Jesus were collected quite early in the life of the church and were later circulated. One of these hypothetical collections is referred to as Q (*Quelle*—German for source). Most scholars feel that it was a source for the evangelists. In particular, Matthew and Luke are believed to have drawn on Q for their respective "sermons" of Jesus, each one providing his own context for the various sayings. We may classify these sayings into the *apophthegm*, *proverbs*, *legal sayings*, and *prophetic sayings*.

The **apophthegm** or pronouncement story is a brief episode or event that precipitates a saying of Jesus. It originates in the anecdote about a well-known person. The anecdote climaxes in a significant statement or declaration. The episode or event exists for the saying and not vice-versa. One example is the saying, "I have come to call not the righteous but sinners" (Mark 2:16–17; Matt. 9:10–13; Luke 5:29–32). The setting for the narrative is a meal where Jesus is eating with tax gatherers and sinners. No details, such as time and place, are given about the meal. Such matters were irrelevant since the saying was the focal point; the meal served only as a point of anchorage. Care should be taken not to so concentrate on some hidden meaning in the story as to neglect the saying given birth by it. The story may be nothing more than a pretext for the saying.

The **proverbs**, or **wisdom sayings**, in the Gospels are probably best described as aphorisms—terse, succinct statements easily remembered. The proverb is quite similar to the Old Testament wisdom saying. Examples are:

> For those who want to save their life will lose it (Mark 8:35).

> No one tears a patch from a new garment and sews it on an old garment (Luke 5:36).

> Many who are first will be last, and the last will be first (Matt. 19:30).

A proverb is open-ended. It demands contemplation because it is filled with universal applicability or speaks of a universal principle of truth. Frequently a proverb uses figurative language such as metaphor, hyperbole, or simile to ensure a broad range of meaning.

The **legal sayings** are those which have a juridical ring to them. They usually have to do with an area of ministry or ecclesiastical order. Below are three examples:

> Laborers deserve their food (Matt. 10:10b).

> If anyone will not welcome you or listen to your words, shake off the dust from your feet as you leave that house or town (Matt. 10:14).

> Truly I tell you, whatever you bind on earth will be bound in heaven, and whatever you loose on earth will be loosed in heaven (Matt. 18:18).

The **prophetic sayings** are usually salvific or judgmental.

> Two women will be grinding meal together; one will be taken and one will be left (Matt. 24:41).

> The days are coming when you will long to see one of the days of the Son of Man, and you will not see it. They will say to you, "Look there!" or "Look here!" Do not go, do not set off in pursuit. For as the lightning

flashes and lights up the sky from one side to the other, so will the Son of Man be in his day (Luke 17:22–24).

Parables

A **parable** is a short narrative comparing one thing to another. In this sense, a parable is an extended metaphor. A parable generally employs familiar situations, persons, or events to illustrate or illuminate an unfamiliar or unrecognized truth. The parable is a successful teaching tool because it is told in terms which people readily understand and remember.

Jülicher separates the parables into four types: the parable as similitude, as story, as example story, and as allegory.[11] When the parable is a similitude, it has a customary sense about it in that it draws attention to some commonly recurrent event, for example, the growth of the mustard seed, the leavening of bread, or the properties of salt. In this type of parable, the reader must ascertain the relationship between the event and the more abstract issue being illuminated.

The parable as story is a pericope with beginning, middle, and end. It will usually revolve around one or two characters engaged in some action and will be marked by a brevity of detail. The action will move swiftly to a conclusion, inviting the reader to make a single comparison between the culminating action and the "point" of the story. Examples of such parables are the parable of the Two Sons, the parable of the Friend at Midnight, and the parable of the Lost Sheep.

Jülicher's third parable type is the example story. In this type, the central character exhibits exemplary behavior. The central point is "look at this person and act likewise." One of the most familiar example stories is the parable of the Good Samaritan. His moral behavior is exemplary and should thus be emulated.

The final of the four types is the parable as allegory. Actually this type is nothing more than a series of metaphors, which means that this parable (unlike the others) necessarily has a number of comparative points. For an example of this type see the discussion of allegory in chapter 4. Examples of this type include the parable of the Tares, the parable of the Net, and the parable of the Sower.

By the time the parables were recorded in the Gospels, their original settings had been lost. Therefore, the idea that a parable focuses on a single

---

[11] Adolf Jülicher, *Die Gleichnisreden Jesu*, vol. 1 (Tübingen: J. C. B. Mohr, 1910).

comparison must be qualified. Most of the parables told by Jesus concerned the kingdom (reign) of God, which itself is presented as a parable.[12] While parables do offer a comparison, the comparison is told in terms of imagery, necessitating a consideration of multiple images and themes.

When readers encounter a parable in the Gospels, they need to ask not only what Jesus' point is, but what literary function the parable has for the evangelist. For instance, in Mark's version of the parable of the Sower (Mark 4:1ff.) and Matthew's parable of the Tares (Matt. 13:24ff.), each original parable is given an allegorical interpretation by the evangelist. The original settings of these parables cannot be discovered and indeed are irrelevant to their interpretation as they now stand in their present contexts. Furthermore, in Mark's Gospel the parables function almost exclusively to separate the insiders from the outsiders. Mark accomplishes this by reversing the parable's purpose. Whereas the parable is supposed to make some point more easily understood, the parables in Mark become a means by which information is clothed in mystery as far as the disciples and those outside are concerned. This use is illustrated in Mark 4:10-13:

> When he was alone, those who were around him along with the twelve asked him about the parables. And he said to them, "To you has been given the secret of the kingdom of God, but for those outside, everything comes in parables; in order that 'they may indeed look, but not perceive, and may indeed listen, but not understand; so that they may not turn again and be forgiven.'" And he said to them, "Do you not understand this parable? Then how will you understand all the parables?"

The disciples, who should understand the parables, are the very ones who do not. The astute reader of Mark's Gospel soon recognizes that the disciples consistently do not understand the parables and that those who think themselves to be insiders may actually be outsiders. This understanding of Mark's use of the parables at once causes modern readers to examine their own status within the circle of Christ.

Poetry

Since we have already discussed poetic parallelism, suffice it here to say that the evangelists were quite adept at its use. An excellent example is the two-stanza poem in Luke's instruction concerning prayer:

---

[12] Hans Conzelmann and Andreas Lindemann, *Interpreting the New Testament*, trans. Siegfried S. Schatzmann (Peabody: Hendrickson, 1988), p. 78.

Ask, and it will be given you;
Search, and you will find;
Knock, and the door will be opened for you.

For everyone who asks receives, and
Everyone who searches finds, and
For everyone who knocks, the door will be opened (Luke 11:9–10).

Hymns

While most New Testament hymns are in the Epistles, there are a few in the Gospels—the Magnificat (Luke 1:46–55), the Benedictus (Luke 1:68–79), the Nunc Dimittis (Luke 2:29–32), and the Song of the Angels (Luke 2:14). All the hymns have a distinct and pervasive lyric quality. They consist of language which is highly structured, cadenced, compressed, intense, economical, and with unusual grammatical features. These qualities become significant for interpretation.

Midrashim

When scholars use the word **midrashim** in reference to the New Testament, they usually have in mind those instances where the author interprets an Old Testament passage in light of contemporary circumstances. Since the term "midrash" actually has a plethora of definitions, however, to tease out a common one is problematic. What one scholar means by midrash is not necessarily what another one means. For this reason, our discussion of midrash is a bit more involved than our discussion of most of the other sub-genres. First we review the possible definitions of midrash, finally focusing upon one of these in some detail. And second, we offer some illustrations of the use of midrash in the New Testament.

The term "midrash" is generally used in one of three ways. First, it may refer to an exegetical method of interpreting the Hebrew Bible. This method may include the rewriting of a text within a new situation or the explaining of a text or portion of it within a new situation. Examples of the former are the chronicler's rewriting of the history in Samuel and Kings and the translation of the Hebrew Scriptures into Greek (Septuagint). In the Hebrew text of Exodus 24:10, we read that Moses and Aaron "saw the God of Israel." In the Septuagint's rendering of the same verse, however, it is paraphrased to read that Moses and Aaron "saw the place where the God of Israel stood." Why the change? It was probably an attempt by the translators to convey in Greek Israel's unspoken assumption concerning the impossibility of seeing God and remaining alive.[13] An example of explaining a text or portion of it within a new situation is the exegesis of Old Testament texts at Qumran. Notice the prophetic application of the following interpretation of Numbers 21:18.

> But God remembered the Covenant with the forefathers, and He raised from Aaron men of discernment and from Israel men of wisdom, and He caused them to hear. And they dug the Well: the well which the princes dug, which the nobles of the people delved with the stave.
>
> The *Well* is the Law, and those who dug it were the converts of Israel who went out of the land of Judah to sojourn in the land of Damascus. God called them all *princes* because they sought Him, and their renown was disputed by no man. The *Stave* is the Interpreter of the Law of whom Isaiah said, *He makes a tool for his Work* (Isa. liv, 16); and *the nobles of the people are those who come to dig the Well with the staves with which the Stave ordained that they should walk in all the age of wickedness—and without them they shall find nothing—until he comes who shall teach righteousness at the end of days.[14]*

Second, it may refer to the fruit of the method, i.e., to a compositional unit resulting from exegesis (e.g., the above exegesis of Num. 21:18). Two or more of these compositional units are called "midrashim." And third, the collection and arrangement of these midrashim into a compilation may also be called midrash. It is the first two of these definitions that we want to expand upon and illustrate.

Underlying the midrashic exegesis of Scripture are two crucial presuppositions: (1) The Scriptures were given by God and are consequently relevant for all subsequent generations; and (2) each part of the Scriptures (sentences, phrases, words, even single letters) has an autonomy independent of the whole. These two presuppositions then have an interesting corollary: Since the Scriptures were given by an infinite God, a particular passage in part or whole may have an infinite number of applications.

There are basically three approaches within midrashic exegesis. Jacob Neusner calls them paraphrase, prophecy, and parable.[15] Paraphrase is simply a rereading of a particular passage. This type of midrash is designed to amplify or clarify a passage in which the meaning is unclear. Clarification may be made by supplying a synonym, telling an

---

[13] Jacob Neusner, *What Is Midrash?* (Philadelphia: Fortress, 1987), p. 25.

[14] G. Vermes, *Dead Sea Scrolls in English*, rev. ed. (Baltimore: Penguin, 1968), pp. 102–3.

[15] Neusner, *What Is Midrash?* pp. 7–11.

illustrative story, giving a word-for-word explanation, or introducing another verse. In the first five verses of the Gospel of John we find a rereading of the first few verses of Genesis. This is an example of midrash by paraphrase.

Prophecy as midrash (according to Neusner) identifies a contemporary event or situation with a scriptural passage. The original meaning or historical frame of reference is not lost, but the reference does inform the present or the future. Thus we may find in Scripture (even historical sections) the meaning of what is happening now. As Neusner explains, "Midrash as prophecy treats the historical life of ancient Israel and the contemporary times of the exegete as essentially the same, reading the former as a prefiguring of the latter."[16]

In the New Testament, Matthew is known to engage in midrash as prophecy. For example, quoting from Isaiah 7:14 he says, "All this took place to fulfill what had been spoken by the Lord through the prophet: 'Look, the virgin shall conceive and bear a son, and they shall name him Emmanuel' " (Matt. 1:22–23). Another example involves the interpretation of a historical reference from Hosea as applying to an event in the life of Jesus: "Then Joseph got up, took the child and his mother by night, and went to Egypt, and remained there until the death of Herod. This was to fulfill what had been spoken by the Lord through the prophet, 'Out of Egypt I have called my son' " (Matt. 2:14–15). Of particular note is that Hosea 11:1 is referring to the exodus of Israel as a nation (the son) from Egypt!

A special type of midrash as prophecy is called *pesher*. This type of midrash assumes that what was written in the Scriptures was intended specifically for the contemporary situation. A given statement in Scripture has its significance in a contemporary event. In a classic example of a pesher interpretation, Peter interprets a prophecy of Joel in Acts 2:16–21 to refer to the events of Pentecost ("This is that . . . ").

Midrash as parable is similar to if not identical with allegorical interpretation. The more profound or authentic meaning of a statement or event is not the obvious historical or literal one. Scripture is interpreted in terms which the author never intended. This is possible because of the presuppositions mentioned above. The real meaning of Scripture is hidden beneath the literal one and must speak in such a way as to offer guidance to everyday living. This last type is probably the most characteristic of rabbinic midrash. While these three types of

---

[16] Ibid., p. 7.

midrash differ some in method and results, they share a common purpose: All midrash attempted to interpret the Scriptures in order to make them authoritatively applicable and therefore binding upon the smallest everyday details of the life of a people. "Thus the task of midrash is never merely reproductive; it is always productive of new understanding. It is a way of keeping the Bible open to the histoires of those who answer its claims."[17]

While we will discuss the literary forms within the Epistles below, to avoid repetition, it should be said that midrashim are also present among the New Testament epistles. Examples include Romans 10:5-13, 1 Corinthians 10:1-11, and 1 Peter 2:4-8, to name a few. The authors of the epistolary literature also compiled Scriptures together in a midrashic fashion (cf. 1 Pet 2:4-8). Perhaps the most obvious midrashim appear in the epistle to the Hebrews. Passages from the Psalms, the Pentateuch, and the Prophets are so radically applied to Jesus and the new covenant that the original context has completely disappeared. Passages that originally referred to Yahweh, David, and others are now applied to Jesus (e.g., Heb. 1:5-14; 5:4-6; 7:11-22). If modern exegetes recognize that the ancient authors were using an acceptable exegetical method, they will be in a better position to allow the authors to communicate their messages in their own exegetical medium.

Other literary forms, such as controversy stories, genealogies, Old Testament quotations, apocalyptic addresses, extended discourses, and Beatitudes, should become part of the reader's repertoire. Excellent discussions of these can be found in almost any good New Testament introduction.

Epistolary Literature

Since matters such as authorship, destination, and audience were dealt with in unit I, attention will be given here only to the literary character of the epistles. Obviously, once we move from the Gospels and Acts into the epistles, we are hard pressed to find what we have previously referred to as a narrative world or the world of the text. Terms such as characterization, plot, setting, story line, and narrative time become inappropriate if not meaningless. We are in a different genre. Nonetheless, just as the Gospels as narrative have uniquely definable

---

[17] Gerald L. Burns, "Midrash and Allegory: The Beginnings of Scriptural Interpretation," in Alter and Kermode, *Literary Guide to the Bible*, p. 629.

structures, so does the genre of New Testament epistolary literature. That the epistles are not mimetic history does not diminish their literary qualities. The qualities are simply of a different sort.

Letter writing in the hellenistic tradition followed a stereotypical form:

(1) *Opening or Prescript.* This consists of three parts: the author, the addressee, and a greeting. The greeting is often a wish for good health, a prayer-wish; and various other information may be offered concerning the writer or addressee.

(2) *Body.* Here the purpose of the letter is elaborated. It may be exceptionally brief or rather long. The body proper is quite often prefaced with a prayer to the gods, an expression of thanksgiving, mention of the author's circumstances, or some mention of a favorable remembrance of the addressee. These preliminary statements serve as a transition from the opening to the body and lay the basis for the relationship between the writer and the addressee. However, in many instances, these transitional matters are foregone, and the writer moves directly to the body. Attached to the end of the body proper may also be a request for reciprocal communication, notification of a prospective visit, or a challenge to action.

(3) *Closing.* The closing usually consists of a final greeting. It may also include a second wish for health for the addressee and/or other persons. A word of farewell (*errōsthe*) is usually placed at the end along with the date.

Before discussing the letters in the New Testament and their similarities to and differences from the hellenistic letter, we need to examine some characteristics of the hellenistic letter besides its form. The letter expressed a relationship of friendship between two parties. The letter was to have a certain "presence" about it, substituting for the actual presence of the writer. Thus a person would write to someone as if he or she were present.

The hellenistic letter is extremely stereotyped. The salutation, final greeting, and prayer (or wish for health) appear in hellenistic letters with almost predictable wording. David Aune, describing what he calls the private or documentary letter with its three-part structure, observes that the basic structure of the letter varied only slightly over the centuries.[18] Within the basic three-part structure, however, there was room for modifications. For example, within the *prescript* of the typical letter occur three elements—the superscription, adscription, and salutation. Each of these could be expanded; and epithets, titles,

---

[18] Aune, *New Testament in Its Literary Environment*, p. 162.

geographical references, a health wish, or a prayer might be added. Aune goes on to describe two other categories of Greco-Roman letters, which he calls official letters and literary letters. Official letters were from a government official to someone else, often in a government position. They were very similar to the private letter. Literary letters were apparently "preserved and transmitted through literary channels and were valued either as epistolary models, as examples of literary artistry, or as vignettes into earlier lives and manners."[19] These letters are further categorized into: (1) Letters of recommendation written by educated persons who had no intention of publishing them. These allowed an influential person to recommend a friend for a particular political or civil position. The framers of such letters made their recommendations on the basis of moral traits rather than on vocational ability. (2) Letter-essays are properly treatises rather than formal letters, because they use the standard epistolary structure in a limited fashion. While they may display the customary opening and closing, these letters are actually philosophical or ethical treatises (e.g., Quintilian's *Institutes* and Plutarch's *On Tranquility*). Epicurus, Diogenes Laertius, and even Plato and Aristotle used the letter as a means of philosophical instruction. (3) Pseudepigraphical letters were fictional presentations of stories about great men of the past.[20] Other fictional letters, which Aune terms imaginative letters, were written in the names of the past, often in an explicit attempt to capture the world-view of people from the past.

While it seems that the personal letter was the norm in Hellenism, there were instances (Epicurus, Seneca) where ethical questions were addressed in the form of the letter. Actually these were treatises and not letters in the strict sense, and they were probably written with the intention of producing a highly literary document. This observation has led some scholars to make a distinction between **letter** and **epistle**.[21] This distinction is based upon the private or public audience; a letter is seen as being nonliterary and written for an individual or particular audience, whereas an epistle is regarded as literary and written for posterity or the public. Second Peter, 1 John, and James are cited as examples of the epistle. For instance, neither James nor 2 Peter has a final greeting or a specific addressee. Gabel and Wheeler

---

[19] Ibid., p. 165.

[20] Ibid., pp. 165–69.

[21] Cf. Gabel and Wheeler, *Bible as Literature*; and Fee and Stuart, *How to Read the Bible*.

suggest that genuine letters differ from epistles in that "an epistle is an artificial or make-believe letter, written for publication rather than for mailing."[22] These scholars feel that the most distinctive aspect of New Testament letters is their occasional nature. They were not written for posterity but were intended to address the particular and actual situations of the audience. Like their Greek and Roman counterparts, their basic purpose was to convey information between two people or audiences. They are not essays. As Ryken explains, "It would be wrong, therefore, to regard the epistles as systematic and expository. Like letters in general, the New Testament epistles (with the exceptions of Romans and Hebrews) are not systematic arguments."[23]

Most scholarship today, however, has reached what Doty calls a balance. The letters of the New Testament fall somewhere between documents as purely occasional responses to local situations and documents as purely theological treatises intended to express Christian theological ideologies that extend beyond historical situations.

The Structure of the New Testament Epistle

Paul's letters are the earliest in the New Testament and set the standard epistolary form. While both formal and conceptual variations are found in the New Testament epistles, they generally follow the basic Pauline structure:

I.   Salutation (sender, addressee, greeting).
II. Thanksgiving (may be a blessing or accompanied by intercession).
III. Body (may include introductory formulae and statement of future plans).
IV. Paraenesis (ethical exhortation and instructions).
V.   Closing (peace wish, greetings, benediction, writing process).

In order to understand how Paul adapted and expanded the form of the hellenistic letter, we need to examine each of the parts of the genuine Pauline letter.

Opening. The standard Greek **salutation** often contained the word *chairein* (greeting) followed by a formulaic wish for well-being. Paul

---

[22] Gabel and Wheeler, *Bible as Literature*, p. 216.
[23] Ryken, *Words of Life*, pp. 90–91.

changed the word to *charis* (grace) and expanded the salutation to include references to his apostleship and fellow-workers. He might also refer to the status of his addressees:

> Paul, called to be an apostle of Christ Jesus by the will of God, and our brother Sosthenes, To the church of God that is in Corinth, to those who are sanctified in Christ Jesus, called to be saints, together with all those who in every place call on the name of our Lord Jesus Christ, both their Lord and ours: Grace to you and peace from God our Father and the Lord Jesus Christ (1 Cor. 1:1–3).

Notice that Paul has not only substituted *charis* for *chairein* but also inserted "peace." *Shalom* (peace) was the traditional Jewish epistolary greeting. So Paul has expanded and modified the traditional formulaic hellenistic salutation to include both his Jewish and Christian heritage. In the opening of Romans, Paul's expansion includes a summary of his gospel. Since Paul did not found the church at Rome and had not visited it, he probably felt the need to establish his authority to speak.

Thanksgiving. Most work done today on the Pauline thanksgivings is little more than commentary on the efforts of Paul Schubert.[24] Schubert contends that the **thanksgiving** serves three functions: it terminates the salutation, gives the basic purpose of the letter, and may offer an outline of the primary topics in the body of the letter. Hellenistic letters frequently have thanksgivings where the writer gives thanks to the gods or informs the addressee that mention is made of him or her before the gods. With the exception of Galatians, Paul follows this tradition. In that letter, Paul is anxious to move on to the problem and therefore contravenes the convention. But in 1 Thessalonians, Paul's thanksgiving section is so disproportional to the rest of the letter (it consumes well over half the letter) that the letter seems convoluted. While Paul follows epistolary custom with the inclusion of a thanksgiving, he does inject modifications based upon his religious perspective. For instance, the thanksgiving becomes the occasion to offer praise for the faithfulness of the addressees and to express a wish that this faithfulness will continue.[25]

As indicated above, the Pauline thanksgiving tends to announce at least some of the major topics of the body. Consider the thanksgiving in 1 Corinthians 1:4–9:

---

[24] Paul Schubert, *Form and Function of the Pauline Thanksgivings* (Berlin: Alfred Töpelmann, 1939).

[25] See Jack T. Sanders, "The Transition from Opening Epistolary Thanksgiving to Body in the Pauline Corpus," *JBL* 81 (1962), pp. 352–62.

> I give thanks to my God always for you because of the grace of God that has been given you in Christ Jesus, for in every way you have been enriched in him, in speech and knowledge of every kind—just as the testimony of Christ has been strengthened among you—so that you are not lacking in any spiritual gift as you wait for the revealing of our Lord Jesus Christ. He will also strengthen you to the end, so that you may be blameless on the day of our Lord Jesus Christ. God is faithful; by him you were called into the fellowship of his Son, Jesus Christ our Lord.

Notice that Paul refers to the charismatic gifts of speech and knowledge and to the "day of our Lord." Both of these subjects are primary concerns in the body of 1 Corinthians, where Paul puts the charismatic enthusiasm in perspective by emphasizing the eschatological nature of the day of the Lord.

Paul also seems to include in his thanksgivings liturgical elements, such as the note in the thanksgiving of 2 Corinthians: "Blessed be the God and Father of our Lord Jesus Christ" (2 Cor. 1:3). So, as James Robinson has successfully demonstrated, while Paul follows the general epistolary form, he also adapts elements from his liturgical tradition to it, resulting in some essentially new patterns.[26]

Body. The material within the bodies of the Pauline letters is diverse. The controlling factor is a need or problem of the recipients. The reader would not logically expect any rhyme or reason within the variegated Pauline landscape called the **body** of the letter. But this is only partially the case. Among the variety of topics in Paul's letters, there is a recurring pattern of formal features. Here are some of these formal features:

(a) The request or injunction formula. Look at the following example:

> Now I appeal to you, brothers and sisters, by the name of our Lord Jesus Christ, that all of you be in agreement and that there be no divisions among you, but that you be united in the same mind and the same purpose (1 Cor. 1:10).

A verb occurs, followed by a direct address and the actual request. This request or appeal formula, however, also occurs in other places within the body of the letter, especially where new material is introduced.

(b) The disclosure formula. Examples are: "I want you to know that" or "We do not want you to be unaware" (Rom. 1:13; 2 Cor. 1:18;

---

[26] James M. Robinson, "The Historicality of Biblical Language," in *The Old Testament and Christian Faith,* ed. Bernhard W. Anderson (New York: Harper & Row, 1963), pp. 132–49.

1 Thess. 2:1; Phil. 1:12; Gal. 1:11). According to Doty, this formula (as well as the request formula) provides a heading "for the following paragraph(s) and states briefly its contents, analogous to a newspaper headline and subtitle."[27] As with the request formula, the disclosure formula introduces new material within the body of the letter (e.g., 1 Cor. 11:3; 1 Thess. 4:13; 1 Cor. 10:1; 12:1; Rom. 11:25).

(c) The joy formula. Expressions of joy ("I have indeed received much joy") were usually a result of some pleasing information which the apostle had received. An example is Paul's joy over Philemon's Christian progress.[28]

(d) Autobiographical notes. Near the beginning of the body in most of his letters, Paul remarks on his activities. Paul recollects his former ministry among the Corinthians in 1 Corinthians 1:10-17, and in Philippians 1:12-26, he talks about an imprisonment (cf. Gal. 1:10-2:21 and 2 Cor. 1:8-2:12). These autobiographical notes are not unrelated miscellany but have integral meanings within his arguments. They reinforce Paul's demands upon his addressees.

(e) The **travelogue**. Toward the end of the body of the letters (with the exception of Galatians), Paul alludes to a possible future visit by himself or an emissary (cf. Rom. 15:14-33; 1 Cor. 4:14-21; 2 Cor. 12:14-13:13; Gal. 4:12-20; Phil. 2:19-24; 1 Thess. 2:17-3:13; Philem. 21f.). Roetzel suggests that the function of the travelogue is to add punch to the message of the letter by promising an apostolic visit.[29]

Paraenesis. Paul was especially adept at tailoring general ethical materials to specific situations. That Paul utilizes traditional materials (from Jewish and hellenistic sources) should not obscure the fact that he did not intend to develop a new Christian moral system. As Roetzel observes, "these act not as a rulebook for solving every problem, rather, they are examples or illustrations of how the gospel is to take effect. These ethical sections, or **paraenesis**, provide practical guidance, but they also convey information, make requests and issue reminders."[30]

The paraenetic sections consist of three types of ethical materials. First, Paul combines various moral statements which have very little inherent connection. For example, Romans 12:9-13 encompasses the topics of love, hate, evil, good, brotherly affection, the bestowing of

---

[27] William G. Doty, *Letters in Primitive Christianity* (Philadelphia: Fortress, 1973), p. 34.

[28] Ibid., p. 35.

[29] Calvin J. Roetzel, *The Letters of Paul: Conversations in Context* (Atlanta: John Knox Press, 1982), p. 35.

[30] Ibid., p. 36.

honor, zeal, spiritual aliveness, service, hope, patience, constancy in prayer, liberality in giving, and hospitality. Paul presents each topic in the form of a moral injunction. Most probably Paul received this material from an existing tradition.

The second type of material is found in lists of virtues and vices, where there is borrowing from both Jewish and hellenistic traditions. The lists vary in length and do not necessarily reflect the situation at any particular church (e.g., Rom. 1:29–31; 1 Cor. 5:10–11; 2 Cor. 6:6–7, 14; Gal. 5:19–23; Phil. 4:8). A list of vices may stand alone, as in Romans 1:29–31, or it may be paired with a list of virtues, as in Galatians 5:19–23. Doty suggests that rules for the household which offer specific domestic duties (*Haustafeln*) should be included in this type of paraenesis.[31]

Third, Paul employs what can be called homiletical exhortations centering around a particular topic. Most of 1 Corinthians 5–15 is taken up with a series of homiletical exhortations on a variety of topics. Another example of this type of paraenesis is Paul's discussion of the resurrection in 1 Thessalonians 4:13–18. More will be said about the forms within the paraenetic sections when we discuss the literary forms in the New Testament letters.

Closing. The **closing** normally includes a peace wish, greetings, a benediction, and sometimes an apostolic pronouncement. Most often these are prefaced with a list of final instructions. The greetings occur between the peace wish and benediction. While these may be stock meanings within the conclusion of the Pauline letter, they are not simply meaningless formalities. In the peace wish, Paul returns to the major concern(s) of the letter. Note this return in 1 Thessalonians 5:23: "May the God of peace himself sanctify you entirely; and may your spirit and soul and body be kept sound and blameless at the coming of our Lord Jesus Christ." The coming of the Lord and the readiness of the saints are major concerns of the letter. The peace wish in Galatians 6:16 ("As for those who will follow this rule—peace be upon them, and mercy, and upon the Israel of God") returns to Paul's concern with the bondage of circumcision versus freedom in Christ and the true Israel.

The benediction ("the grace of the Lord Jesus be with you") varies little in Paul's letters, but it has taken on a distinctly Christian perspective. However, sometimes Paul prefaces the benediction with a warning or exhortation (see 1 Cor. 16:22; 1 Thess. 5:27; and Gal. 6:17).

---

[31] Doty, *Letters in Primitive Christianity*, p. 58.

Conceptual Differences in the Epistles

In addition to the formal variations already mentioned, scholars recognize that there are also conceptual differences among New Testament epistles. Such differences are due in part because of differences in originating circumstances, the use of amanuenses, and changing conditions in the life of the church. For example, the **Pastorals** (1, 2 Timothy and Titus) are recognized by most scholars today as the products of a church well on its way to becoming an institution. The outlook of the Pastorals is advanced in their concern for the survival of the institution. In the earlier Pauline letters, the author is constantly on the offensive, where both internal and external problems are confronted with an almost fever-pitched debate. In the earlier Pauline letters, faith is defined as a trust in God, a belief in Jesus as the Messiah, while faith in the Pastorals is a body of received truth to be defended. Furthermore, in the earlier Pauline letters, the Parousia, or coming of Jesus, is imminent, whereas in the Pastorals it becomes more distant.

Not only is the outlook in the Pastorals different from the earlier letters, but linguistic differences also exist. Approximately twenty percent of the vocabulary in the Pastorals is *hapax legomena* (lit., terms "being said once") and about thirty percent of the vocabulary in the Pastorals is not found in the earlier letters. When we add to this the absence in the Pastorals of very key words of the earlier letters, we get the sense that we are without a doubt in a world with highly different theological interests from the earlier letters.

Along with the differences in outlook and vocabulary, we may also make reference to a difference in form. The paraenetic, or ethical, section virtually dominates the Pastorals.

Some of the same observations pertaining to vocabulary and outlook given above for the Pastorals could be applied to Ephesians, Colossians, and 2 Thessalonians. In Ephesians (which contains about one-third of Colossians) we find a summary of Pauline theology while 2 Thessalonians modifies Paul's eschatological thought.

The **Catholic letters** have the character of more conscious literary production. Second and 3 John appear in traditional letter form while 1 John has moved entirely away from the traditional letter toward the form of an essay on Christian love. James, Jude, and 2 Peter retain little of the letter form. For example, James retains the salutation, but this is followed by a list of moral admonitions and exhortation. It appears to be a moral tractate and not a letter.

While 1 and 2 Peter and Jude employ epistolary conventions, they also move in the direction of the theological tractate. Doty remarks,

> these writings are best understood as tracts expressing support for those undergoing persecution for their religion—persecution both from the state and from deviant Christians. Theological reflections now revolve around the sacred Christian traditions, not around the necessary shaping of the religion in specific contexts.[32]

Sub-Genres in the New Testament Epistolary Literature

When we examine the literary forms of the New Testament letters, it becomes obvious that the authors were well-versed in the broad spectrum of hellenistic and Jewish literary practices. An acquaintance with these forms is indispensable for the hermeneut, especially since content (and therefore, message) must be tailored to form. The catalogue given below is intended to introduce the student to the literary forms in the epistles. The discussion is by no means comprehensive, but perhaps enough interest will be sparked to encourage further specialized study.

The Topos

The *topos* was a particular rhetorical device used by hellenistic Cynic and Stoic itinerant preachers. These itinerant preachers developed standardized responses to frequently asked questions on certain topics. Most often the topic concerned vice or virtue. These *topoi* (plural) could be strung together with no apparent controlling principle or arranged by the use of some *Leitwort*. David Bradley has identified two *topoi* in Paul's letters—Romans 13 and 1 Thessalonians 4:9–5:11.[33]

Lists of Vices and Virtues

We have already referred to these lists above, so only a few comments are necessary here. Attempts to identify **lists of vices and virtues** with particular ecclesiastical communities will probably result in frustration or at best be nothing more than speculation. More likely the

---

[32] Ibid., p. 70.

[33] See David G. Bradley, "The *Topos* as a Form in the Pauline Paraenesis," *JBL* 72 (1953), pp. 238–46.

authors adapted these lists to describe general moral behavior and problems. An example of a list of vices is 1 Corinthians 5:10–11:

> Not at all meaning the immoral of this world, or the greedy and robbers, or idolaters, since you would then need to go out of the world. But now I am writing to you not to associate with anyone who bears the name of brother or sister who is sexually immoral or greedy, or is an idolater, reviler, drunkard, or robber. Do not even eat with such a one.

An example of a list of virtues is Colossians 3:12–14:

> As God's chosen ones, holy and beloved, clothe yourselves with compassion, kindness, humility, meekness, and patience. Bear with one another and, if anyone has a complaint against another, forgive each other; just as the Lord has forgiven you, so you also must forgive. Above all, clothe yourselves with love, which binds everything together in perfect harmony.

Other lists include: Romans 1:29–31; 1 Corinthians 6:9–10; 2 Corinthians 6:6–7; Galatians 5:19–23; Ephesians 6:14–17; Philippians 4:8; Titus 1:7–8; James 3:17; 1 Peter 4:3; 2 Peter 1:5–8; Revelation 9:20–21.

List of Circumstances

These lists reflect details about careers of the apostles. For example in 2 Corinthians 12:10 we find this list: "Therefore I am content with weaknesses, insults, hardships, persecutions, and calamities for the sake of Christ; for whenever I am weak, then I am strong." Another such list is found in 2 Corinthians 11:23–28.

Lists of Rules for Behavior within the Christian Community

These lists show a concern with articulating how Christians should live in the world on a day-to-day basis. These lists of relationships are not unique to the New Testament writings, but as part of the general hellenistic cultural milieu, they became part of the daily life of the church. Most of these lists occur in the later letters of the church (e.g., Eph. 5:21–6:9; Col. 3:18–4:1; 1 Tim. 2:1–15, 5:1–21; Titus 2:1–10; 2 Pet. 2:13–3:7).

Proverbs

Since **proverbs,** or **wisdom sayings,** have been discussed in the Gospel section above, I simply list some examples here.

A little yeast leavens the whole batch of dough (Gal. 5:9).

Bad company ruins good morals (1 Cor. 15:33).

Making the most of the time, because the days are evil (Eph. 5:16).

Confessional Statements

These formulaic statements are professions of belief. They are compact summaries of theological understanding and doctrine which were most likely used and recited within liturgical situations, like baptism. Terms such as "confess" or "believe" suggest confessional statements. Also a rhythmic quality may indicate a **confessional statement** (but this is also a quality of a hymn or what Ryken calls patterned rhetorical prose). The following typify the confessional statement.

> Because if you confess with your lips that Jesus is Lord and believe in your heart that God raised him from the dead, you will be saved (Rom. 10:9).

> He was revealed in flesh,
>   vindicated in spirit,
> seen by angels,
>   proclaimed among Gentiles,
> believed in throughout the world,
>   taken up in glory (1 Tim. 3:16).[34]

Hymns

The present discussion by scholars on hymnic material within the epistolary literature of the New Testament is considerable and far too extensive to discuss at any length here. Therefore, I give the general qualities of the New Testament hymn. The hymnic material is marked by a pronounced and recognizable rhythm. The reader should also look for types of parallelisms. For example, in the confessional statement above (1 Tim. 3:16 might be considered a hymn) the aorist passive is used in every verb. Also in every expression except one, *en* (in) precedes a noun in the dative singular. The rhythmical quality and the parallelism are unmistakable. Again, there is a fine line (often an invisible one) between confessional statements, hymns, and patterned rhetorical prose (to be discussed below).

---

[34] Because of the rhythmical quality of the latter example, it might also fall within Ryken's definition of patterned rhetorical prose.

Metaphor

The epistles are saturated with metaphor evidencing a poetic impulse. Some examples are:

You are God's field, God's building (1 Cor. 3:9b).

These are waterless springs and mists driven by a storm (2 Pet. 2:17b).

The tongue is a fire (James 3:6a).

Do you not know that your body is a temple of the Holy Spirit? (1 Cor. 6:19a).

Paul especially attests to a distinct trust in the power of metaphor to convey meaning. As P. C. Sands observes, the diction of Paul "is continually enlivened by metaphor, 'gluing yourselves to the good,' 'boiling with the spirit,' 'buying up the opportunity,' 'let the love of Christ make its home in you,' 'let the peace of Christ be umpire in your hearts.' "[35]

Diatribe

A **diatribe** is a type of argument in which a writer/orator creates a hypothetical inquirer or objectioner (a dialogue partner, often referred to as the interlocutor). The writer or orator then proceeds to answer the objections of this imaginary questioner. While the inquirer may be hypothetical, the issue at stake is not. An example is in Romans 6. Here the inquirer asks, "What then are we to say? Should we continue in sin in order that grace may abound?" Paul then goes on to answer this challenge in verses 2–14. Apparently this inquirer is persistent, because another question is asked in verse 15: "What then? Should we sin because we are not under law but under grace?" The answer is recorded in 6:14c–7:6. This type of argumentation continues with further questions in 7:7, 13 and 9:14, 19, 30. Another example is James 2:18–22, which begins with, "But someone will say, 'You have faith and I have works.' " The author then proceeds with an elaborate retort. The hypothetical opponent may even be an abstract personification, as in 1 Corinthians 12:15–21 (the speakers are body parts) and Romans 2:21–22 (the speaker is righteousness).

---

[35] P. C. Sands, *Literary Genius of the New Testament* (New York: Oxford University, 1932), p. 153.

Captatio benevolentiae

In *captatio benevolentiae,* the author offers flattery by assuming that the reader will be familiar with a particular corpus of knowledge. Note the flattery and assumption in Romans 7:1: "Do you not know, brothers and sisters—for I am speaking to those who know the law—that the law is binding on a person only during that person's lifetime?" The same assumption underlies 1 Corinthians 9:24: "Do you not know that in a race the runners all compete, but only one receives the prize?" (cf. Acts 24:2–3).

Word Chains

By linking concepts together (usually in some causal manner) in a **word chain** the author produces a climatic effect. In Romans 5:3–5 we read,

> And not only that, but we also boast in our sufferings, knowing that suffering produces endurance, and endurance produces character, and character produces hope, and hope does not disappoint us, because God's love has been poured into our hearts through the Holy Spirit that has been given to us.

A similar chain is found in 2 Peter 1:5–7:

> For this very reason, you must make every effort to support your faith with goodness, and goodness with knowledge, and knowledge with self-control, and self-control with endurance, and endurance with godliness, and godliness with mutual affection, and mutual affection with love.

Other literary devices such as rhetorical questions (e.g., Rom. 8:31–32), personifications (James 1:15), and patterned rhetorical prose are common. The last of these is illustrated especially by the author of Ephesians:

> There is one body
> and one Spirit,
> Just as you were called
> to the one hope
> of your calling
> One Lord,
> One faith,
> One baptism,
> One God and Father of all,
> who is above all
> and through all
> and in all (Eph. 4:4–6).

And again, by Paul:

> For I am convinced that neither death,
>   nor life,
>   nor angels,
>   nor rulers,
>   nor things present,
>   nor things to come,
>   nor powers,
>   nor height
>   nor depth,
>   nor anything else in all creation,
> will be able to separate us
> from the love of God
> in Christ Jesus our Lord (Rom. 8:38-39).

In the first example, the word "one" occurs a seven times. It has the effect of a drum beat—one body, one Spirit, one hope, one Lord, one faith, one baptism, one God. The word "all" has the same effect at the end of the passage—of all, above all, through all, in all. The immediate context of this passage is concerned with unity within the body of Christ. By repeating the word "one" followed by the repetition of "all," the author drives home the point of doctrinal unity within the church.

In light of the many literary forms in the epistles, it is no wonder that recent scholarship has recognized the high literary nature and creative artistry of the New Testament epistolary literature. Ryken neatly capsulizes this view:

> The New Testament epistles represent a mingling of the traditional and the innovative. Like ordinary letters, they exist to convey information to an audience and are prompted by a specific occasion. Their religious focus makes them distinctive. They also differ from other ancient letters by being more consistently literary in their form and style, but this very quality makes them similar to other literature and actually enhances their accessibility for a modern reader.[36]

Apocalyptic Literature

The third literary genre in the New Testament is **apocalyptic literature.** While apocalyptic passages exist in the Gospels, the single sustained apocalypse is the final work in the New Testament canon—the book of Revelation. The Gospels may remind modern readers of a

---

[36] Ryken, *Words of Life*, p. 97.

novella; the epistles of modern letter correspondence; but when modern readers enter the world of apocalypse, they usually find themselves stumbling around amidst lampstands and horses, wondering what this all means! Since apocalyptic writing presents the greatest interpretive difficulties to modern readers, we will briefly examine its basic characteristics and then discuss the artistry of the book of Revelation.

Apocalyptic literature occurs in both the Hebrew Bible and New Testament. Portions of Ezekiel, Isaiah, Zechariah, and the book of Daniel are apocalyptic. Since most readers are more familiar with the book of Revelation, however, I have chosen to discuss apocalypse here in the New Testament section and encourage the readers to examine apocalypse in the Hebrew Bible at their own leisure.

Characteristics of Apocalypse

Although apocalypse is not a modern literary genre, it was a common type of writing in Judaism during the middle hellenistic period (second century B.C.–second century A.D.). *Second Esdras, Ethiopic Enoch,* and the *Syriac Apocalypse of Baruch* are the purest representatives of this genre outside of the Bible. Since apocalyptic as a genre is generally unfamiliar to modern readers, a brief discussion of the major characteristics of apocalyptic should be helpful.

First, the scope of apocalypse is cosmic, having characters moving with ease between heaven, earth, and hell. Conflict involves angels and immense human armies pitted against the powers of deity. This conflict and ultimate victory by the deity is most commonly a result of a small group's persecution and vindication. After this minority experiences a time of extreme, hyperbolized suffering, the deity will eventually rescue them, replacing this present age with a utopian one.

Second, apocalyptic cosmology is dualistic. Working within the universe are an evil and a good force, almost equally matched. In the end, however, the good force triumphs over the evil. The personification of this evil force is typical of apocalypse.

Third, apocalypse is generally, but not always (e.g., the *Shepherd of Hermas*) eschatological; that is, its focus is on the end of history, the final stages of human existence. However, a discrete distinction should be maintained between eschatology and apocalypse. Whereas eschatology is concerned exclusively with the doctrine of the end of the age, apocalypse refers to a revelation and a particular type of writing which discloses that revelation. In addition, apocalyptic could be used to communicate a body of knowledge which had nothing to do with end time concerns. An apocalypse of this type is the *Shepherd of Hermas*, which is concerned with proper Christian living. In other words, the symbolism of apocalyptic might be used without its eschatological character.

Fourth, the mode of presentation is usually an ecstatic vision, dream, or supernatural journey experienced by the author, who is normally a great person from Israel's history. This vision is filled with images (usually very concrete in nature), which incarnate meaning through symbolism and allegory. For example, in Daniel chapter 8, the visionary observes a male goat with one horn, which breaks off and is replaced by four other horns. This is followed by the appearance of a small horn growing out of one of the previous four. This small horn then overthrows the other horns. When the vision is explained in 8:19ff., the goat represents the Greek kingdom and its horn is the first Greek king, Alexander the Great. The horns represent the four kingdoms into which Alexander's kingdom is divided, and the little horn is the most fierce king from among these four kingdoms.

Finally, and most significantly, apocalyptic literature is extremely symbolic. In fact, the basic sub-genre in apocalypse is symbolism. Accordingly, throughout apocalypse, the author uses metaphoric images and events to point to something else. Christ, for example, is represented as a lamb or a lion in Revelation. Apocalypse is imagery at its best.

No other genre of the Bible has been so fervently read with such depressing results as apocalypse, especially the books of Daniel and Revelation. This genre has suffered from a disastrous history of misinterpretation due to a fundamental misunderstanding of its literary forms, structure, and purpose. Because of its very claim to reveal what is shortly to happen, apocalypse has been viewed as a road map into and a blueprint of the future. The tragic flaw in this view is the assumption that the book's frame of reference is the reader's contemporary age rather than the author's. This misguided approach to apocalypse (particularly Revelation) treats the work as if it were a cryptogram by which contemporary events can be used to interpret the symbol of the text.[37]

With the above characteristics and observations in mind, some basic guidelines for reading apocalypse in general and Revelation in particular can be offered.

---

[37] Johnson, *Writings of the New Testament*, p. 513.

Guidelines for Interpreting Apocalyptic

First, the interpreter must recognize that apocalyptic communicates its messages through symbolism. To interpret a symbol literally when it is metaphoric is simply to misinterpret. The issue is not whether the events in apocalyptic are historical. The events may be historical; they may have really happened, or might happen. But the author presents events and communicates meaning through images and archetypes. In chapter twelve of Revelation, we find the following:

> A great portent appeared in heaven: a woman clothed with the sun, with the moon under her feet, and on her head a crown of twelve stars. She was pregnant and was crying out in birthpangs, in the agony of giving birth. Then another portent appeared in heaven: a great red dragon, with seven heads and ten horns, and seven diadems on his heads. His tail swept down a third of the stars of heaven and threw them to the earth. Then the dragon stood before the woman who was about to bear a child, so that he might devour her child as soon as it was born. And she gave birth to a son, a male child, who is to rule all the nations with a rod of iron. But her child was snatched away and taken to God and to his throne (Rev. 12:1–5).

A careful reader recognizes this passage as a description of the incarnation of Christ. The woman with the twelve-starred crown is Israel, the child who will rule the nations is Christ, and the dragon is Satan who was unsuccessful in his attempt to destroy Christ and his mission. To view the symbols and images in such passages as self-referential is to consign interpreters to a literalist prison. The writer does not describe the incarnation here literally, but figuratively, symbolically, calling to mind the historical or spiritual reality. The extra-referentiality of the symbols in general (e.g., the horses in 6:1–8, the soiled garments in 3:4, and the sword of Jesus' mouth in 2:16) can be taken as a rule of interpretation or decoding for the book of Revelation and for apocalypse as a genre.

A second guideline: Look for archetypes. Apocalyptic literature in general and Revelation in particular will also be pregnant with what in literature is called the archetype. As we have already seen, an archetype is an image, plot, motif, character type, or concept which appears with repeated regularity. It becomes a master image around which reality in the literary imagination is organized. Explanation of the significance of archetypes is usually unnecessary because the master images themselves immediately elicit a whole world of perception and understanding. Archetypes such as light, darkness, blood, lamb, water, sea, throne, war, gold, and bride organize meaning in apocalyptic literature.

Third: Recognize that apocalypse always originates in periods of oppression or persecution imposed upon the Hebrews by foreign powers. The literature that emerges is intended to encourage faith and hope. Regardless of how hopeless things may now seem, according to apocalyptic, God is going to bring about the redemption of his people by intervening on a cosmic level. Even though God's people are undergoing persecution, God will eventually manifest his justice and mercy by vindicating his chosen people. The hermeneut must keep this redemptive and vindicative purpose in mind when explicating apocalyptic.

A fourth guideline pertains to the interpretation of the book of Revelation: Look for Old Testament allusions. Since symbols in Revelation have roots in the Hebrew Bible, the reader will find a thorough knowledge of the Hebrew Bible to be indispensable. The book of Revelation is a creative reworking and reapplication of the Hebrew Scriptures. Revelation is heavily dependent upon the canonical prophetic texts and especially upon apocalyptic works like Zechariah, Daniel, and Ezekiel.

The following chart illustrating some examples of this grounding in the Old Testament imagery should be helpful.

Most of the symbols and concrete images in Revelation actually had a long history of literary significance before they were adapted by the author of Revelation. We also may assume that the Apocalypse's original audience had a sufficient familiarity with the symbols and their history of conventional use. Even if we assume that Revelation is a report of historically grounded visionary experiences, these experiences have been artfully crafted into apocalyptic conventions.

One final observation concerning apocalypse is necessary. Apocalypse is one literary genre while classical Hebrew prophecy is another. To interpret apocalyptic as prophecy is simply to misinterpret. The following distinctions should be kept in mind. First, prophecy carries with it a contingency: the outcome in prophecy depends upon the actions of a certain group of people. This is not the case with apocalypse. In apocalypse, this evil age is so far beyond redemption that a predetermined and unchangeable course has been mapped out for human history. Second, the prophetic future is a continuation of the present and is itself part of the course of history. In apocalypse the future is a decisive break with the present age brought about by the direct intervention of God. History will in fact terminate. And third, at least in written form, prophecy is poetic while apocalypse is narrative—albeit highly figurative—prose.

Old Testament Imagery in Revelation		
Item	OT Reference	Revelation
Archangel Michael	Dan. 10:13, 21; 12:1	12:7
Vision of God	Dan. 7:9, 13, 22; Ezek. 1:26–28	4:2–9
Lamb imagery	Isa. 53	5:6–14; 7:9; 13:8; etc.
Heavenly beings	Ezek. 1:10; 10:14	4:6–8
Shadowy horses	Zech. 1:8; 6:1–6	6:1–8; 19:14
Locusts	Joel 1:4–2:11	9:1–11
Resurrection of dead for judgment	Dan. 12:2–3	20:4–6
The holy city	Ezek. 40:1–48:35	21:2–22:5
Horns	Dan. 7:7–8; Zech. 1:18–21	9:13; 12:3; 13:1; 17:3, 7, 12, 16

CHART 6-3

Summary

In this unit we have discussed the world of the text and have found that the storehouse from which the authors pull their material is large, diversified, and well-stocked. Without some knowledge of the materials, modern travelers of this textual world will soon become lost, unable to read, much less follow, the road signs, and they will eventually find themselves groping for meaning and direction. A familiarity with genre, sub-genre, conventions, and strategies by which the author engages the reader must receive as much consideration as the world behind the text. This world of the text is constructed by and must be understood in relationship to its constituent parts. But the parts must be interpreted under the scrutiny of the whole. The individual literary units of a writing are meaningful only in the context of the literary whole. Thus if the individual literary unit has meaning, it is at once dependent upon and in the service of the whole. The biblical text must be interpreted as a structural unity, with each part seen as integral to the whole and as modifying the meaning of the whole. McKnight observes:

Interpretation, then, involves bringing all parts of the text into a meaningful relationship to the entire text. Whenever possible, one unit in the text is seen as standing in metaphoric relation to other units and to the total work.[38]

A reader makes sense of words, sentences, and paragraphs of a text only to the degree that the codes or conventions of the natural language have been mastered. In a similar fashion, readers ascertain the literary meaning or significance of a text only through a mastery of the codes or conventions of the literary languages which co-exist with the codes of the natural language. Consequently, a reader must see a text as the interaction of the types of codes—those of the natural language plus those of literary languages in genre and sub-genre. This means that different readers, depending upon their competence in these languages, may construe meaning at different levels. The best-equipped readers feel at home in the genres and sub-genres, and, when confronted simultaneously by the multiple levels of the linguistic and literary structures, they are capable of applying the multiple codes. The reader thus is not an innocent bystander upon whom the text acts. Rather, the reader plays an integral role in actualizing the meaning of a text. The reader is neither disinterested nor inactive. The text means nothing until someone means something by it. It is to this complex role of the reader in the production of meaning that we now turn.

REVIEW & STUDY

Key Terms and Concepts

Biography	Thanksgiving
Romance	Body
Torah	Travelogue
Apophthegm	Salutation
Proverb	Closing
Legal saying	*Topos*
Prophetic saying	Wisdom saying
Parable	List of vices and virtues
Midrashim	Confessional statement

---

[38] McKnight, *Post-Modern Use of the Bible*, p. 132.

Epistle	Diatribe
Letter	*Captatio benevolentiae*
Catholic letters	Word chain
Pastorals	Apocalyptic
Paraenesis	

Study Questions

1. Read the resurrection narrative in all four Gospels, noting the differences. What do these differences suggest about the authors' use of traditional material and about the mimetic quality of the Gospels?

2. Suggest some explanations for the differences discovered in the above question.

3. In *An Introduction to the New Testament* (Peabody: Hendrickson Publishers, 1989), Charles Puskas sets up the following scenario: Suppose that you were working in the great Ptolemaic library in Alexandria in the first century A.D. Upon receiving copies of the four Gospels, the head librarian instructed you to catalogue and shelve these works according to genre. Puskas suggests three categories—biography, history or tragic drama. We might add a fourth—romance. How would you catalogue the Gospels and what would guide you in your decision?

4. Read Genesis 14:17–20. Now read Hebrews 6:16–7:17. What type of midrash is the author of Hebrews offering on Genesis 14:17–20?

5. Basing your response upon the New Testament writers' practice of midrash upon the Hebrew Bible, what implications do you see for the modern interpretation of the New Testament?

6. Read 1 Thessalonians and 1 Timothy. Identify the paraenetic sections in each. In what ways do they differ? What conclusions might be offered based upon your observations?

7. Both the book of Revelation and the prophecy of Ezekiel contain a vision of a holy city. Read both accounts (Ezek. 40:1–48–45 and Rev. 21:2–22:5) and note the main characteristics of each. There is at least one glaring omission in the vision in Revelation. Try to identify it and offer an explanation for it.

Based upon your comparison of the two visions, do you think
that the vision might be a literary device capable of being
modified by the author?

8. Many scholars have recognized that the author of Mark consistently portrays the disciples as "insiders," but he consistently
depicts women and Gentiles as "outsiders." Read the Gospel of
Mark and see if you can identify the treatment or characterization of each group. What might such characterization
suggest about Mark's theological purpose?

Suggestions for Further Reading

Aune, David. *The New Testament in Its Literary Environment*. Philadelphia:
Westminster, 1989.

Doty, William G. *Letters in Primitive Christianity*. Philadelphia: Fortress,
1973.

Johnson, Luke T. *The Writings of the New Testament: An Interpretation*.
Philadelphia: Fortress, 1986.

Neusner, Jacob. *Invitation to Midrash: A Teaching Book*. San Francisco:
Harper & Row, 1989.

_____. *What Is Midrash?* Philadelphia: Fortress, 1987.

Petersen, Norman. *Literary Criticism for New Testament Critics*. Philadelphia: Fortress, 1978.

Shuler, Philip I. *A Genre for the Gospels: The Biographical Character of
Matthew*. Philadelphia: Fortress, 1982.

Talbert, Charles. *Literary Patterns, Theological Themes, and the Genre of
Luke–Acts*. SBLMS 20. Missoula: Society of Biblical Literature and
Scholars Press, 1974.

UNIT III

THE WORLD IN FRONT
OF THE TEXT

What Happens When We Read?

This unit is devoted to examining aspects of the world in front of the text (the world of the reader). In this chapter, we look at the complex process of reading. In chapter 8, we observe the role of the reader's preunderstanding and presuppositions. This discussion is continued in chapter 9, with an examination of the vital role that methodological presuppositions play in the hermeneutical enterprise. Chapter 10 will use a test case from the Gospel of Mark to show how the three worlds of author, text, reader intersect to produce meaning.

Without an author, there is no text; without a reader, a text does not communicate. In a real sense, an unread text carries no meaning, because it can mean nothing until there is a mutual engagement between reader and text. Meaning involves a process of signification in the act of reading. The creative role of the author has already been established in unit I. In the same unit, I argued for the essential adjunctive role of historical research. The reader, however, is the person who must make key decisions about what the text says. Perhaps Robert Morgan and John Barton overstate their case, but their metaphor speaks to the problem:

> A text has no life of its own. It "lives" only as an electric wire is alive. Its power originates elsewhere: in a human author. There is another point of comparison: however powerful the author's act of creation, the text lies impotent until it also comes into contact with a human reader. Only then can the human power, imagination, and intellect carried by the marks on a page strike a light, communicate warmth, or give a nasty shock. The medium itself is important, and determines how much of the source's power is communicated. Old wires can give unreliable service and cause accidents. But it is the source that gives the wire its potential for illumination or destruction. Without this, there is no live wire. Once this is present, however, those at the receiving end are in control. It is they who decide what to do with the powerful resource they possess— whether and how to use it. They have all power in their hands.[1]

[1] Robert Morgan with John Barton, *Biblical Interpretation* (New York: Oxford University, 1988), p. 269.

If written discourse is communication between author, text, and reader, then what role does the reader play in determining meaning at the receiving end of the process? Communication has not occurred until the message (text) has reached its final destination.[2] For this reason, the reception of a text by the reader should be a primary consideration in any hermeneutic.

Just as the author (sender) brings his or her world-view and understanding of reality to a text, allowing the text to mirror at least some elements of that world-view and reality, so the reader (receiver) brings to the text his or her world-view and conception of reality. Texts must be read and made sense of within the reader's complex and multifaceted world. We understand another person's discourse only by relating it to what we already know and by putting questions to the text from within our own world. As we read a text we infer meaning, and that meaning is in some measure determined by our understanding of our own world. The interpreter's world intrudes into the process of actualizing meaning. We may recognize just how significant this circumstance is when we realize the gulf of time, language, and culture, and when we acknowledge the presuppositions that exist between the biblical texts and ourselves. This means that all sorts of values, preunderstandings, and presuppositions impinge upon the reader and the interpretive process. Consequently, the reader's world is as constitutive of textual meaning as the world of the author. These observations are summarized in the chart below:

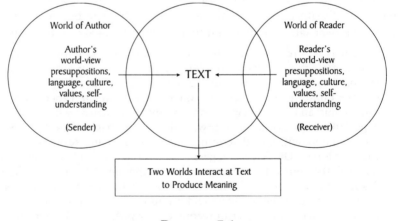

DIAGRAM 7-1

---

[2] Bernard C. Lategan and W. S. Vorster, *Text and Reality: Aspects of Reference in Biblical Texts* (Philadelphia: Fortress, 1985), p. 68.

These observations lead to a number of perplexing but legitimate questions: Does meaning exist within the text apart from the subjective reception of the reader? How does one interpretation of a text influence subsequent interpretations of the same and other related texts? If every reader approaches the text with varying viewpoints, presuppositions, aims, preunderstandings, and methodologies, does a text have only one meaning? If, on the one hand, the answer to this last question is *yes*, then we are faced with what Japp calls a hermeneutic of reduction, i.e., a text has only one objective meaning. If the answer, on the other hand, is *no*, then we must be willing to accept what Japp calls a hermeneutic of unfolding, which allows the text in dialogue with the reader to have a multiplicity of possible meanings.[3]

Without question the biblical texts were born within specific historical contexts. There is also no question that authors of the biblical texts directly refer to and allude to specific historical events within their real world. But do the texts refer only to historical facts? Do they not also refer to realities which transcend historical events and facts? If they do, then the texts refer to realities which must be "construed by the readers in their situation (ancient readers as well as modern ones)."[4] This means that a biblical text has at least two levels—an original meaning and a contemporary significance.[5] We might go so far as to suggest that authors even expect readers to construe meaning based upon the readers' own circumstances and needs. When this happens, meaning becomes in part the significance construed by the reader. The early church not only told and wrote the stories of Jesus, they also retold and rewrote them. The existence of four Gospels is evidence that Jesus and his message could be applied in a variety of ways, each with a particular emphasis. Simply put, the story and message were dynamic. The events in Israel's history were also told and retold, applied and reapplied by subsequent generations in such a way that the events spoke to these generations. The "meaning" of the texts for these readers was the significance which spoke to their lives. The texts were more than mere repositories of historical information; they were living organisms capable of interpretations that reached beyond their own historical and cultural milieux. Depending

---

[3] U. Japp, *Hermeneutik: Der theoretische Diskurs, die Literatur, und die Konstruktion ihres Zusammenhanges in den philologischen Wissenschaften* (Munich: Fink, 1977), p. 47.

[4] McKnight, *Post-Modern Use of the Bible*, p. 107.

[5] Ibid.

upon the needs of the readers, the texts contained an overflow, a surplus of meaning significance.

While readers may enhance the reading experience through excursions into the author's world, we should never naively suppose that we as readers can divorce ourselves from the influences of our own worlds. Just as authors assimilate, internalize, and then synthesize their cultural experiences, adding to these experiences individual evaluations and expressions, so readers do the same.

Reading is not a pure activity. Readers are not simply innocent bystanders, sponges who soak up a text. The text at the **artistic pole** (composition) of the communicatory continuum may be complete, but the work at the **aesthetic pole** (reading) must be created with the help of the reader. A passive reading never allows room for the active participation of the reader in the creation of meaning.

Reading is not a monological process (i.e., a process by which the text speaks to the reader), but a dialogical one (i.e., reading is a process through which the text and reader engage in an ongoing dialogue). What readers do to a text is just as constitutive of meaning as what the text does to the readers. The text and reader question and answer each other, just as in most forms of dialogue. The reading process is diachronic, that is, it takes place through time. When we consider that this diachronic process is affected both by textual and by reader-responsive considerations, we suddenly come face to face with the realization that the reading process is anything but static. Reading is dynamic, open-ended, always subject to modification, change, evaluation, and rereading.

The Dialectics of Discourse

Before examining the particulars of the reading process and the implications for hermeneutics, an understanding of the **dialectics** of discourse will help clarify some of the issues involved. In oral discourse, a speaker addresses a message to a hearer. The oral message has at least two levels of meaning—the speaker's and the speech's. The two meanings may or may not be identical, for the speech's meaning may not objectively represent the speaker's conceptualization. A gap is then created between the speaker's conceptualization and the speech's meaning. This gap is the first dialectic in oral discourse. The conceptualization is private, while the speech becomes public.

If we concentrate only on the utterance's meaning, there arises a second dialectic—the dialectic between meaning and **reference.** The meaning of a sign (whether the sign is a single word or an entire discourse) is the object, event, or concept which the sign names in the real world, while the reference of a sign is concerned with the thing to which the sign refers. For example, if I utter the word "snake," the meaning of the sign "snake" is a crawling reptile, while the reference may be to a particular person with a particular personality trait. Paul Ricoeur states that "meaning is *what* a statement says, reference is *that about which* it says it."[6] A major problem in hermeneutics is that the term "meaning" is also used in the same sense as reference, especially in the case of written discourse; what a text means is synonymous with what a text is about. This double use of meaning is perhaps unavoidable (as has been the case in this text). Therefore, I will continue to use the term "meaning" to refer to the actualization by a reader of what a text is about. The distinction of the two terms should be kept in mind, however, because the distinction has serious implications for interpretation. For example, if a text's (sign's) reference has to be construed by a reader, then there exists the possibility of multiple interpretations.[7] Further, if a sign has multiple referents, then there will be multiple interpretations, depending upon which referent the reader assigns the sign. The Gospel of Matthew includes individuals, events, and places which existed or happened in first-century Palestine. The meaning (on the first level discussed above) of the text occurs in first-century Palestine. But to whom do the Pharisees, disciples, publicans refer? To what do the events and places refer? What is the reference of the text? Or I suppose we might ask about the "real" meaning of the text.

A third dialectic concerns the reader in written discourse. We have already suggested that there is not necessarily a one-to-one correspondence between an author's conceptualization (the original intentional object) and the inscripturation (the literary concretization) of that conceptualization. The former is private, while the latter is public. A similar dialectic exists on the reader's part between understanding (the reader's conceptualization of the text) and subsequent explanation. The former is private, while the latter is public. There simply is no guarantee that a reader's explanation adequately represents the reader's understanding. This dialectic is further complicated since different readers understand texts differently due to a wide range of elements within readers' worlds. With the above remarks in mind, we are now ready to examine two other

---

[6] Paul Ricoeur, "Biblical Hermeneutics," *Semeia* 4 (1975), p. 81.
[7] See Lategan and Vorster, *Text and Reality*, pp. 27–65.

dialectic pairs within the reading process which more directly impinge upon interpretation.

First, there is the dialectic between the original languages and the translations. Biblical hermeneutics involves a special problem: the languages of the texts are not the same as those of modern readers. If readers use a translation, they are already working with an interpretation, because all translations are themselves interpretations. It is impossible for a translation to have a one-to-one correspondence to the original. Therefore, any interpretation of a biblical text based upon a translation is actually an interpretation of an interpretation; i.e., the interpretation based upon a translation is an interpretation of the translator's understanding of the original. There always exists a linguistic gap between any translation and the original text. Why is this the case? In any society there exists a system of phonological, morphological, and syntactical rules. Most of these rules are not objects which are consciously analyzed by the members of the society, but are simply learned, internalized, and then used intuitively. The system that makes any act of speech possible and comprehensible is called *langue* (in this case Hebrew or Greek; see the discussion of structuralism in chapter 9). The system that makes particular speech acts *(parole)* possible can never be completely mastered or internalized by an individual within a culture, much less by someone outside that culture.

> Hence the *full* meaning of a language is never translatable into another. We may speak several languages, but one of them always remains the one in which we live. In order completely to assimilate a language, it would be necessary to make the world which it expresses one's own, and one never does belong to two worlds at once.[8]

Obviously, if the individual speech act has its meaning only against this *langue*, and if this *langue* can never be completely assimilated by an individual outside the culture, then no translation can completely capture that nonverbal dimension of another language. Of course the nonverbal dimension of language is crucial in the formation and meaning of individual speech acts. No natural language can ever be equivalent to another, thus no individual speech act within one system can ever be the exact equivalent of a speech act within a translation.

As we explained earlier (chapter 4), every literary text actually employs a multiplicity of languages—the natural language, which is

---

[8] Maurice Merleau-Ponty, *Consciousness and the Acquisition of Language*, trans. Hugh J. Silverman (Evanston: Northwestern University, 1973), pp. xv–xvi.

governed by syntactical and linguistic conventions, and literary languages, which likewise involve literary conventions. As readers we acquire levels of competency in the codes and conventions of a text's natural language. A familiarity with grammatical, lexical, and syntactical conventions enables readers to determine what a sentence, unit, or entire text says. It is at this level that readers also give attention to historical events, persons, and places within the real world of the text. In literary texts, however, literary languages are superimposed upon the natural language. This entails, consequently, that readers of literary text must coordinate the conventions of the natural language and the conventions of the literary languages. This balancing act by the readers is described well by Edgar McKnight:

> Readers are confronted simultaneously by the multiple levels of the linguistic and literary structures of the writing being read, and they must apply multiple codes. In the case of letters, for example, readers must keep in mind the first-century letter form and the form of the smaller units (the "hymn," for example) used within the letter. In addition, the systematic ordering on the basis of content must be considered. Since appeal is being made to the reader's will as well as to his or her intellect, rhetorical structures (not necessarily ordered by, but not unrelated to, ancient rules of rhetoric) coexist with structures related to subject matter and the different levels of literary genre.[9]

As we saw in unit II, genres and sub-genres carry their own poetics, their own literary languages. A reader lacking any appreciable understanding of the dynamics of these literary languages tends to read primarily on the level of the natural language. This type of reader will generally unconsciously make no distinction between what the text says and what it is about, i.e., the meaning and the reference are not perceived as differing. The failure to recognize the literary languages within the texts of the Bible has generated questions such as, Why did Eve not think it strange when the serpent talked to her? When was "in the beginning"? What kind of fish could have swallowed Jonah? These types of questions derive from a failure to understand that the biblical texts are literary documents, which by their nature overcode the natural languages with literary ones. More literarily competent readers (those readers familiar with the literary languages) approach the biblical texts open to the texts as potential literary documents.

---

[9] McKnight, *Post-Modern Use of the Bible*, p. 137.

This brings us to the final and most significant dialectic for the reading process and to its impact upon meaning. This is the dialectic between text and work. No other theorist has been more successful in explaining the dynamics of the reading process than Wolfgang Iser. According to Iser, the meaning which readers infer from texts results from the tension between "the role offered by the text and the real reader's own disposition."[10] The following discussion of this process of production is based upon the model offered by Iser.

When approaching a literary text, the reader must take into account two factors: the text and the response to the text. The **literary work** is not synonymous to the text, but is created in the act of reading. The work exists somewhere between the artistic pole (the text created by the author) and the aesthetic pole (the realization accomplished by the reader). The text exists on paper; the work is born out of the interaction between the text and the reader. Since dispositions of readers vary and since a single reader's disposition may change between readings, the literary work can never be precisely pinpointed.

Iser asserts that **gaps of indeterminacy** and the completion of these gaps by the reader is *the* central factor in literary communication. Language is such that it allows itself to be broken up and then reconstructed. The place where the language is broken up and reconstructed "is marked by gaps in the text—it consists in the blanks which the reader is to fill in. . . . Whenever the reader bridges the gap, communication begins. The gaps function as a kind of pivot on which the whole text-reader relationship revolves."[11] As we observed in unit II, authors engage in the process of selection when producing texts. This process of selection leaves some things unsaid. An author cannot possibly incorporate every detail from the real world into the text, for the text would become unmanageable. There are, therefore, gaps of silence within the text. In fact, if a narrative does not leave enough blank spaces through which to engage the reader's imagination, the reader's interest is lost. Because of these gaps, readers of texts are required to "fill them in" by drawing from their own repertoires.

Iser speaks of gaps existing in different textual elements and on different levels: syntax, semantics, pragmatics, narrative flow, character action, even the role assigned to the reader. Iser describes the reading

---

[10] Wolfgang Iser, *The Act of Reading: A Theory of Aesthetic Response* (Baltimore: Johns Hopkins University, 1978), p. 37.

[11] Ibid., p. 169.

process as establishing connections—filling the gaps—among these different levels and phases of the text. Before discussing in more detail Iser's theory of "gap filling," some examples of the basic types of gaps readers are required to fill should be helpful.

Grammatical and Syntactical Gaps

Many of the gaps occurring in texts are due to the inherent ambiguity of language. In Galatians 1:16, Paul states that God "was pleased to reveal his Son to me. . . . " In what sense are we to understand the sense of Paul's statement: "to me," "through me," "in my heart," or "to me in particular"? The dative case of the preposition *en* (trans. NRSV as "to") may indicate any of these relationships.[12] When statements such as "the love of God" occur, are we to treat them as objective (God being the object of love) or subjective (God's love) genitives? Thus, does this phrase refer to the love a person has for God, or the love that God has for a person? The text does not always supply the answer, and this means that the reader must make a decision to fill in the grammatical gap; the reader must solve the **ambiguity** of (disambiguate) the text.

Other instances of gaps due to grammatical ambiguity occur when a particular word may be translated in two or more ways. For example, a word may in form be either indicative or imperative. In 1 Corinthians 12:31a, should we translate the word *zēloute* as an indicative ("you are striving for") or an imperative ("strive for")? The manner in which the reader fills this grammatical gap affects the interpretation of the rest of the passage.

Another example of gap filling due to syntactical ambiguity arises from the pronoun and its antecedent. In Luke 11:8, the reader is confronted with a barrage of pronouns: "I tell you, even though he will not get up and give him anything because he is his friend, at least because of his persistence he will get up and give him whatever he needs." If we concentrate on the first few words of the last clause—"yet because of *his* persistence *he* will get up"—who are the antecedents for these two pronouns? Notice the question: "Who are?" This question itself assumes that the two pronouns have different antecedents. This assumption is based upon the word "persistence." The man outside the house asking for bread must be the one who is persistent. Further, the man outside the

---

[12] For an excellent discussion of such examples, see McKnight, *Post-Modern Use of the Bible*, pp. 223–35.

house is thought to be persistent because the reader will read back into the parable the persistence usually associated with the poem which follows. If, however, the word translated "persistence" (a *hapax legomenon*) were to be translated "sense of integrity," then both pronouns would refer to the man inside the house! As McKnight suggests:

> Normally, the ambiguity involved in the subordinate grammatical and syntactical structures can be handled by the reader because one actualization fits the total linguistic and literary context better than the others. When different actualizations fit the same context equally well, the reader may process the text in different ways allowed by the ambiguity.[13]

The antecedent of a pronoun is not always easily determined. In John 3:2, Nicodemus says to Jesus, "Rabbi, we know that you are a teacher who has come from God." What is the antecedent for "we?" Is Nicodemus referring to the Sanhedrin, to his colleagues, or to some other group? The antecedent is unclear.

Poetic or Literary Gaps

Generally, filling gaps created by literary structures is not as easy as filling those created by the ambiguities of syntax and grammar. James 1:13b reads: "For God cannot be tempted by evil, and he himself tempts no one." The reader may want to add to the end of this sentence the words "with evil." The context seems to suggest that the reader should supply what is only hinted at by the text. This is an example of poetic omission. Intentional omission of words or even phrases is part of the stock and trade of literary artists. The result is the involvement of the reader in the completion of the sense of the text. When the writer in Ephesians 5:21–22 says, "Be subject to one another out of reverence for Christ, wives . . . to your husbands as you are to the Lord," the reader must supply the missing verb in the second part of the sentence, since it is not present in the original language.

In Hebrew poetic parallelism, verbs are often omitted and must be supplied by the reader: "They shall beat their swords into plowshares, and their spears into pruning hooks" (Isa. 2:4). The reader must understand that the same verb "beat" is understood in the second clause. There are also times when the reader must supply information not discernible from the immediate context. Such information includes religious, cultural, and geographical matters.

---

[13] Ibid., p. 226.

There are also paratactic constructions with which the reader must deal. Paratactic constructions include grammatical clauses joined with no indication of their syntactic relationship. In the New Testament, phrases and clauses are often joined by the conjunctive *kai* ("and"), and the reader must determine whether the relationship between the clauses is causal, circumstantial, conditional, etc. Consider Psalm 23:1: "The LORD is my shepherd, I shall not want." The second clause is the result of the first. The reason that the Psalmist lacks nothing is because the Lord is his shepherd.

Literary devices such as simile, hyperbole, and metaphor (discussed in chapter 4) may also be ambiguous. Hyperbole, if taken literally, certainly results in misreading. Indeed, if the reader does not hold a body of information in common with the author, the hyperbole may not have its desired effect. The same is true for simile and metaphor. Both forms are comparative figures of speech; i.e., simile and metaphor require that a reader compare two objects that are in real life incongruous. In Matthew 5:13–14, Christians are called light and salt, the latter metaphor being partially unintelligible to the modern reader. Peter Cotterell and Max Turner observe:

> The use of metaphor is a creative act, and there can be no certainty that the interpretation of the metaphor will follow the intention of its creator. The receiver must search through his own experience, and must employ his own imagination, and if necessary engage his own research, and only so can the meaning of a metaphor be realized. But that experience and that imagination are his, and not those of the creator of the metaphor, so that the use of metaphor inevitably opens up the way to misunderstanding.[14]

In order for metaphor or simile to operate, there must exist a commonality of perception between the metaphor's creator and the hearer. Without this commonality, the reader or hearer may misunderstand the force of the metaphor or simile. Cotterell and Turner offer a striking example illustrated by the metaphor of "burning coals" in Romans 12:20: "You will heap burning coals on their heads." This metaphor demands a comparison where both the *vehicle* and the *tenor* of the metaphor are not immediately apparent to the modern reader.[15] If the reader bases the interpretation of this metaphor upon other references to burning coals in the Bible, judgment is perceived to be the primary idea (e.g., Gen. 19:24; Lev. 10:2; Ps. 11:6). But does the idea of judgment fit

---

[14] Cotterell and Turner, *Linguistics and Biblical Interpretation*, pp. 300–301.
[15] Ibid., pp. 302–5.

the context of the metaphor? The force of Romans 12:14–21 concerns forgiveness, not judgment. In the *Stories of the High Priests of Memphis*,[16] a repentant person is depicted as going to the person he had wronged, bearing a clay dish containing burning coals on his head. This better explains the source of the metaphor in Proverbs 25:21–23:

> If your enemies are hungry, give them bread to eat;
> and if they are thirsty, give them water to drink;
> for you will heap coals of fire on their heads,
> and the LORD will reward you.
> The north wind produces rain;
> and a backbiting tongue, angry looks.

Since the last verse describes the rain pattern in Egypt, the origin of the metaphor of "burning coals" probably has its source in Egypt also. With this in mind, the meaning of the metaphor in Proverbs is that if a person acts in a forgiving way towards an enemy, the enemy will come to repent. This is almost certainly the meaning of the metaphor in Paul's usage. Without this contextual background, the modern reader may very well assign to the metaphor a meaning of retribution instead of forgiveness.

According to Iser, the various **textual segments** (sentences, lexical units, etc.) present different perspectives within the text. But the segments point to something beyond what is said. This something is what is left unsaid. This is the "unwritten text" and is actually the unstated connections between the textual segments or components. The reader must infer these unstated connections. As a reader joins these segments, a referential field results in which the reader holds the segments in tension. This tension gives rise to the need for a common framework that allows the reader to grasp the similarities and differences according to a pattern. To some extent, the text provides no such framework; the reader must supply it; however, things are not quite this simple.

Meaning is the result of a dialogue between a reader and a text. This dialogue depends on a pair of structures—structures of effect and structures of response. While readers clearly bring their unique individual symbolic worlds to the text, responses are not entirely arbitrary because the structures of response as well as the structures of effect are textually determined. Since these structures are interactive, we will not attempt to discuss them separately but in their dialogic relationships.

---

[16] See William Klassen, "Coals of Fire: Sign of Repentance or Revenge?" *NTS* 9 (1962–63), pp. 337–50.

First, we must consider the relationship between reality and thought systems. Every age has its own dominant thought system that reduces the contingencies and complexities of reality to a meaningful and manageable structure. What any one epoch considers to be reality is not reality in its totality, but rather an order imposed upon reality. Every system imposes an order upon contingent reality, thereby providing a framework for living as well as for a set of social norms that lays claim to a universal validity. But when a system becomes dominant, it does so through a reduction of the complexity of reality. While it foregrounds some possibilities, it necessarily backgrounds or excludes others. The negated or neutralized possibilities are not eliminated, but only deactivated, waiting to be resurrected or reactivated. Literature is the means of resurrection. Literature attempts to bring to light the possibilities neutralized or excluded by the dominant system. Literature interferes with the existing ordering of reality, drawing attention to its deficiencies. The result of such an interference is the bringing to light of the system's inability to deal with the multifarious nature of reality. Once literature attacks the system at its seams, a rearrangement of the meaningful structures of the system is called for. The excluded possibilities are the focus of literary works.[17] But how does a literary text accomplish the work of a gadfly?

What Iser calls the repertoire of a text consists of schemata and strategies. The schemata consist of social norms and literary allusions while the strategies consist of narrative techniques (especially perspectives) and gaps of indeterminacy.

Social Norms

The negated or neutralized possibilities of the dominant thought system constitute the focal point of a literary text. At the same time, however, in order to establish this focal point, the text must incorporate implicitly the framework of the contemporary system. The text accomplishes this by "explicitly shading in the areas all around that system."[18] On the one hand, when a text incorporates elements of the current thought system, these elements are recoded in such a way that the familiar elements lose their validity. On the other hand, the text does not formulate an alternative validity, but presents the elements in such a

---

[17] Iser, *The Act of Reading*, pp. 71–78.
[18] Ibid., p. 73.

way that readers must discover or construct the intention of recoding. Consequently, the readers are called upon to be partners in constructing meaning. Now if the readers are contemporary with the text, they are provided with the possibility of a fresh look at the system that they have to this point accepted without question. If the readers, however, are no longer involved in the thought system of the text, they are able to reconstruct the framework from the text, to experience the system's deficiencies, and to discover the alternative answers implicit in the text. So the historical distance between a text and later generations of readers does not vitiate a text's power. The contemporary reader is confronted with defamiliarized norms, necessitating a reassessment of the norms and possibilities negated by such norms. The result is the construction of meaning. Later readers experience a reality that is not theirs and are able to transcend their own world or *Sitz im Leben,* resulting in a reassessment or broadening of their reality.[19]

Literary Allusions

The schemata of the text also consists of past literary elements and entire traditions that are intertwined with the social and cultural norms.

> If the function of the incorporated norms is to bring out the deficiencies of a prevailing system, the function of literary allusions is to assist in producing an answer to the problems set by these deficiencies.[20]

These literary allusions offer the reader past answers to the problems presented by the social norms, but answers that are no longer valid. So what is the value of the allusions? Since the allusions are now stripped of their original context, the reader should assume that their function is more than simple reproduction but that they serve as guides or points of orientation for discovering a new meaning. Since the literary elements are depragmatized by a new context, the original or old context recedes into the background, but does not disappear. The old context serves as a backdrop that throws the now implied significance into relief. It is only against the background of the old context that the reader is able to construct new possibilities and their significance.

The repertoire of the text (schemata and strategies) constitutes the context for the dialogue between the text and the reader. The repertoire provides the reader with the wherewithal to produce an answer to the

---

[19] Ibid., pp. 78–79.
[20] Ibid., p. 79.

questions raised in the text. But before we move to textual strategies, it is necessary to make a more thorough examination of the relationship between the schemata and the role of the reader.

The social norms incorporated within a text originate in a historical thought system, while the literary allusions have their origin in past reactions to problems. Since the norms and allusions are not equivalent, a problem for the reader arises when the norms and allusions are joined together. The fact that they are joined together suggests that they are related in some fashion. So the reader is called upon to look for a system of equivalences between the two even if their marriage is designed to highlight differences. The reader is called upon to create a system of equivalences between the two systems, but since a text always refers to something beyond itself, the reader is also called upon to create a system of equivalences between the work and the real world. The role of the schemata is to organize the reader's reaction to the problem implied within the text. But the schemata's structure must be realized through reading. The degree to which the structures of meaning are optimized will depend upon the reader's awareness of these structures and the degree to which the reader is willing to open up to an unfamiliar and sometimes threatening experience. But according to Iser, "the meaning must inevitably be pragmatic, in that it can never cover all the semantic potentials of the text, but can only open up one particular form of access to these potentials."[21] This is tantamount to saying that the schemata present a range of organizational possibilities, and these can be realized in a number of ways. It is here that the reader's unique individual disposition and background come into play. Meaning originates, then, from the interplay between the reader's own decisions and the attitude that the text provokes in the reader toward the problems that the text implies. Nevertheless, the organizational structure of the schemata guards against indiscriminate meaning assembly by the reader by providing the context for meaning assembly.

For Iser the most determinate guide relating to the schemata is negativity, which is actually a basic form of what he calls gaps of indeterminacy (a concept that we will discuss in detail in relation to textual strategies). For Iser, negativity is "the basic regulator of the human condition."[22] Human beings are incapable of knowing how they experience one another. Because of this basic knowledge gap, we create

---

[21] Ibid., p. 85.
[22] Iser, *Prospecting*, p. 142.

our own conceptions of how others experience us and then substitute these conceptions for reality. Indeed, we even base our actions and reactions to others upon our projections. We create an imaginary picture and base all our communication upon this fiction. But projections are exactly that—projection—and not reality. Consequently, we spend our lives bridging a fundamental double gap by formulating imaginary projections based upon imaginary perceptions.

Negativity is responsible for stimulating the processes of imagination that can bridge the knowledge gap. When applied to the text and reader, negativity must be understood in terms of negation. When a text incorporates familiar social norms and literary allusions, it does so in order to negate them, to cancel them out. These negated norms and allusions, however, remain in the background and serve to stimulate the reader to assume a posture or attitude toward the text. In other words, when the norms are negated, the reader is expected to look for the positive "elsewhere than in what is negated and this demand is nearly always accompanied by a number of signposts to point the way."[23] The alternatives to the negated norms and literary conventions are only implicit in the text and the reader must discover what they are. This is where the concept of negativity is important, for there is, Iser assumes, a hidden motive behind the many negations and deformations within the text. This motive is negativity, and it can be discovered only by the constitutive activity of the reader in recognizing that something is being withheld that must be discovered. There is no doubt that the negative slant given to the knowledge offered induces the reader to ideate the as yet hidden cause governing the negation—and in so doing he formulates what had been left unformulated.[24]

The meaning of the text is never that which is manifest, but exactly that which is latent. But what is stated serves as the primary context for what is unstated. So the reader is engaged in a constant switch between what is manifest or present and what is unstated or absent. It might be said that the reader must always distinguish between what a text says and what it might actually be about. And that "aboutness" is never explicit, but will always come into being through the protracted attempts of the reader to initiate and engage in the play of the text. Such an engagement should not strike readers as an unfamiliar process, for it is exactly this process that ensures everyday instances of communication.

---

[23] Ibid., p. 140.
[24] Iser, *The Act of Reading*, p. 214.

What is spoken or manifest is always accompanied by the unspoken. In other words, absence is always co-present with presence. The spoken is always impregnated with associations that cannot be dispensed with, and every object to which the spoken refers is one that has already been described in countless ways, so that whatever is said about it can only be a selection from the possibilities, thus defining itself by what it excludes.[25]

So when we as readers are sucked into the text through negativity, we are engaged in a drama that mirrors the drama of life itself. More complex texts tend to make the signposts that point the reader to discovering the hidden motive more ambiguous, thus dismantling any specific frame of reference from which the reader is to view the negations. When this occurs, the play of the text manifests itself in a multiplicity of possibilities.

Strategies

While the repertoire of the text consists of the social norms and literary allusions that produce negativity, it also includes textual strategies. On the one hand, the schemata create the context within which the reader must actualize a system of equivalences between the norms and allusions and between the text and the real world. On the other hand, the textual strategies function to organize the readers' actualization, without making them feel as if they are being led by the nose. As Iser puts it:

> [The strategies] provide a meeting-point between the repertoire and the producer of those equivalences, namely the reader himself. In other words, the strategies organize both the material of the text and the conditions under which that material is to be communicated.[26]

The strategies not only govern the structures of the text but also the acts of comprehension triggered in the reader. Put another way, it is the function of the strategies to carry the schemata (the primary code of the text) to the reader and to guide the reader's creation of the aesthetic object (the second code) by providing the meeting place for the schemata and the individual reader's own social and cultural code.

The textual strategies include those devices normally associated with the conventions of genre. For Iser, however, the emphasis falls

---

[25] Iser, *Prospecting*, p. 102.
[26] Ibid.

upon the unmanifested dimension of the text, which we refer to as seams, but which he refers to as gaps. Literary texts offer readers only enough information to keep them "oriented and interested." Inferences that are to be drawn from the information are left up to the imagination of the reader. The resulting empty spaces or gaps within the text must be filled by the reader.

> The gap functions as a kind of pivot on which the whole text-reader relationship revolves. Hence, the structured blanks of the text stimulate the process of ideation to be preformed by the reader on terms set by the text.[27]

How are such gaps strategically created and subsequently filled by readers? To answer this question, we must look at Iser's treatment of textual perspectives.

There are generally four perspectives in a literary work (especially the novel)—the perspectives of the narrator, the characters, the plot, and the implied reader. The point of their convergence is the meaning of the text. This point of convergence is not provided by the text, but must be supplied by the reader. In other words, the convergence of the perspectives must emerge from a vantage point beyond the four perspectives, but pre-structured by the text. The real reader, then, is a mediator between the various perspectives, including that of the implied reader. This mediating activity is created by gaps between the perspective, gaps that Iser refers to as blanks. Between perspectives there is a "suspension of connectability," an empty space that must be filled by the reader.

> In other words, between the "schematized views" there is a no-man's land of indeterminacy, which results precisely from the determinacy of each individual view in its sequence. Gaps are bound to open up, and they offer a free play in the interpretation of the specific ways in which the various views can be connected with one another. These gaps give the reader a chance to build his own bridges, relating the different aspects of the object which have thus far been revealed to him.[28]

These blanks function to impede textual consistency or coherence. While they are actually empty spaces, they do stimulate the reader's involvement; indeed, they are responsible for the very dialogue between reader and text. The blanks between the perspectives also serve as the referential field for the reader's attention in any one moment of the reading

---

[27] Iser, *The Act of Reading*, p. 86.
[28] Iser, *Prospecting*, p. 9.

process. When two or more perspectives must be related by the reader, it is the blank that makes such a relation possible.

The perspectives have the function of stimulating the production of the aesthetic object. Consequently, the aesthetic object is never congruent with a single perspective. The aesthetic object is produced through the consistency-building activities of the reader. Since all the perspectives are interactive and this interaction is continuous throughout the work, the reader is called upon to mediate between the shifting perspectives in order to produce a consistent viewpoint.

> Authorial comment, dialogue between characters, developments of plot, and the positions marked out for the reader—all these are interwoven in the text and offer a constantly shifting constellation of views.[29]

As the readers are confronted with the shifting and interacting perspectives, they are faced with the task of making them consistent. When we consider that this task is one carried out during the time flow or on the temporal axis of reading, the real reader's role is actually that of a wandering viewpoint. As the reader's attention shifts in the time flow of reading from one perspective to another, it is incapable of embracing all the perspectives at once. The perspective with which the reader is involved at any one moment is the "theme." But this theme is set in relief by the previous perspectives with which the reader has been concerned. The previous segments constitute what Iser calls the "horizon." "It [the horizon] is made up of all those segments which had supplied the themes of previous phases of reading."[30]

These complementary concepts of theme and horizon point up a strategic element in literary texts pertaining to the wandering viewpoint—the relationship between expectation and memory, or protension and retention. Every segment or perspective **(theme)** is viewed within the context of a horizon; but in the time flow of reading, a theme is immediately transformed into the background, thus becoming part of the horizon from which the next theme will be viewed. Therefore, while the horizon influences the theme, the theme will also modify the horizon. The horizon always arouses expectations of things to come (e.g., how a problem will be resolved), while the theme will either satisfy the expectations or frustrate them. In addition, each new theme not only answers or frustrates expectations, but gives rise to new ones. In

---

[29] Iser, *The Act of Reading*, p. 96.
[30] Ibid., p. 97.

most literary texts, the theme serves to modify the expectations of the horizon or even to frustrate them. As a result, the theme has a retroactive influence upon the horizon, because the reader must go back and reconsider the previous segments and their relationship. So reading becomes an interplay between protension and retention. It is through this process of protension and retention that the wandering viewpoint continually seeks to relate the perspectives. Iser describes the process as follows:

> Every articulate reading moment entails a switch of perspective, and this constitutes an inseparable combination of differentiated perspectives, foreshortened memories, present modifications, and future expectations. Thus, in the time-flow of the reading process, past and future continually converge in the present moment, and the synthesizing operations of the wandering viewpoint enable the text to pass through the reader's mind as an ever-expanding network of connections. This also adds the dimension of space to that of time, for the accumulation of views and combinations gives us the illusion of depth and breadth, so that we have the impression that we are actually present in a real world.[31]

Since the shifting perspectives challenge the reader to produce a consistent viewpoint (i.e., create meaning), consistency building is a configurative, productive activity. The wandering viewpoint travels through the text of interconnecting perspectives making connections that will (at least for the reader) result in a mediated, consistent meaning. In other words, the wandering viewpoint seeks patterns of consistency. Now since readers differ in terms of memory, mental capacity, training, and interest, patterns of connections may be realized to varying degrees. Hence, the intersubjective structure of the text is capable of generating a multiplicity of subjective actualizations. As Iser puts it:

> This network of connections potentially encompasses the whole text, but the potential can never be fully realized; instead it forms the basis for the many selections which have to be made during the reading process and which, though intersubjectively not identical—as is shown by the many different interpretations of a single text—nevertheless remain intersubjectively comprehensible in so far as they are all attempts to optimize the same structure.[32]

Iser, however, is careful to guarantee a modest degree of determinacy created by the gaps of indeterminacy. He does this by redescribing

---

[31] Ibid., p. 116.
[32] Ibid., p. 118.

the concept of horizon by calling it a vacancy, thus transforming the horizon into a type of controlling or governing gap (a determining indeterminant). While the blanks are the empty spaces, the missing links between perspectives, the vacancies develop when a segment fades from relevance, thus forming the background for the next theme. Against this background of the vacancy, each new thematic segment must be approached.

> As the vacancy is structured by the sequence of positions in the time-flow of reading, the reader's viewpoint cannot proceed arbitrarily; the thematically vacant position always acts as the angle from which a selective interpretation is to be made.[33]

What Iser actually wants to ensure is a dialogic balance between the text and the reader, a free-play that produces an aesthetic object that is a product of both the governing structures of the text and the creative imagination of the reader. Perhaps this is no better stated than in his famous essay, "The Reading Process":

> Thus, the reader, in establishing these interrelations between past, present and future, actually causes the text to reveal its potential multiplicity of connections. These connections are the product of the reader's mind working on the raw material of the text, though they are not the text itself—for this consists just of sentences, statements, information, etc. . . . The literary text activates our own faculties, enabling us to recreate the world it presents. The product of this creative activity is what we might call the virtual dimension of the text, which endows it with its reality. This virtual dimension is not the text itself, nor is it the imagination of the reader: it is the coming together of text and imagination.[34]

The aesthetic object is not a well-defined kernel of meaning placed in some manner by the author into a text. Neither is the aesthetic object the result of the free-play of the reader's imagination. In terms that recall Gadamer's definition of meaning, the aesthetic object is given birth when the horizons of reader and text converge (and perhaps sometimes clash). Until that convergence takes place, the meaning of the text (if indeed we should even be referring to the meaning of the text!) is only virtually present. It is not that the reader activates the meaning structures of the text to formulate meaning. Nor is it that the text simply activates the creative activities of the reader. The aesthetic object comes into being through the mutual interaction of the text's structures and the reader's

---

[33] Ibid., p. 202.
[34] Iser, *The Implied Reader*, pp. 278–79.

imaginative activities. Without either there simply is no aesthetic object produced. When either pole of this dialogue is absent, communication between a piece of literature and a human mind is impossible. Where there is, on the one hand, no strategic provision on the part of the text for the free-play of the creative human imagination, or, on the other hand, no willingness on the part of the reader to allow the imagination to play (and to be played by) the text, the game of literary communication never gets off the ground.

Iser's central idea of gaps of indeterminacy has been progressively adopted and applied by biblical scholars. For example, McKnight observes:

> A reader makes sense of one segment and then confronts another segment. What is the relationship between the first segment and the succeeding segments? The text itself does not fill in the connections. The reader must progressively fill in the gaps or blanks and thereby form the segments of the text. The reader is provided potential by the text, but the reader must determine or actualize meaning.[35]

McKnight then offers John 7:1–9 as an example which necessitates the filling of gaps. Jesus is portrayed as going about in Galilee instead of Judea because of danger in Jerusalem. When his brothers encourage him to "leave here and go to Judea so that your disciples may also see the works you are doing" (v. 3), Jesus responds, "Go to the festival yourselves. I am not going to this festival" (v. 8). In the very next segment, however, the text indicates: "But after his brothers had gone to the festival, then he also went, not publicly but as it were in secret" (7:10). A reader will make sense of the first segment by assuming that Jesus simply did not want to go. The next segment forces a complete reevaluation of what the reader considered the only possible reading of the initial segment. What the reader encounters in the second segment demands that the first segment and its meaning be reconsidered.

Perhaps the most notable proponent of gap filling in the area of biblical studies is Meir Sternberg.[36] He suggests that reading is a copy of life. Just as we move through life groping and stumbling, trying to make sense of events, constructing some pattern by which all the events fit together into a meaningful whole, learning through trial and error, so we do the same thing in reading. The omniscient narrator knows everything, but refuses to tell the reader everything. The narrator creates gaps between segments which the reader must fill by perpetual introspection

---

[35] McKnight, *Post-Modern Use of the Bible*, p. 237.
[36] Sternberg, *Poetics of Biblical Narrative*, pp. 186–229.

and **retrospection,** constantly engaging in a process of evaluation and reevaluation of the partial information supplied by the narrator. Reading thus becomes a drama, a drama similar to that of living, in which the reader is the principal character. For example, if one reads the sordid story of David and Bathsheba in 2 Samuel 11, the manner in which the gaps are filled is central. Why does Uriah not go down to his house after David brought him home from the war? Does Uriah know about his wife's affair with David? Does Uriah think David knows that he knows? Does David suspect that Uriah knows about the affair? The text does not allow an unequivocal answer. The gaps may be filled legitimately by both affirmative and negative answers. Each hypothesis is supported by a number of arguments, but other arguments indicate a flaw and support the opposite answer. This situation, according to Sternberg, is deliberate. The text demands that both hypotheses be utilized to shed their different light on details in the text. The text requires the reader to maintain both hypotheses simultaneously. The text and the reader profit from such an interaction. Sternberg concludes that the meaning of a text is inexhaustible because no context can provide all the keys to all of its possibilities.[37]

Wallace Martin's summary of the effect that readers experience during the process of reading is well stated:

> When a perspective on life proves inadequate, the reader tends to question the entire repertoire of conventional assumptions on which it is based. If open to the experience the text provides, we are likely to find negations of some of our own views; as a result, the self that begins reading a book may not be quite the same as the one that finishes it.[38]

Reading in this sense is a transforming experience, a confrontational dialogue with the possibilities offered by the text. Reading is an engaging, life-changing, rebirthing phenomenon.

Obviously, within this view of the actualization of meaning (where the work is a function of the text), the reader actively participates in the process of communication and in the construction of meaning. If different readers bring different dispositions, skills, preunderstandings, competencies, and traditions to the reading of the text, different readers will experience the text and actualize the work differently. This observation, along with the above description of the reading process, obviously has the potential to introduce a certain amount of subjectivity into the

---

[37] Ibid., p. 228.

[38] Wallace Martin, *Recent Theories of Narrative* (Ithaca: Cornell University, 1986), p. 162.

hermeneutical enterprise. This leads us to the flip side of the coin. Just as a reader has a repertoire from which to draw (to be discussed in chapters 8 and 9), texts as written discourse also have what might be called a **literary repertoire.** As Lategan points out,

> inscripturation implies the molding of the message in a specific form. Syntactic and semantic relationships become fixed and cannot be altered at will. Genre, point of view, minor and major stylistic features—all imply a definite choice to the exclusion of other possibilities.[39]

The process of communication operates under the direction of rules which are part of the literary repertoire. A communicatory act simply cannot mean what the rules will not allow. Since written discourse is also communication, with the reader being the author's counterpart in the communication process, there are limitations that the text itself imposes upon the reader. While we may claim that readers can never discover the author's intention, we may, however, assert that any author makes assumptions about the reading audience. The assumptions include knowledge about the author's symbolic world and how that symbolic world is reflected in the language. Authors assume that readers bring with them a level of competency. Umberto Eco refers to this body of competency demanded by the text as the text's "encyclopedia," each element of which places restrictions on the reader. We close this chapter with a discussion of Eco's concept of the text's encyclopedia as a means of offering a balance to the tendency towards subjectivity inherent in Iser's process of reading.

Eco is quite aware that literary texts (as well as other artistic productions) are open, lending themselves to a multiplicity of interpretations:

> We see it (the work of art) as the end product of an author's effort to arrange a sequence of communicative effects in such a way that each individual addressee can refashion the original composition devised by the author. . . . As he reacts to the play of stimuli and his own response to their patterning, the individual addressee is bound to supply his own existential credentials, the sense conditioning which is peculiarly his own, a defined culture, a set of tastes, personal inclinations, and prejudices.[40]

The openness of a text does not mean that the text will allow any interpretation whatsoever. The text dictates (at least for the competent readers) the limits of interpretative creativity. What are these textual encyclopedic restraints on the reader? Eco offers seven of them.[41]

---

[39] Lategan and Vorster, *Text and Reality*, p. 75.
[40] Eco, *Role of the Reader*, p. 49.
[41] Ibid. pp. 18–23.

Constraints upon the Reader

Basic dictionary. In our discussion of "gap filling," we learned that the text requests that readers supply information in order to fill out the text. This process begins at the most elementary level of words or the reader's **basic dictionary**. In Luke 7:12 we read, "As he approached the gate of the town, a man who had died was being carried out. He was his mother's only son, and she was a widow." When confronted with the word "widow," the reader immediately knows that the widow is a woman. But a word like "widow" is more complex. For instance, not only is a widow a woman in the physical sense, she is also a woman whose husband is deceased. "At this point the reader does not know as yet which of these *virtual* properties must be *actualized*."[42] The reader will make a decision only based on further information offered by the text. The terms within a sentence imply properties commonly associated with the terms, and these associations imply still others. When a text involves a highly technical vocabulary, the reader will make associations within strictly defined parameters. Authors are aware of this imposition upon readers and consciously choose their vocabulary in order to place readers within a particular frame of reference.

Rules of co-reference. Since words within any language can have multiple meanings (think of the various meanings of the word "lot"), the meaning of a word at any point within the text must be determined by what Eco calls **rules of co-reference**. Initially, the reader makes sense of terms based upon co-textual relations, i.e., upon the relationships which a word has with the other words within a sentence. As reading progresses, terms that remain ambiguous will be disambiguated through other textual clues.

Contextual and circumstantial selections. As we saw in chapter 1, co-text is concerned with the relationship between words, sentences, and units of a text in the text's linear development. Eco defines contextual selections as "coded abstract possibilities of meeting a given term in connection with other terms belonging to the same semiotic system."[43] Thus, a term may have one connotative meaning in one language system while having a different meaning within another.

Circumstantial selections relate a term with external circumstances. The reader is asked to connect the term or phrase with circumstances in the "extraverbal environment." "Thus 'aye' means 'I vote yes' in the

---

[42] Ibid., p. 18.
[43] Ibid., p. 19.

framework of certain types of formal meetings and 'I will obey' in the framework of the Navy."[44] The reader is to infer information implicit within the text but not explicit. The reader fills in the gap, but the **contextual and circumstantial selections** limit the possible inferences which the reader can make.

Rhetorical and stylistic overcoding. When a reader approaches the literary devices of a text, some literary competence is expected. Figures of speech and rhetorical devices require that readers avoid naively applying literal interpretations to these devices and figurative constructions. While figures of speech may lend themselves to polysemy, they also limit denotative interpretations.

Along with the rules governing rhetorical constructions, we may include here the rules of genre. Since we have discussed these rules in some detail in unit II, they should not detain us here. We should be reminded, however, that there is an inseparable link between the way something is said (genre) and what is said (content). The reader should recall the distinction between the natural language and the literary languages of genre and sub-genre that are superimposed or overcoded upon the natural one. By employing a particular genre, or literary device—**rhetorical and stylistic overcoding**—an author sets parameters within which interpretation must take place.

Inferences from common frames. A frame refers to a situation in life which is generally understood throughout a particular culture. Authors may assume that some information or knowledge pervades a culture. Possible frames of common, cultural references include rules of etiquette, agricultural practices, religious traditions and practices, legal concerns, and literature. If an author either consciously or unconsciously refers to one of these frames of reference, it enables the informed reader to recollect an entire body of knowledge. The reader may then perform a correlation between the frame of reference and the elements within the text. A single term may find its significance within a particular frame of reference. When the New Testament authors use the term "circumcision," the entire historical and religious matrix of the practice of circumcision is immediately called to mind. **Common frames of reference,** thus, may supply the context, which limits the reader's interpretation.

Inferences by intertextual frames. As Eco claims, "no text is read independently of the reader's experience of other texts."[45] While com-

---

[44] Ibid.
[45] Ibid., p. 21.

mon frames of reference are usually limited to an individual's culture, **intertextual frames of reference** are the result of an amalgamation of the various literary traditions with which the reader is familiar. When an author alludes to another text or literary tradition, the reader is asked to make inferences based upon a tradition outside the author's own tradition. Through allusions to another tradition or text, the author asks the reader to "overcode" a secondary frame of reference upon the primary one. When the author of 2 Peter makes reference to Isaiah 53, the reader is expected to overcode the present frame of reference with inferences originating in the context of the suffering servant theme in Isaiah. The reader is in a sense guided in the process of filling in the gaps by the author's intertextual frame of reference.

Ideological overcoding.   Every reader confronts a text under the influence of some ideological perspective. The reader may be unaware of this influence, but it is there nonetheless. The counterpart to the structures of the reader's ideological perspective are the structures of the text's ideological perspective. The convergence of these two can be termed **ideological overcoding.** The ideological orientation of the reader is always present and can no more be absent from the interpretive process than stripes from a zebra. They may be suppressed, but not dismissed. An informed reader, however, is aware of the influence that the ideological orientation of the author has upon interpretation. The ideological perspectives of a text are reflected in both textual structure and language. The vocabulary of a text may be such that it seeks to persuade or dissuade a reader in specific areas. In this way, a text shapes and to a great extent seeks to determine a reader's response.

Summary

In developing his theory of the reader's role in relation to the text's encyclopedia, Eco focuses on what he calls the "model reader." The fact is, however, none of us are model readers. Moreover, no two readers are identical; neither are we ever individually the same reader twice. While some readers may share common areas of agreement, each reader has an individual imagination and as such fills out a text in individualistic ways. To compound this sense of subjectivity, literary texts are self-referential. Given this self-referential quality of literary (what we have already referred to as mimetic) texts, the reader is invited, indeed, required to become intimately involved in creating the literary *work*. This is a requirement because the literary *work* (the aesthetic object) comes into being only through the imaginative interaction between the text (the artistic object) and the reader. Some readers, however, are more informed and therefore more competent than others; i.e., some readers are more cognizant of the restraints placed upon the process of reading by the linguistic, figurative, and ideological structures of the text. Authors of truly mimetic texts know their trade well. They know that competent readers read in particular ways, and therefore structure their presentation in ways that either validate the poetics of reading or frustrate them. They can impose one intertextual frame of reference upon another one, demanding that the reader make the connection; they can withhold information at strategic places in the plot; they can provide information in order to foreshadow some other event further along in the story; they can deliberately decontextualize a literary device.

Perhaps we have reached something close to a balance here. It may be a disturbing balance, however, to those who tend to demand something of literary texts and language that is simply unachievable—complete objectivity. Literary texts as specific instances of *parole* have an inherent **polyvalence** because the systems (*langue*) from which they originate are polyvalent. The best which we may claim for such texts is that they establish parameters which may constitute one interpretation more or less legitimate than another. Not all interpretations are equally plausible, just as not all readers are equally skilled. While we assert that readers confront texts with a given repertoire, we may also claim that these same readers should be cognizant of the text's repertoire. If a reader ignores the text's repertoire, an aesthetic object will be actualized, but it will be an inferior one.

REVIEW & STUDY

Key Terms and Concepts

Reference	Polyvalence
Parole	Retrospection
Langue	Concretization
Literary work	Literary repertoire
Artistic pole	Basic dictionary
Aesthetic pole	Rules of co-reference

Dialectics
Gaps of indeterminacy
Ambiguity
Textual segments
Progressive actualization
Theme
Anticipation

Contextual and circumstantial
  selections
Rhetorical and stylistic
  overcoding
Common frames of reference
Intertextual frames of reference
Ideological overcoding

Study Questions

1. Read Genesis 2:4–8 in the RSV. Notice the words in verse 8, "And the LORD planted a garden in Eden." What creative order do you notice in verses 8 and 9? Now read the same reference in the NIV, noting the words in verse 8, "Now the LORD had planted a garden in the east, in Eden." What creative order do you notice here? Why do you think the translators of the NIV changed the tense? What does this suggest about translations?

2. Read Judges 5:24–31 in the RSV. Based upon our discussion of gaps, what are some of the types of gaps you as a reader must fill in this passage? Now read Judges 4:17–22. Notice that this is a prose account of the events described in 5:24–31. Now reread 5:24–31. In what ways does your second reading differ from the first one?

3. What reasons can you give for judging an interpretation (reading) of a text better than another interpretation?

4. What are some reasons you might give for the importance of genre considerations in the process of reading?

5. In terms of common frames, how might a familiarity (or lack of it) with an author's world influence interpretation?

6. In terms of intertextual frames, what value for interpretation is there in a person being versed in a variety of literary traditions?

7. In concluding this chapter, I have suggested that interpretations of a text might be multiple. I have also suggested that the parameters imposed by the text upon reading make one interpretation more plausible than another. We might refer here to a limited subjectivity. In terms of an individual reader and a text, construct a diagram that illustrates this limited subjectivity.

Suggestions for Further Reading

Croatto, Severino. *Biblical Hermeneutics: Toward a Theory of Reading as the Production of Meaning.* Maryknoll: Orbis, 1987.

Eco, Umberto. *The Role of the Reader.* Bloomington: Indiana University Press, 1979.

Iser, Wolfgang. *The Act of Reading: A Theory of Aesthetic Response.* Baltimore: Johns Hopkins University Press, 1978.

_____. "The Reading Process: A Phenomenological Approach." In Jane Tompkins, ed., *Reader-Response Criticism: From Formalism to Post-Structuralism.* Baltimore: Johns Hopkins University Press, 1980.

Lategan, Bernard and Willem Vorster. *Text and Reality: Aspects of Reference in Biblical Texts.* Philadelphia: Fortress, 1985.

McKnight, Edgar V. *The Bible and the Reader.* Philadelphia: Fortress, 1985.

What the Reader Brings to the Text:
The Role of Reader Presuppositions

According to Heidegger, interpretation is always grounded in three things—something we have in advance, or "a fore-having," something we see in advance, or "a fore-sight," and something we grasp in advance, or "a fore-conception."

> Whenever something is interpreted as something, the interpretation will be founded essentially upon fore-having, fore-sight, and fore-conception. An interpretation is never a presuppositionless apprehending of something presented to us. If, when one is engaged in a particular concrete kind of interpretation, in the sense of exact textual interpretation, one likes to appeal to what "stands there," then one finds that what "stands there" in the first instance is nothing other than the obvious undiscussed assumption of the person who does the interpreting.[1]

Any interpreter brings to the act of interpretation a **fore-structure**. This fore-structure includes the interpreter's preunderstanding, a vast array of presuppositions, and the purpose and aim for interpretation.

The Role of Preunderstanding

Every reader approaches a text under the guidance of a perspective. Any text is read, perceived, and interpreted within a preexistent structure of reality. All understanding and interpretation proceed from a prior understanding or a system of making sense of reality. There is no such thing as a pure reading, an objective interpretation. Since reality is infinite, no person can reach outside the realm of time and space to give an objective account of reality. As part of the structure of reality, I can never completely escape the present. I am always being affected by my

---

[1] Martin Heidegger, *Being and Time*, trans. John Macquarrie and Edward Robinson (New York: Harper & Row, 1962), pp. 191–92.

present horizon of understanding, a horizon within which and from which all things are intelligible to me. Without this horizon of understanding, this world of **preunderstanding**, discovering meaning would be simply impossible. Without a preunderstanding, understanding is impossible.

A reader may approach a text without presupposing the results of reading, but the same reader will never engage a text without some preunderstanding, some specific questions about the text, or some idea about what the text itself is about.[2] Readers always wear tinted glasses and make sense of a text according to the particular shade of the lenses. New Testament exegete Günther Bornkamm recognizes this:

> Only the bearing of life on relevant matters that makes itself felt in preunderstanding can establish communication between the text and the interpreter and make possible a proper examination of the text, allowing the interpreter to ask himself about the text and to revise it on the basis of his own self-understanding.[3]

This is especially true for canonical texts, because they impose upon readers a receptivity that other texts do not.

> When the believer and believing community read the Scriptures, they do so as "believers." This means they already accept the faith presented and presumed by the text and thus hear the sacred text in light of the prior faith. The text is thus approached with a "preunderstanding." The text is heard within the context of the faith. A secondary consequence of this preunderstanding and contextual hearing is the tendency to ignore or indulge differences, inconsistencies, and problems within the text. The reader fills out and smooths over differences and difficulties within the text in light of the overall cohesion of the canon and in terms of the community's faith perspective.[4]

The community of faith provides the colored lenses through which the reader views the text.

Reader Presuppositions

Perhaps Terry Eagleton is correct in his idea of textual rewriting.[5] Every time a text is read, it is in essence unconsciously rewritten by the

---

[2] Rudolf Bultmann, *Existence and Faith*, ed. and trans. Schubert Ogden (London: Hodder and Stoughton, 1961), pp. 289–96.

[3] Günther Bornkamm, "The Theology of Rudolf Bultmann," in *The Theology of Rudolf Bultmann*, ed. Charles W. Kegley (London: SCM, 1966), p. 7.

[4] Hayes and Holladay, *Biblical Exegesis*, p. 123.

[5] Eagleton, *Literary Theory*, p. 12.

reader under the pressures of presuppositions attending the reader's horizon of understanding. The **presuppositions** through which any act of perceiving and interpreting reality is filtered are many. Since it is not within the purview of this text to enumerate the almost infinite number of possible presuppositions, I simply offer several categories of presuppositions and then discuss two of these categories: theological and methodological.

Presuppositions might be more appropriately called assumptions. Presuppositions, however, are not synonymous with beliefs or convictions. Presuppositions are axiomatic, a priori, unconscious assumptions. They are not generally subjected to examination or exegesis, but they impact exegesis and interpretation profoundly. Once a reader realizes that he or she holds a certain presupposition, then it may become a belief which is open to examination and modification. Nevertheless, the presupposition which becomes a belief still exerts a powerful control on interpretation. When these presuppositions and beliefs are taken as a whole at any one point in the hermeneut's career, we have the framework within which all texts are perceived and interpreted. This **interpretive framework** consists of presuppositions, beliefs, and attitudes that are ethical, doctrinal, denominational, philosophical, theological, and methodological. Obviously, these classifications constitute the elements of a person's world-view; they are not consciously categorized but exist in an ever-changing process of interrelatedness.

Theological Presuppositions

The biblical texts speak to different people in different ways in each historical period because people hold different world-views. Also, biblical truth is discovered and expressed within a particular universe of meaning. Interpretations, therefore, must be consistent with the established interpretive framework of the interpretive community. The world-view of the interpretive community sets the parameters within which interpretations are accepted or rejected.

Theological presuppositions are varied and numerous. Traditionally, however, they have focused on the Bible itself. This focus, therefore, crucially influences interpretation. Some of the areas of central focus have been the concepts of faith, revelation, word of God, and inspiration, including issues of authority and history.

Faith

Duncan Ferguson makes the following claim:

Faith is the necessary preunderstanding for the interpretation of the Christian faith. . . . Faith is firmly rooted in historical probability, though it is born not of historical knowledge but of God. Historical evidence may suggest that God is present and acting in the events of history, but it cannot supply the personal experience of trust in and commitment to the risen Lord.[6]

What allows Ferguson to make such a claim? Central to his view is the idea that faith originates in an experience. This experience is confrontational. A person experiences deity on a personal, mystical level, thereby receiving a knowledge of God; not a cognitive knowledge, but an experiential knowledge, a participatory knowledge. An individual does not receive this faith knowledge through a study of God or the Bible. The assumption, however, is more complex than this. The faith knowledge originating in God centers in the Christ event. The assumption is that knowledge of God comes from God's self-disclosure in Jesus Christ. But the Christ event *is* historically grounded. Further, the primary source for understanding this historically grounded Christ event is the Bible. Faith knowledge obviously influences how we will read and interpret the biblical account of the Christ event. Therefore, from this perspective, a person must necessarily claim that faith knowledge and historical study are standard assumptions for doing hermeneutics. These two assumptions obviously create a circularity. A pre-posture of faith means that we read with a predetermined attitude; and what we read impacts our faith knowledge by enlarging, modifying, or changing it in a variety of ways.

Not all interpreters accept the idea that faith is a necessary presupposition to interpretation. It is suggested that a person does not require (or desire) an experience of God in order to interpret rationally a written document. Even if the author claimed such an experience, the written document generated by the experience communicates with literary, religious, and philosophical categories of the author's culture. To interpret requires only a knowledge of those categories, not an experience similar to the author's.

Revelation

In the context of biblical hermeneutics, **revelation** is understood as the process of God's self-disclosure to humans. This initiative by God

---

[6] Ferguson, *Biblical Hermeneutics*, pp. 63–64.

presupposes in humans the capacity to respond. The concept of divine revelation has been categorized in numerous ways—historical, temporal revelation, natural revelation (God has revealed himself in the world of nature), and personal revelation, which constitutes the faith knowledge discussed above. The concept of revelation, however, is closely associated with the Bible. This is especially the case if the Bible is in one way or another equated with the **word of God.**

Word of God

A common position is that God's revelation is his word. But how does this concept relate to the Bible? First, I might assume that the word of God (the content of revelation) is the same as the Bible. In this view, the Bible is the standard for the Christian's faith and practice.

A second position concerning the relationship between the word of God and the Bible depends upon the identification of God's word and God's saving activities throughout history, culminating in the Christ event. These activities are recorded in the Bible, and God speaks through these activities. Actually, the Bible is a record of God's redemptive activities, and human response to them. According to this view, the Bible is not God's word, but gives access to it. God speaks to humanity through the Bible, but the Bible is not God's word.

Third, there is the position that Jesus is God's ultimate revelation, the living Word of God. The Bible is the essential historical witness to this supreme revelation of God in Jesus, but it is not itself God's revelation. The Bible constitutes *the* access to God's supreme revelation or word in Jesus.

A fourth position claims that the Bible *becomes* the word of God in proclamation. As the Bible is proclaimed, so it is assumed, the Spirit of God uses it to produce a faith response. A faith-hearing results in a movement towards conformity to a distinctive Christian lifestyle (which is, of course, defined by the particular community of faith in its interpretation of the Bible).

Each of these positions affects how an individual community interprets the Bible. If I assume that the Bible is synonymous with the word of God, my interpretive approach may be characterized by a sense of literalism along with the deification of the Bible. If the Bible is a record of God's word to humans in history, I will probably fall squarely within the historical-critical camp. If the Bible is the primary access to God's supreme revelation in Jesus Christ, my interpretive method will concentrate on the New Testament and those passages in the Hebrew Bible which I perceive to pertain to Jesus as the Messiah. If the Bible becomes the word of God in proclamation, then the interpretive community must define a proper pedagogy for proclamation. An interpretive community cannot countenance just any proclamation. There must be a proclamational canon. But where does one secure such a canon? From the Bible, of course. Further, if proclamation creates a response, how do we judge the difference between an acceptable and unacceptable response? By recourse to the Bible, naturally.

Inspiration

The assumption that the Bible is "inspired" centers in the claim that in some manner, God superintended the writing of the Scriptures. Just what this idea of superintendence entails is a debated issue. Terms such as "infallible," "inerrant," "plenary inspiration," "verbal inspiration," and "clarity" are used to describe this superintendence or the result of it. To claim **verbal inspiration** for the Bible presupposes that God dictated each and every word of Scripture to each individual author and that they wrote Scripture in a robotic fashion, faithfully and inerrantly recording exactly what was received. Each author simply functioned as a stenographer. Part of this view assumes that the Scriptures are clear in their presentation and that the goal of all interpretation is to articulate this plain sense.

A second view of inspiration might be called **conceptual inspiration.** According to this view, God communicated a message to an individual through a dream, vision, mental impression, or some other means, and left the author free to choose the form in which this message would be conveyed. Between the divine act of inspiration and the human act of inscripturation, there exists a gap. This gap allows for the creativity of the author in choice of genre, literary devices, and strategies. This also allows for the different levels of authorial competence and takes into account that human agents differed in personality and historical setting. Each author composed by choosing from a personal vocabulary, literary repertoire, and experience those words, forms, and genres that best conveyed the message.

One interesting assumption relating to divine inspiration is that since God is the author of language, the language of God's revelation (the Bible) is transparent and unambiguous. Those who claim such transparency and non-ambiguity for divinely inspired texts usually do not make the same claim for other, secular texts. These assumptions force the interpreter to further assume that sacred texts must be interpreted differently than secular ones. Other scholars, however, ask on what basis we should presume to interpret sacred texts differently from secular ones if the authors of the former did not consciously write with such a view in mind. Indeed, if we assume that God is the "ultimate" author, why should we also assume that God reveals or speaks through language any differently than any human author? Why should the poetics of a sacred text be different from that of similar secular texts of the same historical matrix? Even God himself cannot transcend the conventions of communication if he wishes to be understood. Why claim linguistic transparency for sacred texts and ambiguity for secular ones? If God is *the* author of language (as some claim) and if language is ambiguous (as most claim), then why would we ever assume that God would transcend his own authorial ambiguity?

Summary

Theological preunderstanding and presuppositions as components of a person's world-view are constitutive of meaning. Any single understanding and explanation of a text proceeds from a prior understanding and set of presuppositions. In a sense, then, all interpreters peer "through a glass darkly."

The range of theological presuppositions is as varied and extensive as the range of religious communities. Concepts such as scriptural authority, the Bible's relation to history, progressive revelation, and canonicity are part of a long and growing list. A discussion of theological presuppositions, not to mention the other presuppositional categories, would fill volumes. Nevertheless, since methodological presuppositions exert such a powerful influence upon interpretation, a detailed treatment of these follows in chapter 9.

REVIEW & STUDY

Key Terms and Concepts

Fore-structure	Preunderstanding
Presuppositions	Interpretive framework
Revelation	Word of God
Verbal inspiration	Conceptual inspiration

Study Questions

1. In the Apocrypha, read Judith 13:1–26. Now read Judges 4:17–22 and 5:24–27. Did you read these texts differently? If so, was it due to presuppositions concerning the nature of the two books? Explain.

2. Suppose a person were to ask you the following: "Do you believe the Word of God is inspired?" How would you answer? If you were to answer *yes*, can you be certain that you both mean the same thing? Why or why not?

3. Speculate on the following statement: There is something inherently unique about the writings of the Bible that requires that they be interpreted differently than other writings.

Suggestions for Further Reading

Barr, James. *The Bible in the Modern World*. New York: Harper & Row, 1973.

Childs, Brevard S. *Biblical Theology in Crisis*. Philadelphia: Westminster, 1970.

Ferguson, Duncan. *Biblical Hermeneutics: An Introduction*. Atlanta: John Knox, 1986.

Merleau-Ponty, Maurice. *Consciousness and the Acquisition of Language*. Trans. by Hugh J. Silverman. Evanston: Northwestern University Press, 1964.

Morgan, Robert with John Barton. *Biblical Interpretation*. New York: Oxford University Press, 1988.

How Methods Affect Interpretation

D ecisive in interpretation is the aim of the interpreter. A text has no rights except those allowed by the interpreter. The text, we have already argued, exercises controls over interpretation, but this is true only to the degree that the interpreter chooses to permit such controls. There is obviously the case where the interpreter is not even aware of the text's literary repertoire.

Interpreters use texts to fulfill their interests or aims. This means that often interpretive purpose differs from authorial intent. Consequently, given the possibility of this difference, hermeneutics must give appropriate attention to interpretive aims, for differences in interpretation may be due as much to differing aims as to textual ambiguity, interpretive competence, and matters of genre. As Robert Morgan points out, "Leviticus is read as religious law by Jews, as a source of religious history by historians and anthropologists, and by Christians maybe as typology or outdated theology coupled with some moral exhortation."[1] Depending upon what the aims might be, a text may mean different things to different readers at different times.

How does the issue of aims pertain to methodology? Literary aims or interests require literary methods; historical aims require historical methods; and theological aims may require a variety of methods. Interpretive aims dictate interpretive methods. These methods in turn influence the way in which interpreters perceive and use the data of the text.[2] We make sense of texts against the backdrop of our own world by employing methods determined and validated by that world. Every method is in turn anchored to a set of underlying presuppositions that determine the questions to be put to the text; and the answers are those expected in advance.

---

[1] Morgan, *Biblical Hermeneutics*, p. 12.
[2] McKnight, *Post-Modern Use of the Bible*, p. 58.

Interpretive integrity should certainly require the hermeneut to articulate aims and examine methodology. The method should be consistent with aims. Aims may pertain to moral instruction, historical knowledge, the justification of a liturgical practice, doctrinal support, or simply aesthetic enjoyment. There should be a viable relationship between the genre of the text, aims, and methodology. If the method of interpretation does not suit aim and genre, interpretation will be based upon presuppositions that are consistent with neither the aims nor the character of the text.

To interpret a text means to interpret in one way and not another. The hermeneut has no choice in this matter; interpretation proceeds from some method. The only choice that the hermeneut has is either to remain ignorant of the interpretive method and the attendant assumptions or to select consciously a particular methodology after examining the feasibility of the other alternatives. Since to interpret at all is to do so from one perspective rather than others, interpreters should be aware of the particular method they have selected and why.

Finding the most suitable method for interpretation is not an easy task. Sorting through the number and diversity of critical methods can be frustrating, especially to beginning hermeneuts. We find historical critics, feminists, Freudians, existentialists, structuralists, deconstructionists, narrative critics, reader-response critics, Marxists, redaction critics, canonical critics, New Critics, and formalists. How do we find our way through such a maze of competing and sometimes disparate methods?

In the introduction, I stated that interpretive theories can be categorized into three groups, depending upon their locus of meaning: author-centered, text-centered, and reader-centered. For the sake of clarity, I will discuss these groups individually. After discussing the nature of each broad interpretive area, I will summarize the specific theories which have profoundly influenced biblical interpretation.

Author-Centered Interpretation

Every literary text is created by a communicating mind. The author seeks to communicate meaning to an audience. "Every utterance is an attempt to express something, an idea, a feeling, a set of facts, and is successful to the extent that it effectively communicates what it set out to communicate. A poem, then, would be good if it achieved what its author intended."[3] In author-centered criticism, the meaning of the text

---

[3] Keesey, ed., *Contexts for Criticism*, p. 15.

must be related to the mind which created it. If the author creates a text, then interpretation should concern itself with the relationship between the author and the text. The text is the effect, the author the cause. Author-centered criticism seeks to ascertain as much as possible about the mind and world of the author in order to determine what that mind communicates through the text. The better the interpreters understand the creative mind, the better they will understand the creation of that mind.

Getting into the author's mind, however, is not easy. This holds especially true for ancient authors. If there is anything known at all about an ancient author, it is usually minimal. When the interpreter has other writings by the same author, these are examined to determine as much about the author as possible. In a sense, the author-centered critic seeks to create a profile of the author. In addition to examining other writings by the same author, author-centered critics also attempt to find out about the author's world. The assumption is that if an author is the product of his or her world, then the author's literary creation will reflect that world. The elements within the author's social, political, religious, intellectual milieu are constitutive of meaning. Therefore, understanding the author's world makes for a fuller understanding of the text.

Another important assumption of author-centered criticism is that history is periodic; that is, history can be divided into periods having relatively unique assumptions, values, and beliefs. This assumption permits the study of texts under headings such as "Renaissance," "Medieval," "Romantic," Neo-Classical," or "Elizabethan." The best-equipped interpreter is knowledgeable of the assumptions, values, and beliefs characteristic of each period. Consequently, author-centered criticism has a historical focus. The historical focus supplies a check against overly anachronistic interpretations.

As we discuss text-centered and reader-centered theories, some of the shortcomings of author-centered criticism will come to light; however, we should examine two of them here. First, historical periods are so complex and unpredictable that they produce complex and unpredictable individuals. While it seems a commonplace that authors are affected by their contemporary conditions, obviously not every individual of a particular age is the same. Writers of literary texts can be quite extraordinary and unique individuals within their cultures. This uniqueness makes them stand out. Is it feasible to assume that the individual mind is a microcosm of an interpreter's conception of a corporate mind? Second, always lying just beneath the surface is the interpreter's tendency to use the text to explain something about a culture or a period. When this happens, constructing a picture of a particular historical period becomes the end of interpretation.

Author-Centered Theories

Source Criticism

Source critics seek to identify earlier traditions and documents within a text. Since authors do not compose texts within literary vacuums, we should expect to find adaptations of earlier traditions for current purposes. It was argued previously that the recognitions of such sources may have a significant impact upon interpretation. The way in which an author adapts an earlier tradition or document may witness to the author's purpose.

Source criticism has enjoyed a long and venerable career in both Hebrew Bible and New Testament studies. Source-critical studies of the Hebrew Bible have focused upon the Pentateuch, and more recently have included other parts of the Hebrew Bible. For centuries the Mosaic authorship of the Pentateuch was generally accepted without much question. Gradually, however, scholars began to doubt whether everything in the Pentateuch could be from the hand of Moses. Under the influence of seventeenth-century rationalism, and because of passages which could not have been from Moses (e.g., the account of Moses' death [Deut. 34:5-8], familiarity with the monarchy [Gen. 36:31-39], and the phrase "until this day," which suggests that the passages containing it were written after the time of Moses [Gen. 35:4 LXX and Deut. 34:5-6]), many scholars further questioned Mosaic authorship of the Pentateuch. Based upon these passages and other discoveries such as historical inaccuracies, repetitions, and divergent writing styles, these scholars concluded that the Pentateuch was the product of an extended process of compilation.

In the second half of the nineteenth century, Julius Wellhausen and Abraham Kuenen popularized the view that the Pentateuch is comprised of four sources. Both Wellhausen and Kuenen detected a close relationship between the Pentateuch and the book of Joshua. They, therefore, spoke of the four-source hypothesis as relating to the Hexateuch. Later followers of Wellhausen claimed that the sources of the Hexateuch also formed the basis of the books through Kings.[4] All subsequent source-critical

---

[4] A discussion of the various reactions and challenges to Wellhausen would take us too far afield here. For a concise and informative discussion of these challenges and alternatives, see A. S. Van der Woude, *The World of the Old Testament* (Grand Rapids: Eerdmans, 1989), pp. 166-205.

scholarship is deeply indebted to Wellhausen, and many scholars today feel that the four-source theory is still the best explanation for the composition of the Pentateuch.

The **four-source hypothesis** is really quite simple: The Pentateuch/Hexateuch is composed of four documents (JEPD) or parts of documents which are concerned with the same events. These documents were composed at different times by and for people with different concerns and purposes. Each source thus constitutes a layer within the Hexateuch, and each layer has its peculiar language, style, and theological viewpoint.[5] What follows is a summary of the characteristics of each source.

J (*Yahwist*). The hand of the *Yahwist* is first detected in Genesis 2:4b, where the divine name Yahweh appears. The Yahwist's depiction of God is simple, personal, and highly anthropomorphic. God walks, talks, forms with his hands, and experiments. God differs sharply from the transcendent being in Genesis 1:1–2:4a. Sections coming from the hand of the *Yahwist* include Genesis 2:4b–4:26; 6:1–8; 11:1–9; 12:1–4a, 6–20.

E (*Elohist*). This document favors the name Elohim for God and associates the divine name Yahweh with a revelation to Moses. The hand of the Elohist is found primarily in the patriarchal narratives. The Elohist depicts divine revelation as occurring through indirect means, such as dreams (Gen. 20:3) or a divine messenger (Gen. 21:17). The vocabulary of the Elohist is also distinctly different from that of the Yahwist (e.g., the reference to Mount Horeb instead of Mount Sinai). Elohistic passages include Genesis 20:1–8; 21:8–34; 22:1–19.

P (*Priestly Writer*). The Priestly document differs in many ways from the Yahwist and Elohist documents. The interests of the Priestly writer include cultic and priesthood stipulations, brief historical notations, the sacrificial system *after* Moses, minute details, and calendarizing of events. The style is formulaic and repetitious. God is depicted as a transcendent being, creating and arranging through fiat. The primary concern of the Priestly writer is God rather than human beings. The God of Genesis 1 could never be characterized in the anthropomorphic terms of Genesis 2–4. Included among the Priestly portions are Genesis 1:1–2:4a; 5:1–27; 9:1–17; 11:10–27; 25:7–10.

D (*Deuteronomist*). The bulk of Deuteronomy (chaps. 12–26) is the book of the law found in the temple during the reign of Josiah in the seventh century. The book has its own paraenetic style and vocabulary. Most scholars today, however, agree that Deuteronomy is the product of a

---

[5] Ibid., pp. 188–90.

complex process of compilation and contains much older material. Characteristic of Deuteronomy is the attention given to the Levites and the proclamation and interpretation of the laws in it.[6] Some scholars today propose that Deuteronomy was composed in the courts of Hezekiah and Josiah, receiving its final form in the second half of the seventh century B.C. at the hands of a circle of writers who produced the Deuteronomistic history.[7]

Although source criticism has been applied to all the writings of the New Testament, its primary focus has been upon the Synoptic Gospels. This focus is twofold: a concern for the relationship between two or more texts that suggests some kind of dependence, and the discovery of sources within a single text.

The nineteenth century witnessed a tremendous concern to uncover the history behind the Gospels. A great deal of energy was especially expended in the attempt to reconstruct the life of Jesus. For this reason, the Gospels were treated as sources for reconstructing history. If one Gospel were earlier than the others, then that one should be historically more reliable, for it would have been closer to the actual events. In the first quarter of the twentieth century, B. H. Streeter popularized in the English-speaking world a solution to the relationship between the Synoptic Gospels. His solution was a refinement of Holtzmann's (1832–1910) **two-document hypothesis.** This solution remains popular in source-critical studies today. Simply put, this hypothesis claims that Mark was the first Gospel and was a source for both Matthew and Luke. It also claims that Matthew and Luke made use of another, no longer extant, source which has come to be known as Q (Ger. *Quelle* for "source"), and that Matthew and Luke each had sources, designated M and L respectively.

Recent scholarship has challenged the assumption that the Gospels can serve as sources for reconstructing the life of Jesus. Scholars generally recognize today that not only are the Gospels separated from the events they describe by at least a generation (Mark was composed around A.D. 70, and Matthew and Luke between A.D. 80 and 90), but that the Gospels are theologically rather than historically motivated. We should also recognize that the two-document hypothesis has met with significant criticism. One older hypothesis (the Griesbach hypothesis) claims that Matthew and Luke were written before Mark, and Mark borrowed from Matthew and Luke, especially where Matthew and Luke agreed.

---

[6] Ibid., p. 190.

[7] See M. Weinfeld, *Deuteronomy and the Deuteronomic School* (Oxford: Oxford University, 1972).

Source criticism is also concerned with identifying lost sources within the text. When they encounter a portion of a text thought to be uncharacteristic of the author's style, vocabulary, or ideology, source critics usually suspect that the author has drawn from a source. An example of this is John 21, where the vocabulary differs significantly from that found in the rest of the Gospel (*ischyein* rather than *dynasthai* and *exetazein* instead of *erōtan*). In Romans 3:25–26, we encounter the idea of God "overlooking" past sins. This seems to contradict (not only in vocabulary, but also in concept) what Paul has already claimed in Romans 1–2 (i.e., that God punishes all sin).[8] Some suspect the use of a source.

This brings us to a significant observation concerning source-critical studies: Source criticism assumes that an author's usual or normal vocabulary, style, and ideology can be discovered. But can we sufficiently define an author's normal vocabulary, style, and ideology, and then use that definition as a canon by which to determine whether a passage is or is not the work of that author? Most source critics answer in the affirmative. Care should be taken, however, in assuming that an author cannot use vocabulary, style, and ideologies that seem to differ from those in other contexts. Even if an author incorporated earlier traditions or sources, this suggests that the writer recognized some agreement between his or her ideas and the source.

With the advent of redaction criticism (to be discussed below) and its emphasis upon the author's theological purpose, source criticism has assumed a more adjunctive role. In order to make a statement of the way in which an author uses sources, those sources must be identified. If authors modify or re-contextualize their sources for theological purposes, we cannot know those purposes without identifying the sources.

Form Criticism

Form criticism proceeds upon the premise that parts (e.g., miracle stories, pronouncement stories, and sayings) of the early Christian and Israelite traditions circulated as individual oral units, were finally collected, and eventually became sources for the composition of the biblical texts.

Substantial efforts have been made to identify the individual forms of the biblical texts. This is true of both the Hebrew Bible and the New Testament. For example, the book of Psalms has been sub-divided into

---

[8] Christopher Tuckett, *Reading the New Testament: Methods of Interpretation* (Philadelphia: Fortress, 1987), p. 85.

psalms of lament, thanksgiving, coronation, and hymn, among others. The prophetic books have also come under the scrutiny of form-critical studies—the prophetic address may be, among other things, judgment, exhortation, admonition, or promise. In the New Testament, much of form-critical activity has centered around the Synoptic Gospels. Some of the forms identified by Martin Dibelius, Rudolf Bultmann, and Vincent Taylor[9] include: paradigm (a brief account of an event which is designed to supply the context for a "pronouncement" of Jesus); miracle stories (which Bultmann claimed were designed for propaganda and apologetic purposes); legends (which Dibelius defined as "religious narratives of a saintly man in whose work and fate interest is taken");[10] and "sayings" of Jesus (which Bultmann divided into proverbial sayings, prophetic sayings, legal sayings, and parabolic sayings). Most of these general forms are further subdivided.

Form critics are concerned with the ways in which individual forms were utilized in the ancient culture of Israel and the life of the early church before the forms became fixed in writing. Underlying this concern is the assumption that small units of folk memory are the means by which a people's tradition is preserved and passed on. Form criticism seeks to isolate these small units of tradition and then discover how these units were used within the community. For example, the psalms were produced in Israel within specific social contexts and in turn reflect social aspects of Israel's culture. The epistles and Gospels in the New Testament contain units that reflect the faith and worship of the early church. As the individual stories were told and retold, they tended to be told within common settings, such as preaching, teaching, or worship. As a result, the pericopae assumed discernible forms which fit the settings. The forms, for example within the Gospels, received their shape within the Christian communities. Usage dictated form. This means that by the time the evangelists produced their Gospels, the individual pericopae were already molded into definite shapes. Perhaps recognizing that a single story could assume different shapes in different settings might account for some of the variations of the same story as told by the evangelists.

Form criticism, however, goes further than correlating form with setting. Form criticism is the English translation of the German word

---

[9] Martin Dibelius, *From Tradition to Gospel* (New York: Scribner's, n.d.); Rudolf Bultmann, *The History of the Synoptic Tradition*, trans. J. Marsh, rev. ed. (repr., Peabody: Hendrickson, 1993); Vincent Taylor, *The Formation of the Gospel Tradition* (London: Macmillan, 1960).

[10] Dibelius, *From Tradition to Gospel*, p. 104.

Formsgeschichte. Since *Geschichte* means "history," form criticism is also concerned with the history of the individual forms, the way in which the forms were transmitted and adapted.[11] This concern is sometimes called "tradition criticism." This means that form criticism attempts to inquire as far back into the form as possible, even to the form's origin. Therefore, form criticism concerns itself with a process of development from origin to present context.

The concern with the origin and development of forms and traditions has led many scholars to assume that many of the Gospel stories (or at least details of the stories) did not originate in the life of Jesus, but were "invented" by the church. Debate continues concerning the extent to which early Christians modified existing traditions about Jesus or created new ones.

Form criticism has successfully called attention to the range of forms utilized by the biblical authors. With form criticism's insistence that the forms in the biblical texts were simply metaphors reflecting problems or events in the life of the early Christian communities, attention was diverted away from the text itself. For Bultmann and his followers, what actually happened in the life of Jesus was not important; in fact, historical certitude was impossible to obtain. What became foremost, therefore, was the discovery of the faith of the early believing community and the traditions through which that faith was expressed. This position would say, therefore, that the controversy between Jesus and the Jewish authorities over the Sabbath really describes the controversies between the early Christians and Jews. Positively, however, form criticism concentrates upon the stories and sayings as types of expressions rather than as historical events in the life of Jesus, a prophet, or a patriarch. Consequently, form criticism focuses upon the ways in which ancient religious communities used and shaped forms. Thus, "form criticism allows the interpreter to understand and appreciate the role and significance of the faith and practices of the believing community in the formation of the traditions that the community would hold sacred and declare canonical."[12]

Redaction Criticism

Redaction criticism represents a movement towards a more concentrated focus upon the text as a whole. A basic assumption underlying redaction criticism is that the authors were guided in their adaptation,

---

[11] Tuckett, *Reading the New Testament*, p. 101.

[12] Hayes and Holladay, *Biblical Exegesis*, p. 89.

modification, and arrangement of their sources by theological purposes. The theological purpose of an author can be discovered by examining how that writer uses sources. Writers arranged and altered their sources and traditions according to their own theological purposes or those of their community. This, of course, means that source and form criticism are presuppositions for redaction criticism. Sources and individual units of tradition must be available before an interpreter can determine to what extent and in what ways an author has adapted and reapplied the sources and traditions. It follows that redaction criticism inherently focuses on four concerns: (1) selection of traditional material and sources; (2) adaptation and modification of the material; (3) arrangement of the material; and (4) the extent of the author's own theological contribution to the text.

When a text's sources are available to the interpreter, conclusions about the author's theological purposes reflected in the obvious modifications, selections, and arrangement are relatively simple to make. For example, if Markan priority is assumed when studying Luke, we can easily observe the ways in which Luke modifies his source. Consider the followings passages from Mark and Luke:

Mark 8:27–33	Luke 9:18–22
Jesus went on with his disciples to the villages of Caesarea Philippi; and on the way he asked his disciples, "Who do people say that I am?" And they answered him, "John the Baptist; and others, Elijah; and still others, one of the prophets." He asked them, "But who do you say that I am?" Peter answered him, "You are the Messiah." And he sternly ordered them not to tell anyone about him. Then he began to teach them that the Son of Man must undergo great suffering, and be rejected by the elders, the chief priests, and the scribes, and be killed, and after three days rise again. He said all this quite openly. And Peter took him aside and began to rebuke him. But turning and looking at his disciples, he rebuked Peter and said, "Get behind me, Satan! For you are setting your mind not on divine things but on human things."	Once when Jesus was praying alone, with only the disciples near him, he asked them, "Who do the crowds say that I am?" They answered, "John the Baptist; but others, Elijah; and still others, that one of the ancient prophets has arisen." He said to them, "But who do you say that I am?" Peter answered, "The Messiah of God." He sternly ordered and commanded them not to tell anyone, saying, "The Son of Man must undergo great suffering, and be rejected by the elders, chief priests, and scribes, and be killed, and on the third day be raised."

Some differences are striking—the setting is different: "people say I am"/"crowds say I am." Both rebukes are missing in Luke's account. The redaction critic must ask why the source was modified. Why does Luke soften Mark's treatment of the disciples? Why the different settings for the same event? Why crowds instead of people? Why "one of the ancient prophets has arisen" instead of simply "one of the prophets?" and why the answer, "the Messiah of God" rather than "the Messiah?" The answer most redaction critics quickly offer is that the differences are due to Luke's theological interests. Luke has something to say *through* his narrative that is theologically different from that of Mark.

But what happens if the interpreter has no available sources which underlie that text, or when there is evidence that the author has simply incorporated a unit of tradition without any modification? Mark is a case in point; what are Mark's sources? The answer lies in the more modern approach of redaction critics to view a text as an entity within itself. This approach supposes that a final redactor has produced a final version of a text and the text itself supplies the primary evidence for discovering the author's theological purpose. The interpreter must examine in detail the way in which each individual part of a text relates to the other parts and consequently, the way in which the text as a whole presents its message. This observation obviously vitiates any attempt to harmonize texts which make use of the same or similar traditions. The Gospels should not become only sources for constructing a homogenized Gospel story.[13] Each Gospel is a biased (Ger. *Tendenz*) narrative which has its own message to communicate. In the Hebrew Bible, both the Chronicler and the author of Samuel–Kings have their own messages, and attempts to harmonize these two accounts of the same period stand in opposition to redaction criticism.

Canonical Criticism

Unlike source criticism (which looks for the sources and traditions behind a text), form criticism (which seeks to identify the various forms within a text with their life-settings within the early communities), and redaction criticism (which finds meaning in the author's editorial activity), canonical criticism[14] moves beyond the final redaction of a text to

---

[13] Ibid., p. 105.
[14] The most notable work in the field of canonical criticism has been done by James Sanders, *Canon and Community* (Philadelphia: Fortress, 1984); and Brevard

the point when the texts were accepted as canonical by believing communities. As Terence Keegan sees it, "What is most important is the text which is accepted by the Church as canonical. This canonically accepted text is the starting point of all biblical exegesis. This text is what the Church has taken into its life and what remains with the Church to the present day."[15] Canonical criticism is more concerned with the text as accepted by the believing communities than with what lies behind the text.

For canonical critics, the biblical texts are not merely sources for what lies behind the texts. Meaning in any final sense does not lie in the history behind the text or in the redactional activity of the author. The locus of meaning is the canonical text which was produced within and taken up into the life of the believing communities. For instance, the emphasis within Synoptic studies should not be what happened within the life of Jesus; emphasis rather should be upon the question of what the single text, say of Matthew, means.

In his treatment of the Hebrew Bible, Childs notes that the books of Ezra and Nehemiah do not cooperate well with the historical critic who attempts an accurate historical reconstruction of the period encompassed by the two books. Childs goes on to suggest that such attempts at historical reconstruction simply miss the point of interpretation. The focus should be upon what the canonical texts have to say as Scripture; that is, what do the texts of Ezra and Nehemiah say in their present individual arrangements and why were these texts, as they are, taken into the believing community as inspired texts? Exegetical concern is not *primarily* centered on what lies behind the text, but on the text itself. Also important within canonical criticism is the situation of the reader. Readers produce meaning within their present situations. This idea of reader-produced meaning, however, holds true only for members of the believing community.

Now I should explain the word *primarily* in the last paragraph. Canonical critics are concerned with historical studies pertaining to the biblical texts. As Keegan points out, canonical critics perform historical studies but they do not read the biblical text historically.[16] Canonical critics study the historical processes of canonization. A text

---

Childs, *Introduction to the Old Testament as Scripture* (Philadelphia: Fortress, 1979); idem, *The New Testament as Canon: An Introduction* (Philadelphia: Fortress, 1985).

[15] Terence Keegan, O.P., *Interpreting the Bible: A Popular Introduction to Biblical Hermeneutics* (New York: Paulist, 1985), p. 30.

[16] Ibid., p. 137.

is composed, copied, re-copied, transmitted to subsequent generations, and finally canonized. This process is significant for how the church in every generation should understand and interpret a text. This interest in the canonical process results in two interrelated activities in canonical criticism: (1) the examination of the process by which the biblical texts in a final, stable form were accepted as canonical; and (2) based upon this process, the development of a hermeneutic for the interpretation of these texts within the church today. What follows is a brief discussion of some key observations made by canonical critics concerning the canonical process and some resultant interpretive suggestions.

The canonization process of the biblical canon was always in a state of flux. During this process, what might be termed an orthodox idea of what constituted a sacred piece of writing simply did not exist. The Sadducees, Pharisees, and Essenes all recognized and used varying collections of books. In the process of the canonization of the New Testament books, various Christian communities regarded different collections as authoritative.

In order for a book to be finally accepted into the canon, it had to have a universal quality; it had to be able to speak to the changing situations within the life of the believing community in every age. Flexibility of application was a prerequisite for canonization. The needs of the community and the ability of a writing to speak to those needs resulted in its being selected while others, not able to do this, were rejected. After the canon stabilized, believing communities continued to adapt and reapply the canonized books to the communities' needs.

At every stage of the canonical process, believing communities applied the writings to their own situations. This took place through adaptation, expansion, and interpretation. Believing communities sought to understand the writings through resignification. Modern hermeneuts should study the process of resignification throughout the canonical process in order to produce guidelines for the interpretive process today. To some extent, the interpretive processes extrapolated from the canonical process itself should be used as interpretive guides in today's interpretation and resignification of the biblical texts.

The believing communities adopted and adapted entire texts, not partial ones. Entire texts were resignified so as to speak in toto to the needs of the believing communities. Consequently, canonical criticism advocates a hermeneutic which considers the text as a unified whole.

This focus does not mean that canonical critics are uninterested in historical-critical studies. Indeed, canonical critics employ source, form, and redaction criticism, albeit with an ulterior motive. They are interested in source criticism because it is important to ascertain the ways in which the sources were resignified; they are interested in form criticism because knowing the Sitz im Leben is helpful for understanding how a community shaped and used the form; and they are interested in redaction criticism to the extent that it offers insights into the manner in which writers in the communities reinterpreted and reapplied their sources.

Since the early believing communities resignified the texts, a plurality of meanings is suggested for the texts. Canonical critics do not advocate interpretive license; on the contrary, they insist that their hermeneutics derive from the interpretive activities observable in the stages of the canonical process. Multiple meanings are possible, but only insofar as they flow from the hermeneutics of resignification.

Text-Centered Interpretation

The backbone of text-centered criticism is its spotlight on artistic strategies, literary forms, and textual coherence as these relate to **textual autonomy.** Text-centered criticism has been given several names, such as New Criticism and objective (in the sense of the text being the object of focus) criticism. The latter designation springs from a basic assumption of text-centered criticism—the text is autonomous; that is, it has a life of its own apart from the author or reader. This assumption suggests that the standard by which we can rightly judge any interpretation of the text is the text itself. This second assumption then leads to at least a corollary: the text must be viewed spatially, that is, as a whole. Because of this concept of wholeness, text-centered critics are dedicated to demonstrating how the parts of the text *cohere* in order to produce the whole.[17] But the understanding of the whole conditions our understanding of the individual parts. Since many text-centered theories (those approaches which fall under the umbrella of New Criticism with its emphasis on the text's autonomy as a literary artifact) share a focus on the formal aspects of a text, the designation "formal criticism" has become an appropriate one.

---

[17] Keesey, ed., *Contexts for Criticism*, p. 75.

Text-Centered Theories

Formal Criticism

In formal criticism, lexical, historical, and social meanings become irrelevant, because the literary context dictates meaning. The literary context can create new meanings while eliminating old ones. The meanings of literary forms or strategies such as motif and archetype are conveyed *only* within the context of the text. The only meaning possible for a part of the text thus depends upon its function in the text as a whole. The text may or may not depict reality in the sense of describing accurately the political, social, or religious milieu of its author's time.

Two other assumptions of formalists pertain to the concepts of **complexity** and **congruence**. Literary texts (i.e., literarily coherent texts) are complex constructs employing irony, metaphor, ambiguity, and tension. "The complex poem is better than the simple poem because it appeals to a greater number of our desires and aversions."[18] Obviously, formal critics do not intend to divorce literary texts from human experience. Indeed, texts generate experiences that we recognize as inherently human. The formalists claim that this textual complexity presents us with a story world full of emotional and moral significance, somewhat congruent to our own complex experiences of the real world.

But the assumption of congruence presents a problem. If the text somehow creates a congruence between the textual world and the real one, then the context for interpretation is not the text alone, but includes those typical or definable human experiences of the real world. While the text may be complex, it is also coherent. Can it then really create a congruence between reality and the world of the text? Reality is disorganized, infinite, always in flux. Because of **selectivity** and arrangement, the text can never be more than an imitation of reality, a redefinition of it. Reading a literary work may be similar to the drama of living, but it is never a true copy of life, because selection is made *for* us rather than *by* us.

One last crucial assumption warrants attention. When formal critics refer to form, the referent may be any part of the text—words, literary devices, and so on—in a particular order. What they do not mean by form is literary *type*. Generally they are not interested in genre—whether a satire, a comedy, or an epic. The reason for this indifference towards

---

[18] Ibid., p. 77.

generic categories is that such considerations might distract attention away from the *particular* text to *intertextual* concerns. When we begin to compare an Aristophanean comedy with one by Molière, or Mark's Gospel with Matthew's, we are appealing to an interpretive context outside the text itself. A text constitutes its own interpretive domain, and it neither requires nor desires historical or generic contextualization. The meaning of a literary text is contingent only upon the unique form of the text itself. Meaning is textual meaning and it is inseparable from the unique form.

Structuralism

Source, form, and redaction criticism in one way or another seek to go behind the text to the stages of textual development—the traditions or sources underlying the text, the early believing communities that shaped the text, or the theological intention of the author. Even canonical criticism seeks to articulate meaning in terms of the process of canonical development. The discovery and articulation of meaning (authorial or textual) are central. With structuralism, this changes. Issues such as the author's identity and purpose, original audience, and originating circumstances are bracketed out as areas of concern. Structuralism is not concerned with *what* a text means, but with *how* a text means. Therefore, only the final form of the text is of interest to structuralists.

Structuralism in general is based upon the assumption that all human social activity is nothing more than manifestations of underlying systems of abstract rules or conventions which govern the way humans order their existence into meaningful structures. These systems of rules exist on a subconscious level. For example, when I formulate a sentence, I do not consciously recite beforehand the syntactical and grammatical rules which underlie my sentence, just as I do not consult a commentary on dress codes before I attend a funeral. At a fundamental level, the principles in these systems are universal. In all areas, then, of social activity, "deep structures" can be found common to all human societies, regardless of other culturally identifying specifics.

Another assumption of structuralism is that all human activity is essentially a form of communication. Furthermore, communication is possible precisely because people adhere to basic rules. Language is a form of communication and is, therefore, governed by a subconscious set of rules or conventions.

Structuralism as applied to literary discourse is based upon three concepts, two from Ferdinand de Saussure and one from Claude Lévi-Strauss: (1) the distinction between *langue* and *parole*, (2) the definition of *sign*, and (3) the concept of **binary opposition** as it relates to the concept of myth.

Langue *and* Parole

According to Saussure, meaning depends on an underlying system of conventions and relationships, which Saussure refers to as *langue,* and on the individual instances of actual speech, which he terms *parole.* *Parole* refers to the individual, meaningful act of speech that is based upon the subconscious system of literary conventions and relationships. Now if all human activities are governed by basic systems of subconscious rules, and if all these activities are actually forms of communication, we might assume that literature is a form of communication and thus governed by a set of basic conventions or rules. This can be expressed in the following proportion:

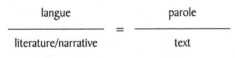

DIAGRAM 9-1

Since **deep structures** (basic underlying conventions) are common to all languages, we can assume that as a form of communication, there are likewise common deep structures within literature in general and the genre of narrative specifically. Since *parole* is an instance of individual speech, based on the underlying enabling system of *langue*, a narrative text is a specific manifestation based on the enabling system of narrative. This means that the limited set of conventions of narrative transcends cultures, literary traditions, time, and space. All narrative traditions share the same basic conventions. It is the explicit task and goal of structuralism to uncover these deep structures within individual narratives, which produce what is referred to as a **meaning effect** upon readers. Since all narratives communicate through a shared system of conventions, interest in individual textual meaning is replaced by an interest in the effect an individual text has on the readers. These deep structures operate at levels of writing and reading alike. Not only have authors of narrative texts internalized these deep structures, but competent readers have also internalized them. This is the only means possible for understanding a narrative text.

According to structuralists, a text actually has three meaning effect levels which correlate to types of structures. The first level is the **structures of enunciation**. These structures are determined by features such as authorial intent, authorial *Sitz im Leben*, and audience (the concerns of the historical-critical method). Second are **structures of culture.** Culture's structures consist of the specific codes of a specific people at a specific time. The third level of meaning effect is determined by the text's deep structures that are universal in all human activity. On the level of any genre of literature like narrative, certain narrative and mythological structures are present. For more conservative structuralists, these three meaning effect levels with their accompanying structures combine to produce a composite meaning effect. Consequently, texts have the potential for a plurality of meaning.

Sign and Its Dual Character

The second of Saussure's concepts that structuralists build upon is that of *sign* and its dual character. Concerning linguistics, Saussure claimed that a language was comprised of a series of "signs" involving relationships between signs and what the signs refer to. Every sign consists of a **signifier** and a **signified.** The signifier is the "immediate object of perception" while the signified is "that which the perception evokes."[19] For example, the word "rose" is a sign signifying a particular flower in the real word. The signifier is the word-sound "rose" and the signified is the flower. We might say that the real-world flower is denoted by the signifier "rose." This brings us to a crucial point for structuralism. The signified may have not only a denotative meaning but also a connotative one. For example, the signifier "rose" may refer both to the real-world flower and to a person who is as lovely as a rose. Now if a text (e.g., a narrative one) is itself a sign, it may also have both denotative and connotative meanings. It is on the denotative level that we would expect to find manifestations of authorial intention. On the connotative level, however, there exists a subconscious system of con-

---

[19] Ferdinand de Saussure, *A Course in General Linguistics*, trans. Wade Baskin, ed. Charles Bally, Albert Sechehaye, and Albert Riedlinger (New York: Philosophical Library, 1959; repr., McGraw-Hill, paperback edition, 1966).

ventions and convictions which precede authorial intention. Actually, it is more accurate to speak of a plurality of levels of connotative meaning. Deep within the text are three levels which structuralists attempt to excavate: narrative structures common to all narratives but manifested culturally at the surface level; universal mythical structures; and an author's semantic universe, a system of convictions which underlies the author's work. The bottom level can be reached only by analyzing the narrative and mythical structures.

Every narrative has a series of three sequences. The initial sequence is the *crisis* describing some disruption of the social order. Following the initial sequence is the *plot* proper which consists of one or more topical sequences involving attempts to restore the social order. In the final sequence, *resolution* (*dénouement*), the hero is successful in restoring the social order. The articulation of these sequences varies on the surface level from narrative to narrative, depending upon culture specifics; but on the deep level of the text, these three sequences will always be found.

Each of the sequences may involve up to six roles which structuralists call **actants.** These actants are related along three different axes. A sender sends an object to a receiver, the object is carried to the receiver by the subject, and finally the subject may receive assistance from helpers and be frustrated by opponents. The relationships among the actants within a sequence can be represented by the following diagram:

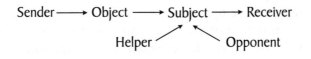

DIAGRAM 9-2

Every narrative can be examined as a series of sequences by using diagrams like the one above.

Mythical Structures and Binary Opposition

Along with examining these endemic narrative structures, structuralists go even deeper in an effort to identify the presence of mythical structures. Narratives may contain mythical elements even though they are not mythical in general; thus, a narrative may contain mythical elements even though the narrative (unlike a pure myth) is a conscious logical argument. Therefore, according to biblical scholars who apply structuralism to the interpretation of the Bible, the Bible can be analyzed according to mythical structures.

The structuralists employ Lévi-Strauss's idea that **myths** are attempts to deal with "binary oppositions" inherent in human existence. These fundamental oppositions cannot be logically mediated. Some of these oppositions are love/hate, life/death, youth/old age, sin/righteousness. Myths attempt to mediate the oppositions by offering parallel oppositions that are proportional to the binary ones and capable of reconciliation. Structuralists seek to uncover these mythic structures and, by arranging them in paradigmatic order, discover the author's semantic universe (the fundamental system of convictions upon which the author operated).

Reader-Centered Interpretation

Formalist critics—those critics who claim that the text itself provides the objective standard of meaning—tend to view the text as static, an autonomous literary object which somehow contains within itself a meaning awaiting to be grasped. In the view of text-centered critics, textual meaning is independent of author and reader. Once the text leaves the hands of the author, the author's intention and entire matrix of originating circumstances lose any claim of being constitutive of meaning. Reader-centered critics, however, have called into question the formalists' presupposition of textual autonomy. The pendulum of interpretive emphasis swings in the direction of the reader's role in the construction of meaning. Affective critics (as some reader-response critics are called) have begun to ask significant questions: Why do we value some texts above others? Why do we continue to read and value texts even if the originating circumstances are irretrievable? Is it really legitimate to talk about meaning apart from a consideration of what happens when we read? What *does* happen when we read? Why do we respond to certain texts in certain ways? Reader-centered theories of interpretation in various ways and degrees attempt to answer these and similar questions as they pertain to the dynamic interaction between text and reader, an interaction with a resultant reader response.

The so-called affective critics constitute a multifarious group. Along a continuum between text and reader, affective critics may be placed according to the relative role which each critic ascribes to the text in the determination of meaning.[20] Perhaps the most successful strategy here is first to summarize briefly representative affective critics along the continuum and then to offer two composite pictures of critical methods—narrative and reader-response—which fall respectively toward the ends of the continuum. I follow these two methods by looking at two others which, on the one hand, place an obvious emphasis on the reader, but, on the other hand, do not lend themselves to easy categorization. These two interpretive methods are feminist and deconstructive criticisms respectively.

Representative Affective Critics

I. A. Richards. In the first quarter of this century, I. A. Richards developed an affective approach to the interpretation of texts. He grounded his approach in a behavioral theory which viewed the individual as a bundle of competing desires and aversions. The individual perpetually attempted to realize desires and to avoid aversions. The degree to which an individual was successful in harmonizing these desires and aversions into some meaningful whole directly correlated with personal mental health. Human beings thus have some inherent need to formulate a worldview which gives structured meaning to their existence. According to Richards, good literary art is a primary catalyst in such a formulation. Good literary works are those marked by, among other things, structural order and symmetry, complex systems of images, and creative verbal texture. These qualities generate a sense of aesthetic satisfaction. Textual complexities, however, are held together within a sophisticated, harmonious whole. These types of texts, with every part fitting harmoniously together, serve as a kind of microcosmic pattern of the individual's need to structure his or her own existence into a harmonious whole. In some manner, therefore, the complex, yet harmonious literary work becomes a balm for our psyches.

What Richards and other affective critics had to face, though, was the possibility of different readings of the same text. They also had to deal with the appropriateness of judging one reading to be more valuable than another one. Richards resorted to the *text* in order to tease out some standard by which a reading might be judged acceptable or not. But to use the text, or some canon extrapolated from it, as the standard for measuring a reading's adequacy is to make meaning (even if meaning is defined as reading experience) a function of the text.

---

[20] See Keesey, *Contexts for Criticism*, pp. 129–37.

Wolfgang Iser. Wolfgang Iser, whom we have already discussed, moves further away from the text toward the reader with his theory of the "implied reader." According to Iser, there exists within a text a potential reader who

> embodies all those predispositions necessary for a literary work to exercise its effect. These predispositions are laid down, not by an empirical outside reality, but by the text itself. Consequently, the implied reader as a concept has its roots firmly planted in the structure of the text; he is a construct and in no way to be identified with any real reader.[21]

The implied reader would possess the necessary competence in the conventions assumed by the text in order to "decode" the text. Within every text there are those "gaps of indeterminacy" which the reader must fill. In the process of such gap filling, the resultant interaction between reader and text produces the "work." But the work is always in a virtual state, because real readers can only approximate the competence of the "implied reader." Meaning, consequently, can never be reduced to a single, objective meaning latent within the text, but exists in the interaction between the text and the reader. According to Iser, however, the text presents several perspectives between which the reader shuttles. Together with the gaps, these perspectives, or textual clues, guide the reader in formulating the "work." Obviously, while Iser moves toward more reader involvement in the construction of meaning, the text remains crucial in its role of establishing parameters for reading. His theory also allows for one reading to be more plausible than another, depending upon how closely the real reader approximates the competence of the ideal reader.

Norman Holland. For Norman Holland, the reader occupies a more central position in the interaction between text and reader. The meaning of the transaction between reader and text depends upon the **identity theme** of each individual reader. The reader absorbs and adapts the content of a text in a way that "is characteristic—and pleasing—for him."[22] But what if the readings of two different readers compare similarly? For Holland the answer is simple: the psychic needs ("identity themes") of both readers so closely correlate that the same is true of the interpretations. At least the possibility exists that a new "work" is created in every reading.

---

[21] Iser, *The Act of Reading*, p. 34.
[22] Norman Holland, *5 Readers Reading* (New Haven: Yale University, 1975), p. 122.

Stanley Fish. While Holland moves very close to the reader's end of the continuum, Stanley Fish represents the most radical break from dependence upon the text as the objective center of meaning. According to Fish, readers actually create the work of art through the process of perception. The text does not guide a reader's response; response and, therefore, meaning are the direct result of the strategies applied to the text by the reader. But what determines a reader's interpretive strategies? For Fish, the answer is to be found in the reader's **interpretive community.** Interpretive communities may adjust and, therefore, correct a reading by bringing it into conformity with the interpretive strategies of the community. These interpretive strategies determine the formal features of the text, not vice-versa. From this perspective, the reader and interpretive community are completely determinative of meaning, and for all practical purposes, the text disappears.

As we might expect, any attempt to extract a single reader-response method of interpretation must be somewhat convoluted. Apart from the concession that the literary work of art comes into being only through the interaction between text and reader, reader-response theories vary sharply with respect to placement of interpretive emphasis. Nevertheless, for purposes of introduction, the following description of reader-response criticism may give the beginning student a more secure handle on (if not a completely pure representation of) the critical method. I discuss reader-response criticism first because narrative criticism is actually a sub-category of reader-response criticism, but more bound by the formal structures of the text.

Reader-Response Criticism

Chapter 7 discussed in detail the reading process. In order, therefore, to avoid duplication, I only summarize the reader-response approach to interpretation.

When a tree falls in the forest, is there a sound produced if there is no one present to hear it fall? The falling tree produces sound waves which must pass over someone's eardrum creating a vibration before sound is produced. This might be expressed in the equation, waves + eardrum = sound. The sound is the result of the interaction of two objects—waves and eardrum. In a similar fashion, reader-response critics view literary meaning as bipolar. Meaning is produced through the interaction between a text and a reader. Until a reader picks up a text and begins reading it, a literary work does not exist. Most reader-response critics define a literary "work" as the product of the interaction between a literary "text" and a reader. This literary work exists only as a potentiality, a virtual entity somewhere between the text (artistic pole) and the reader (aesthetic pole).

Within a narrative, time does not correspond exactly to real time. Neither does narrative sequence necessarily correspond to the actual sequence of events of the real or narrative world. Literary devices— flashback, summary, expansion, or even digression—may confront the reader. The reader is then called upon to sort through this narrative, sequencing it to form a "story." The narrative is the text; the story is the literary work. The equation is similar to the one above: artistic pole + aesthetic pole = artistic work.

Not only does a narrative text require a sequential reformulation by the reader, but authors frame their texts with the intention of involving readers. In a sense, authors expect readers to enter into a literary covenant with them in order to jointly create an artistic work. Most reader-response critics agree that authors allow for reader involvement by creating gaps within the text which readers must fill.

The two ideas of sequencing a text and filling in gaps (discussed in chapter 7) may seem innocent until we realize that this process varies with each individual reader. For reader-response critics, not only does a text exist in a state of indeterminacy, but so does a reader. As the literary work is always coming into being, the reader is also coming into being. Both literary work and reader are only possibilities.

Not only do reader-response critics reject the idea that a text is an autonomous object, they also reject the idea that readers are autonomous, free to read as they please. Readers are always submerged within social contexts exerting profound influences. An individual's entire social context and degree of involvement within that social context profoundly affect the way that person will actualize the text, what questions will be put to the text, and how that individual will perceive and fill in the gaps presented by the text. The end product of this dual indeterminacy (of text and reader) is a plurality of interpretations. If both the artistic and aesthetic poles are ultimately indeterminate, there exists the possibility of an infinite number of "artistic works."

Narrative Criticism

Narrative criticism is a method of studying narratives, emphasizing not only traditional narrative elements such as plot, setting, and characterization, but also the role of the reader. Like reader-response criticism, narrative criticism assumes that the story does not exist autonomously within the text, but comes into being through the interaction between the text and the reader. Employing the concept of sign, narrative critics accept the narrative itself as the signifier and the story (produced through the interaction between the narrative and reader) as the signified. The whole of narrative criticism may be seen as an analysis of the narrative content within the context of relationships between authors, texts, and readers (see diagram 5-1).

The real author is the flesh and blood person who at some point in history crafted the narrative text. The real reader is likewise some flesh and blood person who in time and space reads the text. Each of these persons exists apart from the text; the real author and real reader are not dependent upon the text for existence.

Narrative critics have introduced the idea that there exists a literary entity who is found only within the text. This entity is not the same as the real author, but is only a partial and incomplete reflection of the real author. For example, when I read the Gospel of Mark, the only author I encounter is that one which I may be able to construct from the text alone. Even more revealing is the reading of several Pauline epistles. When I read 1 Corinthians, I encounter one entity; when I read Galatians, I encounter another one. These two implied authors are not the same because the text yields different information about the implied authors. The text of Mark does not present the real flesh and blood Mark, nor does Galatians present the real-world Paul. When Paul authored 1 Corinthians, he donned one hat, but he wore yet a different one when authoring Galatians. Accordingly, it is possible for a real-world person to author several texts, each one having a different implied author. In a sense, the implied author is that composite of discernible ideologies underlying a particular text.

The implied reader, like the implied author, is that entity defined by the text. The implied author may consciously or unconsciously construct the text in such a manner as to provide guidance to a reader. This means that a text contains unspoken assumptions about the reader. It is obvious that the implied author (the real author for that matter) of Mark's Gospel did not have a twentieth-century reader in mind when he or she wrote. Even though the text provides directives (see reader-response criticism above) for the reader by giving definition to the implied reader, the implied reader is not entirely defined by the text. The implied author may assume on the part of the implied reader a set of values, literary competence, and background. But there is simply no way to assure that every reader will satisfy this assumption. As we saw above in reader-response criticism, both the text and the reader are characterized by indeterminacy. On the one hand, even if we assume that the role of the implied reader may be completely defined, no single reader can perfectly and completely conform to the role the text provides for the implied reader. A reader may approach perfectly conforming to the role of the implied reader by consciously or unconsciously accepting the ideology of the implied author inherent within the text, but there is no objective way to measure such conformity. On the other hand, to the degree that the reader fulfills the role of the implied reader provided for by the text, the reader becomes captive to the text and its ideology. Some reader-response critics feel that this captivity results in a new orientation for the reader, a reorientation which in turn produces a new person. The opposite of this may also occur. A reader may discover that the role demanded of the implied reader by the text may be so foreign or ideologically unpleasing that the reader simply refuses to read, i.e., refuses to become the implied reader.

All narratives are told through the voice of a narrator. For the narrative critic, therefore, the person and activity of the narrator occupy a place of special importance in the determination of meaning. A narrative may be told in the first or third person, and the narrator may be outside the action or a character within the story. Further, a narrator may vary in degree of knowledge, from very limited knowledge to virtual omniscience.

The narrator should not mistakenly be identified with the implied author. The narrator is a fictive creation of the implied author and is dependent upon the implied author for any characteristics and abilities which may be discernible from the text. The view of the narrator may or may not reflect the ideology of the implied author. This is true of the third person omniscient narrator or of the narrator who is also a character within the story.

The counterpart of the narrator is the narratee. The narratee is the entity to whom the narrator tells the story. The narratee is distinct from the implied reader in a dramatic way. The narratee, on the one hand, receives the story as it unfolds moment by moment. The implied reader, on the other hand, reads what the narrator tells the narratee. The implied reader is an entity with a set of values and is able aesthetically to complete the work. The implied reader is implied by the text but is not totally defined by it. The narratee, however, has total definition only by the work. Like the narrator, the narratee may be a character within the story, but is usually a person who has no place within the story. The identity of the narratee will determine to a large degree the style and complexity of the narrator's language. If the narratee is uninformed about the subject matter, the narrator may become very detailed, offering extensive explanation. For example, one narratee may have only limited competency in the subject matter of the narrative, while another one might be well versed in the subject.

The narrative critic does not identify the narrative world with the real world. The real world of both author and reader alike is infinite, but observable and present, with all events apparently working together in an immediate system of interconnectedness. The real world exists in time and space. The narrative world is limited, bounded. The only access to this narrative world is through the secondary medium of the text. The objects, persons, and events in the narrative may not correspond to anything in the real world. Narrative criticism rejects any necessary one-to-one correspondence between the real and narrative worlds. In order for the implied reader to reconstruct the narrative world, determinations as to relative importance of events must be made. The implied author highlights some events, subordinates others, and leaves gaps while moving from one narrative segment to another. The responsibility of bridging these gaps belongs to the implied reader. The implied reader is expected to make inferences and judgments based upon the author's narrative techniques.

According to the narrative critic, meaning is in the narrative world, not in the real world. The meaning of the Gospel of Mark is not to be found in considering Mark an objective, historically accurate portrayal of the life and times of Jesus. What Jesus (or any character for that matter) says or does in the narrative must find its significance within the world of the narrative, not within the real world in which he lived. Even if we assume that the text has achieved a one-hundred percent accuracy in relating the events in the life of Jesus, it certainly has not related all the events in his life. The implied author has shaped the story world by selecting some events and excluding others. This process of selectivity immediately excludes the possibility of the narrative world being a complete replica of the real one. All meaning, therefore, must be found in the narrative world, which is a construct of the text. Meaning must be a function of the relationships, experiences, and connections which the implied reader is called upon to create. Everything within the narrative world comes together to create the context for meaning.

Feminist Criticism

A wide variety of interpretive methodology occurs within feminist criticism. In what follows, I attempt to capture the essence of feminist criticism by referring to several of its most notable proponents. Yet while there exists such a variety of methodological emphases, all feminist critics proceed from a common assumption and several underlying principles. The common assumption is that all the biblical texts were written in the contexts of patriarchal cultures and have been subsequently translated and interpreted within patriarchal cultures. These patriarchal contexts have dehumanized and marginalized women, treating them as second-class, inferior beings. Within these contexts, women traditionally function on a secondary level and are significant as human beings to the degree that their actions and lives support and further the superior function of men. Women are treated as a means to patriarchal ends, rather than as ends within themselves. All feminist interpretation in one way or another seeks to depatriarchalize not only the biblical texts but also theological traditions and systems that are based upon patriarchal interpretations of the patriarchal texts. The interpretive principles of feminist hermeneutics are threefold:

First, virtually all feminist critics place extreme importance upon the **feminist consciousness**.[23] Briefly put, this feminist consciousness concerns recognizing women's own unique experience as a way of understanding Scripture. Two primary convictions function within feminist consciousness: equality and mutuality. The conviction of equality demands that women's interests and aims (including interpretive ones) are as valid as those of men. Any inequality in gender must be rejected out of hand. The conviction of mutuality demands that women (indeed all persons) be viewed as both autonomous and rational beings. Each person stands as an individual, but because all are primarily rational, there exists a universal bond between persons, a bond which transcends roles. Any interpretation which vitiates this feminist consciousness is to be rejected as having no binding authority.

Second, all women are fully human and are to be valued as such. Any biblical passage or interpretation which devalues the humanity of

---

[23] See Margaret A. Farley, "Feminist Consciousness and Scripture," in *Feminist Interpretation of the Bible*, ed. Letty M. Russell (Philadelphia: Westminster, 1985), pp. 41–51.

women cannot be accepted as binding revelation. Elisabeth Schüssler Fiorenza states it clearly: "only the nonsexist and nonandrocentric traditions of the Bible and the nonoppressive traditions of biblical interpretations have the theological authority of revelation."[24]

Third, because women have found that traditional interpretations of their identity regularly contradict their own identity consciousness and self-experience, the basic criterion for judging truth is women's experience. "New understandings must be tested for truth (for accuracy and adequacy) against the reality of women's lives as revealed in women's experience."[25] Rosemary Ruether defines women's experience as the premier interpretive key:

> that experience which arises when women become critically aware of these falsifying and alienating experiences imposed upon them as women by a male-dominated culture. . . . Women's experience, then, implies a conversion experience through which women get in touch with, name, judge their experiences of sexism in patriarchal society.[26]

Within that group of feminist critics who see the Bible as a vital part of their faith experience, there exists a plurality of approaches and interpretations.

Katharine Doob Sakenfeld and Rosemary Radford Ruether. Katharine Doob Sakenfeld lists three optional approaches to the biblical texts: (1) Feminists critics may use texts about women in order to offset the famous (or infamous) texts which have been traditionally used "against" women; (2) feminists may refer to the Bible in general (as opposed to specific texts) in order to discover a theological perspective which in turn may be employed against **patriarchalism;** and (3) feminists may look to biblical texts about women in order to "learn from the intersection of history and stories of ancient and modern women living in patriarchal cultures."[27] These are not exclusive options, but rather broad categories within which critics may move back and forth.

---

[24] Elisabeth Schüssler Fiorenza, "A Feminist Biblical Hermeneutics: Biblical Interpretation and Liberation Theology," in *The Challenge of Liberation Theology: A First-World Response*, ed. L. Dale Richesin and Brian Mahan (Maryknoll, New York: Orbis, 1981), p. 108.

[25] Farley, "Feminist Consciousness and Scripture," p. 50.

[26] Rosemary Radford Ruether, "Feminist Interpretation: A Method of Correlation," in Russell, *Feminist Interpretation of the Bible*, pp. 114–15.

[27] See Katharine Doob Sakenfeld, "Feminist Uses of Biblical Materials," in Russell, *Feminist Interpretation of the Bible*, pp. 56–64; and idem, *Faithfulness in Action: Loyalty in Biblical Perspective* (Philadelphia: Fortress, 1985).

Approaches within the first option may reinterpret texts that marginalize women, or they may bring to bear on these texts other texts which seem to portray women in a more positive light. For example, Genesis 2–3 may be reinterpreted in such a way that women and men are seen as equal, and mutual subjection can be claimed as the import of Ephesians 5. Galatians 3:28 may be brought to bear on texts such as 1 Timothy 2:13–14 and 1 Corinthians 14:34–35.

The second option contains approaches that attempt to extrapolate from the Bible in general a perspective which is in its essence Christian. Exactly what this central witness or perspective is varies from critic to critic. One of the best-known approaches is that of Rosemary Ruether. Ruether examines the entire biblical text and discovers a **prophetic principle** (what we might call a prophetic consciousness or prophetic impulse) which is present at different places and times within the biblical canon. According to Ruether, this prophetic principle rejects every "elevation of one social group against others as image and agent of God, every use of God to justify social domination and subjugation."[28] She describes this principle as follows:

> By the prophetic-messianic tradition I mean to name not simply a particular body of texts, which then would be understood as standing as a canon within the canon. Rather, what I mean by the prophetic-messianic tradition is a critical perspective and process through which the biblical tradition constantly reevaluates, in new contexts, what is truly the liberating Word of God, over against both the sinful deformations of contemporary society and also the limitations of past biblical traditions, which saw in part and understood in part, and whose partiality may have even become a source of sinful injustice and idolatry.[29]

Ruether asserts that religion (along with sacred texts and interpretations of such texts) throughout history has sanctioned existing social orders which divide human beings into classes in which the superior rules over the inferior. But this religious sanction of the existing social order is counteracted by an alternative principle—the prophetic principle. God periodically speaks through the prophetic person in order to criticize and condemn the society that, in the name of religion, perpetuates injustices upon some social groups. Therefore, the prophetic principle criticizes both society's injustices and its religious justification of them.[30]

---

[28] Rosemary Radford Ruether, *Sexism and God Talk: Toward a Feminist Theology* (Boston: Beacon, 1983), p. 23.

[29] Ruether, "Feminist Interpretation," p. 117.

[30] Ibid., p. 118.

True religious and divine experience do not support such social injustice, but rather expose structures that lead to injustices. The emphasis of feminist criticism in a very real sense parallels this prophetic principle because of the former's concentration on the structures which perpetuate the **marginalization** of women.

However, the prophets in the biblical texts were limited in their perspective as to precisely who those oppressed persons were. They were, according to Ruether, unaware of the oppression of women and slaves. Or put another way, due to the limited view dictated by the prophets' social context, women and slaves were not included within the prophets' range of perception. The result is a limitation of the prophetic consciousness. Furthermore, after the initial prophetic renewal, because of its limited perspective, the renewed perspective may itself become the catalyst for subsequent social stratification.[31] This recognition that the prophetic consciousness is tied to its social context means that the prophetic consciousness requires perpetual reinterpretation. This is the pattern, in fact, that we see in the biblical texts themselves and in church history (e.g., the initial messianic freedom of the Christian experience was deformed to marginalize Judaism; the freedom-giving servanthood of Jesus is deformed when the language of servanthood is identified with human roles of power).[32] Feminist critics like Ruether correlate the feminist consciousness with this prophetic consciousness and call for the reinterpretation of texts and traditions within new contexts. At the same time, they take steps to guarantee that the fruits of feminist interpretation should always be a viable part of Christian communities.

Within Sakenfeld's third option, all texts (positive or negative) are viewed as speaking realistically to the condition of women as oppressed persons yearning for freedom.

> The Bible is viewed as an instrument by which God shows women their true condition as people who are oppressed and yet who are given a vision of a different heaven and earth and a variety of models for how to live toward that vision.[33]

Elisabeth Schüssler Fiorenza. By observing how women of the past have been treated within androcentric cultures, women today may identify

---

[31] Ibid., p. 119.

[32] Ibid., pp. 120–21.

[33] Sakenfeld, "Feminist Uses of Biblical Materials," in Russell, *Feminist Interpretation of the Bible*, p. 62.

with these women in their oppression and struggle for freedom. Schüssler Fiorenza argues that the Bible has been employed as a weapon against women's struggle for freedom. Accordingly, a feminist hermeneutic challenges the authority of the patriarchal texts and their use as a weapon against women's struggle. It will also examine ways in which the Bible may be employed as a positive resource in women's struggle for freedom. In order to explain how this hermeneutic works, Schüssler Fiorenza has set forth five key elements within it.[34]

First, feminists critics must assume a posture of suspicion rather than acceptance of biblical authority. This task is twofold: (1) The critic must recognize any oppressive, sexist, or racist elements within the Bible and refuse to explain these elements away; and (2) honest attempts should be made to uncover any antipatriarchal undertones in the biblical texts, undertones which may be hidden within the androcentric language of the texts.

Second, critics must evaluate rather than correlate. This means that some texts and interpretations must be rejected if they perpetuate and legitimate patriarchal structures.

Third, interpretation is inseparable from proclamation. Texts or traditions that perpetuate patriarchal oppressive structures should not be proclaimed as "Word of God" for people today. Before texts are translated with inclusive language, a careful selection process should be engaged. Texts that support patriarchal structures should not be allowed proclamational status. Only texts that affirm persons as equals should be allowed into the lectionary.

Fourth, texts that do perpetuate and legitimate patriarchal structures of oppression should not be abandoned. Furthermore, these texts should become resources for remembering how women were oppressed and marginalized. Schüssler Fiorenza refers to this reclamation of suffering as a hermeneutic of remembrance. While feminists may recognize these texts as reflecting reality, they do not equate this with acceptance of the validity of that reality. This hermeneutic of remembrance should allow critics to reconstruct the origin and history of early Christianity from a feminist perspective. The biblical canon retains only scattered remnants of the early nonpatriarchal Christian community, but these

---

[34] See Elisabeth Schüssler Fiorenza, "The Will to Choose or to Reject: Continuing Our Critical Work," in Russell, *Feminist Interpretation of the Bible*; and idem, *Bread Not Stone: Introduction to a Feminist Interpretation of Scripture* (Boston: Beacon, 1985).

remnants give evidence that patriarchal structures were not originally part of the Christian community.

Fifth, interpretation must include celebration and ritual. This actualizes the text into the present. Bible stories are retold from the perspective of the feminist imagination, especially the reconstruction of those nonpatriarchal remnants. Included within this imaginative reconstruction are creative tools such as music, dance, drama, and literary creativity. As the church through history has ritualized parts of the biblical text and traditions in order to celebrate "forefathers," so the present church should engage in the creative formulations of rituals that will celebrate our "foremothers."

Deconstructive Criticism

Up to this point, we have seen that all interpretive activity occurs within a context; outside of a context meaning is not possible or capable of being evaluated. There is a basic assumption here: there exists a world of reality that is beyond and independent of language, a reality, however, that somehow is made "present" through and represented by language. Language is a type of secondary representation of reality, a reality which is ever present prior to the act of representation. This assumption, according to deconstruction critics, underlies all Western philosophical and interpretive traditions. All Western philosophical systems assume that that to which language refers and that from which language originates is some extra-linguistic reality or "transcendental signified." The most influential challenge to this assumption of hermeneutics of "presence" comes from Jacques Derrida, whose influence began in the 1970s and continues today. In summarizing Derrida's approach to interpretation (and by implication deconstructionism's approach in general), Clarence Walhout offers the following evaluation:

> Hermeneutics is, for him [Derrida], the process whereby we encounter the ambiguity in texts and in all cultural products and find in the very ambiguity new possibilities for thought and action.[35]

Derrida consciously rejects any reference to his work as a system. Moreover, in order to militate against the tendency of scholars to define his work as a system, Derrida has adopted a strategy of employing terms in such an ambiguous and inconsistent manner that his critical thought is

---

[35] Walhout, "Text and Actions," p. 35.

not easily classified by terminology. In order to speak at least coherently
about deconstruction, however, I concentrate on select terms (used by
Derrida and other deconstruction critics) that will assist in characterizing
deconstruction.

Almost central to Derrida's thought on meaning is his concept of
"writing" *(écriture).* "Writing" for Derrida is not the inscription of
thought, but the fundamental human activity which precedes such inscription. In most Western hermeneutical thinking, individuals are able
to write a text because they have previously "read the world." Or put
another way, the world of reality that we variously encode within our
texts already exists as a metaphysical reality. It is a given. Derrida rejects
this assumption by claiming that the world we are capable of knowing
comes into being through the act of "writing." There is no world waiting
to be read. Language is not rooted in a perceivable reality that precedes
it; on the contrary, language itself sets the parameters of thought and,
therefore, our world. If this is the case, we cannot be aware of the "presence" of that which is beyond our thoughts, but only of its "absence."[36]

In Derrida's estimation, since all human activity takes place in
time, such activity is historically bound. Now this does not mean that
human activity is in toto historically or culturally determined. Human
activity also determines and perpetually reshapes and redefines culture.
Culture does not exist prior to individual acts of "writing." A priori
assumptions about reality may exist, but these are themselves products
of cultural "writings." This is the reason Derrida can assert that "writing"
precedes speech. It is simply impossible to know something which exists
prior to what is known.

Two other terms which help to explain the concept of "writing" are
trace and **mark**. Each and every human action leaves a mark on culture,
and each and every mark gives witness to its originating human action,
an action which itself escapes complete specification. Therefore, writing's *mark* leaves a *trace* of the indeterminate origin of the writing.

If every human action has both a culturally specific mark and a
trace of the moment of origination, then every human action has not
only a determinate meaning, but also an indeterminate meaning. More
simply put, if every human action is shaped by culture, while at the same
time shaping the culture, the culture is constantly and infinitely undergoing modification and change while in a reciprocal fashion influencing
the actions that change it. This complex of mutual influence gives rise to

---

[36] Ibid., p. 36.

both continuity and discontinuity between the action and the culture. Therefore, interpretations of human actions (including literary ones) must focus on both the way in which an action is shaped by culture (i.e., the action's continuity with the culture) and the way in which an action is discontinuous with the culture.

This brings us to another of Derrida's focal terms—*différance*. This word is a deliberate misspelling of the word différence, combining two other words—*differing* and *deferring*. Using Saussure's definition of *sign*, Derrida says that a text derives meaning in its *differences* from other texts. But every text also evidences the *trace* of an indeterminate origination. Since this indeterminate quality creates change within the culture, meaning is always *deferred*. Interpretation itself becomes an activity laden with ambiguity. Interpretation is a human action with a determinate and indeterminate meaning. Every hermeneut approaches a text within a culture, both influenced by and exerting influence upon the culture. Since this is an infinite process of shaping and reshaping, interpretation is an endless, ever-changing process. Interpretation is an infinite process of creation. All meaning is bound by cultural context, but that context becomes boundless.

Another well-known deconstruction critic, Paul de Man, investigates more narrowly the inherent ambiguity of language and argues that all language is metaphorical and rhetorical. Unlike the formalists, however, de Man does not assume that a text is a unified and coherent whole. Literary language, like all language, is radically rhetorical and metaphorical in nature; thus texts are marked by an indeterminateness.

Actually deconstruction is more a way of analyzing interpretive methods and philosophical systems than a method of interpretation itself. It is a backward analysis of the historical development of a tradition so as to arrive at its hidden presuppositions and bases. Derrida is interested in deconstructing Western philosophy and its metaphysical foundations.

If deconstruction critics are correct in their claims that all language is inherently metaphorical and that there exists no metaphysical reality outside our "writing," then all hermeneutics which seek a grounding either in linguistic objectivity or in a world of reality beyond language, of which language is simply the linguistic representation, are like the proverbial house built upon the sand. But do we really have a choice? Can we communicate (i.e., think and speak) in any other way except through language? Can we interpret outside the confines of some system? The answer to these questions must be negative. Nevertheless, while we may interpret within some system, we should take the reminders of the deconstruction critics in a constructive sense. At the best, interpretive systems rest on theoretical bases. We should be willing to subject our methodological bases to scrutiny, for if the base is faulty, so are our subsequent interpretations.

Summary

Interpreters do not interpret without provocation and purpose. Provocation and purposes (what might be called interpretive aims) are objectified by interpretive methods. The interpreter will consciously (sometimes unconsciously) advocate the method that most nearly correlates with the interpretive aims. Interpretive aims dictate methods. In turn, the method chosen determines what kinds of questions the interpreter will ask the text.

A hermeneut must use some method or a composite of several methods. There is no alternative in this matter; interpretation is based upon method. In many cases, however, the interpreter may be unable to articulate the method. Most often such inability produces haphazard, inconsistent results. The defense against such results, of course, is to examine the labyrinth of available methods and then to choose one or a mixture of methods that takes into account the three worlds of hermeneutics—author-centered methods, text-centered methods, and reader-centered methods. Author-centered methods insist that since a text is the creation of an individual mind, any interpretation will be enhanced that takes into account anything that can be discovered about that mind or the world within which that mind thought. Text-centered methods tend to treat the text as a literary artifact that assumes a reality and life all its own once it leaves the hands of the author. The meaning of a text is exactly that—the meaning of the text, and the standard by which any interpretation of the text is measured is the text. The text is a coherent and complex whole, and any interpretation of the text must treat it as a coherent and complex whole. Reader-centered methods recognize that the text has no power to communicate meaning without the presence of a reader. In a number of creative ways, adherents of reader-centered methods locate meaning somewhere within the interaction between the reader and the text. The reader and text engage in a dialogue out of which meaning is created. These reader-centered methods are particularly interested in what actually takes place when an individual or community reads a text. The best hermeneutic will be the one that pulls from "something old and something new," the one that gives audience to a variety of interpretive approaches.

REVIEW & STUDY

Key Terms and Concepts

Four-source hypothesis	Signifier
Two-document hypothesis	Signified
Quelle	Actant
Textual autonomy	Myth
Complexity	Interpretive community
Congruence	Identity theme
Selectivity	Marginalization
Binary opposition	Patriarchalism
Langue	Feminist consciousness
Parole	Prophetic principle
Meaning effect	*Écriture*
Structures of enunciation	Trace
Structures of culture	Mark
Deep structures	*différance*

Study Questions

1. What are some aims that interpreters might have, and how might such aims influence interpretation?

2. Assuming Mark to be a source for Luke, notice how Luke (23:47) has edited Mark 15:39. Why do you think Luke makes the change?

3. Compare the resurrection narratives in all four Gospels, making a list of the elements in each narrative. Note that the differences are quite striking. What might these differences suggest about the Gospel writers' redaction activities?

4. According to canonical criticism, resignification is central to the interpretation of biblical texts. How does the canonical critic judge between plausible and implausible interpretations? Is theirs a reproductive or productive approach to interpretation? Explain.

5. Develop an actantual (see diagram 9-2) model for the Jephthah narrative in Judges 10:6–11:40. Can you identify a mythical structure that attempts to mediate binary oppositions?

6. Read Galatians and Philemon. Attempt a characterization of the implied author and reader in each. How do they differ?

7. Read Ecclesiastes. What can you ascertain about the narrator and narratee?

8. If meaning is to be found in the narrative world and not in the real world of the author, what assumptions can you make about concepts such as truth, history, and divine inspiration?

9. Letty M. Russell says that "a feminist interpretation of the Bible is rooted in the feminist critical consciousness that women and men are fully human and fully equal. This consciousness is opposed to teachings and sections that reinforce the social system that oppresses women and other groups in society." In light of Ephesians 5:21–33 and Galatians 3:28–29, is it possible, and if so in what way, to interpret 1 Timothy 2:9–15 so that it is less offensive to the feminist consciousness?

10. Suggest a way in which deconstruction might interface with feminist criticism.

Suggestions for Further Reading

Caputo, John D. *Radical Hermeneutics: Repetition, Deconstruction, and the Hermeneutic Project*. Bloomington: Indiana University Press, 1987.

Childs, Brevard. *The New Testament as Canon: An Introduction*. Philadelphia: Fortress, 1985.

Culler, Jonathan. *On Deconstruction: Theory and Criticism after Structuralism*. Ithaca: Cornell University Press, 1986.

_____. *Structuralist Poetics: Structuralism, Linguistics, and the Study of Literature*. Ithaca: Cornell University Press, 1986.

Eagleton, Terry. *Literary Theory: An Introduction*. Minneapolis: University of Minnesota Press, 1983.

Genette, Gérard. *Narrative Discourse*. Oxford: Oxford University Press, 1980.

Holland, Norman. *5 Readers Reading*. New Haven: Yale University Press, 1975.

Hompkins, Jane, ed. *Reader-Response Criticism: From Formalism to Post-Structuralism*. Baltimore: Johns Hopkins University Press, 1980.

Jefferson, Ann and David Robey, eds. *Modern Literary Theory: A Comparative Study*. Ottawa: Barnes and Noble, 1982.

Keegan, Terrance J. *Interpreting the Bible: A Popular Introduction to Biblical Hermeneutics.* New York: Paulist, 1986.

Keesey, Donald, ed. *Contexts for Criticism.* Mountain View, Calif.: Mayfield, 1987.

Martin, Wallace. *Recent Theories of Narrative.* Ithaca: Cornell University Press, 1987.

McKnight, Edgar B. *Post-Modern Use of the Bible: The Emergence of Reader-Oriented Criticism.* Nashville: Abingdon, 1988.

Patte, Daniel. *What Is Structural Exegesis?* Philadelphia: Fortress, 1976.

Perrin, Norman. *What Is Redaction Criticism?* Philadelphia: Fortress, 1969.

Ruether, Rosemary R. *Sexism and God Talk: Toward a Feminist Theology.* Boston: Beacon, 1983.

Russell, Letty M., ed. *Feminist Interpretation of Scripture.* Philadelphia: Westminster, 1985.

Schüssler Fiorenza, Elisabeth. *Bread Not Stone: Introduction to a Feminist Interpretation of Scripture.* Boston: Beacon, 1985.

Tuckett, Christopher. *Reading the New Testament: Methods of Interpretation.* Philadelphia: Fortress, 1987.

Young, Pamela Dickey. *Feminist Theology/Christian Theology: In Search of Method.* Minneapolis: Augsburg/Fortress, 1990.

Mark's Gospel and the Merging
of Three Worlds

I once read an anecdote about a woman who suffered from insomnia. Desperate for sleep, she sought the advice of her pastor, who naturally offered her what he felt to be a foolproof solution. He told her to go home, close her eyes, open her Bible at random, and point to a spot on one of the open pages. The verse to which she pointed would be her answer from God. Complying with her pastor's advice, the woman randomly pointed to a passage. Upon opening her eyes she read, "Behold, I show you a mystery; We shall not all sleep, but we shall all be changed" (1 Cor 15:51). The woman was so pleased with the outcome that she actually laughed herself to sleep! On the one hand, we laugh at the naïveté of such an approach to reading the Bible, for while the woman's problem was solved, we can safely assume that this passage of Scripture has absolutely nothing to do with insomnia. Both the approach and result are ludicrous. On the other hand, it is no laughing matter when we assume that when one person speaks to another, the speaker intends to communicate something to the listener(s). That something may be trivial or profound, but it is something nonetheless. It is an equally safe assumption that authors intend to communicate something to readers. On the one hand, authors may choose to be as clear and precise as possible, diminishing the possibility of misunderstanding; put another way, an author may consciously attempt to erase the gap between intention and understanding. On the other hand, authors may try to be opaque and ambiguous, using language in such a way as to elicit the cooperation of their readers in producing meaning. The latter especially characterizes what I have referred to as mimetic texts. All texts communicate according to genre conventions and presuppose certain kinds of readers. But mimetic texts create a role for the reader which is more complex and imaginative than texts that we might refer to as propositional.

As we have argued throughout this book, literary meaning is the result of a conversation between a text and a reader, but a conversation informed by a knowledge of the author's world. In this chapter we will use the Gospel of Mark as a text case to show how the three worlds of author, text, and reader merge to produce meaning. We intend not to offer a detailed commentary on Mark but only to demonstrate how the three worlds merge. Consequently, we will focus on how the narrative structures of plot (the world of the text) set the stage for a reader to make interpretive decisions (the world of the reader) based upon some knowledge of the world-view of ancient Judaism (the world of the author).

We will argue that Mark's plot (the emplotment of episodes) invites the reader to make a decision about the goal of Jesus' ministry. Nowhere does Mark make the goal explicit. He does, however, through the literary strategies of plot, ask the reader to infer that Jesus is redefining the concept of the people of God. In other words, Mark invites the reader to **assemble meaning**. While Mark's plot creatively implies in a number of ways that Jesus is redefining the people of God, we will demonstrate this assumption by looking at only three narrative strategies: (1) Mark's use of literary allusion, (2) his use of intercalation, and (3) Jesus' relationship to his contemporary world-view as it is assumed by Mark. While all three are strategic elements of the narrative world of the text, the first two create sufficient gaps to engage the reader in making decisions, and the third requires some knowledge on the part of the reader of the author's world. I should emphasize that these plot strategies do not exhaust Mark's literary repertoire. We could have chosen to discuss other plot items such as multiple points of view, protension and retention, and a variety of motifs and structures of openness. Some matters, however, must be left to my readers to pursue.

Mark's Use of Literary Allusion

Any text must be read intertextually. **Intertextuality** refers to the notion that all communication takes place within contexts. All communication occurs in conversation with other texts. These "texts" are not all written ones. Included in what counts for texts here are such elements as prior written texts, oral traditions, social norms, language norms, religious norms, and literary norms. Intertextuality includes both ends of the communication process, both author and reader. Not only do authors communicate within these "texts" but so do readers. Therefore, any writing of a text is intertextual and any reading is intertextual. In other words, everything that goes into defining a culture is part of the text that a writer or reader uses and depends upon in the process of communication. Here we are concerned with the intertexuality of the text in terms of the author's use of prior literary texts.

Mark's Abrupt Beginning

Mark's extensive use of **literary allusion** invites the reader to make inferences about the purpose of Jesus' ministry. From the beginning of his story to the end, Mark alludes to events in the Hebrew Bible that are calculated to suggest to the reader some significance for defining the purpose of Jesus' ministry. Mark opens his story with a reversal of the Exodus story. The original story moves from the wilderness, to the Jordan, to Judea, and finally to Jerusalem (under David). In Mark the action is reversed: "People from the whole Judean countryside and all the people of Jerusalem were going out to him, and were baptized by him in the river Jordan, confessing their sins" (1:5). The reversed movement is Judea, Jerusalem, and the Jordan. In the original story, Israel was tested in the wilderness for forty years, while in the reversed version, Jesus is tested in the wilderness for forty days. Only Jesus seems to take the reversal back as far as the wilderness.[1] Through this allusion, Mark may be giving the reader advanced warning that not only is Jesus reformulating the people of God, but that his reformulation will reverse some of the ways in which the people of God is currently defined. Mark hands the readers this allusion and asks them to make sense of it.

Allusions to Moses

The two feeding episodes (Mark 6:30–44 and 8:1–13) contain four different allusions to the Hebrew Bible. In both episodes, the feeding takes place in a deserted place and Jesus instructs his disciples to give the crowds something to eat; and in both the disciples respond with a question about the feasibility of obtaining enough food to feed such a large number. In the first feeding episode, the disciples seat the crowd in "groups of hundreds and fifties" (6:40). Below are the passages in the Hebrew Bible to which Mark alludes.

---

[1] John Drury, "Mark," in Alter and Kermode, *Literary Guide to the Bible,* pp. 408–9.

Num. 11:13:   Where am I to get meat to give to all this people? (NRSV)

Num. 11:22:   Are there enough flocks and herds to slaughter for them? Are there enough fish in the sea to catch for them? (NRSV)

Exod. 18:24–25 So Moses listened to his father-in-law and did all that he had said. Moses chose able men from all Israel and appointed them heads over the people, as officers over thousands, hundreds, fifties, and tens. (NRSV)

Equally fascinating is the similarity between Jesus' decision to speak in riddles to outsiders but clearly to the disciples (Mark 4:11) and Yahweh's pronouncement about Moses:

> When there are prophets among you,
>   I the LORD make myself known to them in visions;
>   I speak to them in dreams.
> Not so with my servant Moses;
>   he is entrusted with all my house.
> With him I speak face to face—clearly, not in riddles;
>   and he beholds the form of the LORD (Num. 12:6b–8, NRSV).

An Allusion to Elisha

In 2 Kings 4:43 is an account of a miraculous feeding involving the prophet Elisha. The parallels with the two feeding episodes in Mark should be obvious:

> A man came from Baal-shalishah, bringing food from the first fruits to the man of God: twenty loaves of barley and fresh ears of grain in his sack. Elisha said, "Give it to the people and let them eat." But his servant said, "How can I set this before a hundred people?" So he repeated, "Give it to the people and let them eat, for thus says the LORD, 'They shall eat and have some left.' "

An Allusion to Israel as Sheep

In the first feeding episode, the narrator refers to the crowd as being "like sheep without a shepherd" (6:34c). First Kings 22:17, 2 Chronicles 18:16, Isaiah 13:14, Jeremiah 50:6, Ezekiel 34:12, Zechariah 10:2 all refer to Israel as being like sheep without a shepherd.

Allusion to Passover and Covenant

The reader is not surprised by Jesus' meal with the disciples on the first day of Unleavened Bread (Mark 14:12). But Jesus' actions during the meal (14:22–25) give the reader pause, for it suddenly becomes obvious that against the background of the feast that celebrates the very founding and deliverance of the people of God, Jesus is forming a new people. By allowing the bread and wine to symbolize his broken body and shed blood, Jesus identifies himself as the sacrificial lamb. When he says of his blood that it "is poured out for many" (Mark 14:24), the reader (and disciples) should think in terms of the sacrificial lamb at the original Passover (Exod. 12:1–13) and of the blood of the original covenant (e.g., Exod. 24:8 and Zech. 9:11). Both speak of deliverance through death. Jesus becomes both founder and ratifying sacrifice of a new covenant.

The strength of allusion is its power of suggestion. It appears that Mark is inviting the reader to make a connection between what Jesus is doing in the two feeding episodes and what God has done in the past for Israel. Given the parallels between the feeding episodes and the above passages, we might conclude that Mark invites the reader to assume that Jesus is reformulating the people of God.

Mark's pervasive use of allusion creates a wide field of possibilities. As we have seen above, some allusions seem calculated to produce connections that enable readers to assemble meaning. Some, however, seem designed to create interpretive openness. Below are two examples.

An Allusion to Esther

One of the most puzzling allusions in Mark occurs in 6:21–23, the account of Salome's dancing before Herod. The account is an unmistakable allusion to the book of Esther. When compared to the conversation between Ahasuerus and Esther, the counterpart between Herod and Salome reveals some striking similarities:

Mark 6:22b:	*aitēson me ho ean thelēs, kai <u>dōsō soi.</u>*
	αἴτησόν με ὃ ἐὰν θέλῃς, καὶ δώσω σοι.
Mark 6:23b	*ho ti ean me aitēsēs <u>dōsō soi heōs hēmisous tēs basileias mou.</u>*
	ὅ τι ἐάν με αἰτήσῃς δώσω σοι ἕως ἡμίσους τῆς βασιλείας μου.
Esth. 5:3b	*kai ti sou estin to axiōma; <u>heōs tou hēmisous tēs basileias mou.</u>*

καὶ τί σού ἐστιν τὸ ἀξίωμα; ἕως τοῦ ἡμίσους τῆς
βασιλείας μου.

Esth. 7:2b   *kai estō soi heōs tou hēmisous tēs basileias mou.*

καὶ ἔστω σοι ἕως τοῦ ἡμίσους τῆς βασιλείας μου.

Why such an allusion here? Is there really any similarity between
Esther and Salome that would warrant such an allusion? These and any
other questions lead nowhere. The context simply does not justify the
allusion. Perhaps it was this sense of displacement that led Kermode to
look outside the immediate context for the purpose of the allusion.
Kermode finds the allusion connected to Jesus' use of "little girl" and
Jairus (meaning "the awakener"). The former is used of Salome and
Jairus' daughter while the latter occurs in Esther.[2] After observing that
Esther is a story of a beautiful young girl surviving death at the hands of
a sleepless king by enticing him to touch her with his golden scepter,
Kermode asks, "is the story of the little girl a transformation of that
story?"[3] While an interesting observation, it does not make a connection
between Esther, Salome, Herod, and John the Baptist. This is another
example of the power of allusion to invite interpretation.

An Allusion to Joseph

As puzzling as Mark's allusion to Esther is his allusion (14:52) to
Joseph's encounter with Potiphar's wife (Gen. 39). At Jesus' arrest, readers are introduced to a mysterious "young man" who was following Jesus
"wearing nothing but a linen cloth" (14:51b). When the arresting authorities attempt to subdue the young man, he evades them by slipping
out of his linen cloth and fleeing naked. A comparison of this event to
the account of Joseph's escape from the overtures of Potiphar's wife
yields the following parallels:

Gen. 39:12b   *kai katalipōn ta himatia autou en tais chersin autēs ephygen.*

καὶ καταλιπὼν τὰ ἱμάτια αὐτοῦ ἐν ταῖς χερσὶν αὐτῆς
ἔφυγεν.

Mark 14:52   *ho de katalipōn tēn sindona gymnos ephygen.*

ὁ δὲ καταλιπὼν τὴν σινδόνα γυμνὸς ἔφυγεν.

---

[2] Frank Kermode, *The Genesis of Secrecy* (Cambridge: Harvard University,
1979), p. 133.
[3] Ibid.

At this point, interpretation is frustrated. Readers have sought and will continue to seek for significance in this allusion. What possible connection can there be between the circumstances of Joseph and those of this young man? What is the purpose behind such an allusion? Rereading the text, the reader might find a connection between the naked man among the tombs in Mark 6 and this young man, and even between the young man at the tomb (Mark 16), but a connection between the young man in Mark 14:52 and Joseph in Genesis 36 makes no sense.

Mark's Use of Intercalation

Based upon the above examples, we have seen that Mark employs literary allusion to create interpretive openness that requires the reader to make decisions about the narrative in order to assemble meaning in making sense of the narrative. We have also seen that while some allusions suggest that Jesus is redefining the people of God, others generate an openness that is difficult to fill. Mark also uses a literary structural device called **intercalation**. Intercalation is the practice of sandwiching one story within another, or bracketing several textual segments with similar episodes. Mark does not inform the reader of any relationships between the two stories or the bracketing or bracketed episodes. The reader is invited to find the significance of the intercalation. Like his use of allusion, Mark uses intercalation to suggest that Jesus is redefining the people of God and to create a level of interpretive openness that goes beyond such a redefinition.

The Intercalated Stories of Jairus and the Hemorrhaging Woman

Mark 5:21–43 contains the intercalated stories of Jairus and the hemorrhaging woman. Both the woman and Jairus seek a miracle from Jesus, both seem to have faith in Jesus' healing ability, both fall down before Jesus, and in both instances Jesus is ridiculed. But there is one major difference between Jairus and the woman: the woman is ritually unclean, and thus a religious outsider, while Jairus is the ruler of the synagogue and thus a traditional insider. Is Mark's point here that the status of insider is defined not in traditional terms of clean and unclean (i.e., in terms of ceremonial purity) but in terms of faith in Jesus? Such an understanding is certainly plausible.

But some items in the intercalation beg a comparison between the woman and Jairus' daughter. Mark makes it a point to tell the reader that the woman has suffered for twelve years and that the girl is twelve years of age. In the story of the woman, the healing is public, but only the girl's parents, Peter, James, and John witness the second miracle. Jesus refers to the woman as "daughter" and to the girl as "child" and "little girl." What is the reader to make of this? Given that characters in the narrative consistently understand Jesus' activities as instances of teaching, the reader is probably expected to look beyond the surface of the narrative for clues of a deeper significance. The reader may safely assume also that these intercalated stories constitute a parable of the kingdom. While the woman may represent those who have been ceremonially marginalized by the old system, the young girl of twelve may represent the new seed of the kingdom. Out of the old (Jairus, whose faith is never questioned) comes a new seed, a "daughter" in danger of dying. Mark may be suggesting that Jairus, the woman, and the young girl constitute the remnant of the faithful from among the old system. This is especially suggested by Mark's use of the number twelve in the intercalation.

The Intercalated Stories of the Fig Tree and the Cleansing of the Temple

By means of intercalation, Mark does what any good storyteller does; he asks his readers to become involved in the story. The technique of intercalation is so pervasive that the text displays overlapping intercalations and intercalations within intercalations. Below is an outline of three overlapping and embedded intercalations:

11:12–14	Fig tree
11:15–19	Cleansing of the temple
11:20–25	Fig tree
11:15–19	Jesus enters temple
11:20–25	Fig tree
11:27–33	Jesus enters temple
11:1–11	Jesus enters Jerusalem and temple
11:12–25	First intercalation above
11:27–34	Jesus enters Jerusalem and temple

Such complex intercalation shows plainly that the narrative invites the readers to look for a relationship between what happens to the fig tree and what happens to the temple. The narrative also gives the readers pause when the narrator says that Jesus cursed the fig tree because of its lack of fruit even though "it was not the season for figs" (11:13). Just as Jesus rejects the fig tree for its lack of fruit, is he rejecting the temple, the central religious symbol of the people of God? If Jesus is rejecting the temple as God's house, what is to take its place within the redefined people of God? Mark 11:22–25 may suggest that the people of God now have access to God directly instead of having to go through the priesthood and temple. Simple faith in God becomes the central religious symbol of the redefined people of God.

The Intercalated Stories of the Death of John the Baptist and the Disciples' Missions Trip

Just as Mark's literary allusions create interpretive openness that goes beyond the issue of Jesus' purpose, so does his use of intercalation. The placement of the account of John the Baptist's death between the commissioning of the disciples and their subsequent return (6:7–30) is one of the most problematic intercalations in Mark. The text does suggest a variety of associations between the account of John's death and episodes outside the intercalation. But readers have found it difficult even to formulate sensible questions about the intercalation. In what possible way do the two events interpret each other? Is the reader to make some connection between the disciples of Jesus and those of John? Or is the connection between Jesus and John? Does John's death at the hands of Herod foreshadow Jesus' death? Is the lack of fear of John's disciples to be contrasted with the fear of Jesus' disciples? The intercalation invites inferences without foregrounding any.

Jesus' Relationship to His Contemporary World View According to Mark

In Mark 4, Jesus tells the parable of the sower (4:3–9). When his disciples do not understand the parable (4:10), Jesus offers an interpretation (4:11–20); this is followed by a cluster of sayings (4:21–25), the parable of the growing seed (4:26–29), and the parable of the mustard seed (4:30–32). As Burton Mack has noted, the image of sowing seed constituted a popular analogy for teaching culture *(paideia)*.[4] A reader within the hellenistic culture would recognize that Jesus was offering instruction for the inculcation of culture. Similar analogies occur in other ancient writers, such as Hippocrates, Antiphon, Seneca, and Quintilian.[5] The correspondences within the analogy were sower to teacher, sowing to teaching, seed to words, and soils to students. Within the parable of the sower, the emphasis falls upon the acts of sowing and harvest, consequences beyond the control of the sower or reaper, rather than upon cultivation. When we move to the sayings involving the lamp and bushel basket (Mark 4:21–25), there seems to be a correspondence between the seed/word and enlightenment. As Mack points out, "the opposition is between 'hidden' and 'manifest.' "[6] The two parables suggest that while the new culture begins in a rather inauspicious manner, it eventually will become the greatest of all cultures (the image of the scrub from the mustard seed). The seed analogies recall the Greek *paideia,* while the mustard seed's becoming the great shrub whose branches offer habitation for all the birds of the air alludes to the imagery of the great tree of Daniel (Dan. 4:10–12) that represents Israel. Mack is probably right when he observes that the point of the seed parable is that the kingdom will eventually succeed in displacing both Greek and Jewish cultures.[7] In other words, the secret of the kingdom that the disciples do not understand (Mark 4:10) is that Jesus is establishing a new culture, an alternative society in conflict with both Greek and Jewish ones. The movement within 4:13–25 in conjunction with 4:11–12 suggests (1) that the disciples should recognize that Jesus is instituting a new culture, (2) that they should move from hearing about such a culture to understanding its nature, and (3) that such insight is the condition for being a member of the new culture (an **insider**). The disciples are to understand that everything that Jesus teaches and does pertains in some way to the inculcating of the new culture.

Jesus Redefines the People of God by Challenging Social Boundaries

Social scientists have shown that cultures structure social identities by formulating **boundaries** around particular areas (e.g., cosmological,

---

[4] Burton Mack, *A Myth of Innocence: Mark and Christian Origins* (Philadelphia: Fortress, 1988), p. 159.

[5] Ibid., pp. 159–60.

[6] Ibid., p. 164.

[7] Ibid., p. 165.

social, bodily). Ancient Mediterranean cultures often formulated these boundaries in terms of the categories of clean and unclean. As long as an action or event remained within the boundaries of its area, it was clean. When an action or event crossed its prescribed boundaries, it was unclean. Jerome Neyrey has shown that the boundaries of cleanness within Judaism focused on places, people, things, and times.[8] For example, for Judaism, the land of Israel was holier than any other land; the Holy of Holies was more holy than the other parts of the temple; the high priest (who alone has access to the Holy of Holies) was more pure than priests, who were more pure than Levites, who were more pure than Israelites. Animals and people with blemishes or deformities were unclean.[9] Body fluids such as spit, blood, and semen were unclean because they belonged inside the body. A woman was unclean throughout her menstrual period. Lepers were unclean because their bodies broke out in fluid that belonged inside. Most of these boundaries— cosmological (God on earth is located in the Holy of Holies), social (Jew vs. Gentile, male vs. female, orthodox vs. sinner), and bodily (abstinence from certain foods, avoiding contact with certain people, and ritual worship)—are referred to indirectly in Mark. Mark's plot presents Jesus as not only challenging these boundaries, but as erasing them. Jesus thus foregrounds possibilities that were backgrounded or even negated by the system founded upon the socio-religious categories of clean and unclean.

In Mark Jesus as Son of God empowered by the Holy Spirit is not confined to a specific location, but comes in contact with uncleanness, replacing it with wholeness (exorcisms of unclean spirits [6:7–13]). In addition, the plot presents the reader with John's claim that his successor is "mightier" (1:7), with Jesus' temptation by Satan (1:12–13), and with Jesus' parabolic claim that he is binding Satan and plundering his house (3:22–30). Taking as a cue Mark's reference to God's ripping open the heavens and empowering Jesus with the Holy Spirit (1:10–11), the reader can assume that the boundary between heaven and earth is abolished and that God's holiness is evidenced not in ritual protection, but in the bringing of new life to individuals, freeing them from the power of unclean spirits.

---

[8] See Jerome Neyrey, "The Idea of Purity in Mark's Gospel," *Semeia* 35 (1986), pp. 91–128.

[9] See David Rhoads, "Social Criticism: Crossing Boundaries," in *Mark and Method*, ed. Janice Chapel Anderson and Stephen D. Moore (Minneapolis: Fortress, 1992), pp. 151–53.

Thus far (Mark 1:1–8:33) the plot shows Jesus redefining socioreligious boundaries up to 8:27–33 by means of (1) miracles and (2) his controversies with the Jewish leaders or by his actions that lead to controversies. Jesus' healing miracles involve either those **marginalized** by society (i.e., those who are in some way unclean) or those not in compliance with ritual regulations:

1:29–31	Jesus heals Simon's mother-in-law on the Sabbath.
1:40–43	Jesus heals a leper.
3:1–6	Jesus heals on the Sabbath.
5:25–34	Jesus heals a hemorrhaging woman.
5:35–43	Jesus raises a dead girl.
7:24–30	Jesus heals the daughter of a Syrophoenician woman, a Gentile.
7:31–37	Jesus heals a deaf man with spittle.
8:22–26	Jesus heals a blind man.

Instances in which Jesus' actions deviate from the socio-religious norms in controversy with the Jewish teachers are summarized below:

2:14	Jesus calls a tax collector as his disciple.
2:15–17	Jesus eats with sinners and tax collectors.
2:18–22	Jesus rejects the whole socio-religious system in his defense of not fasting.
2:23–28	The role of the Sabbath is reversed in Jesus' defense of his disciples plucking grain on the Sabbath. There are life situations which take priority over ceremonial norms.
3:31–35	Jesus redefines the family.
7:1–23	Jesus disagrees with the Pharisees over the tradition of the elders. He redefines cleanness in terms of morals rather than in terms of diet.

Until Mark 8:26, the plot presents Jesus as an itinerant teacher whose actions and conflicts with religious leaders are supplanting the culture of the day. Rather than avoiding those ritually unclean, Jesus and his disciples replace their uncleanness with wholeness. Jesus teaches a system that breaks down the boundaries. This is represented in the first half of Mark by Jesus' encounters in the synagogue and by his conflicts with the leaders of Judaism. The boundaries are either erased or extended to include those people, actions, and things traditionally excluded (e.g., women, Gentiles, lepers, sinners, tax collectors, physically afflicted, certain foods, Sabbath regulations). The plot invites the reader to consider this reformulated people of God.

The Redefined People of God Is Inclusive

Following the second feeding miracle in Mark 8, Jesus responds to the disciples' question about bread by firing a volley of questions at the disciples, questions that have to do with the numbers of the two crowds, the loaves of bread, and the baskets of fragments. Jesus caps this interrogation with the question, "Do you not yet understand?" (8:21). The disciples' silence suggests that they do not recognize the significance of the numbers. But the reader should know that the numbers twelve and seven have a history of symbolic significance. Twelve is the number of tribes that constituted the Jewish nation; and in Jewish reckoning, seven represents the number of nations from which Gentiles originated. Furthermore, Mark might expect the reader to correlate this symbolism with other items implicit in the text. Is there an instance in the text where the number twelve occurs? In 3:13–19 Jesus chooses from among his followers twelve whom he commissions as apostles and who will participate in and perpetuate Jesus' teaching and healing. The plot suggests that this group of twelve represents the core of a new people of God. Jesus is formulating a new Israel, a new culture that will replace the old (itself symbolized historically by the twelve tribes). Furthermore, given the significance of the numbers 12 and 7, it is interesting that the first feeding takes place in Jewish territory while the second (where seven baskets of fragments were collected) takes place in Gentile territory. It is possible that Mark is suggesting through the **narrative emplotment** that Jesus is reconstituting the people of God to include both Jews and Gentiles.

The People of God Redefined through Jesus' Controversies with Religious Leaders

Immediately after the first passion prediction (Mark 8:31), Jesus assumes the role of teacher in 8:34–9:1. Much of his teaching, however, takes place within controversies with the religious authorities. In each controversy, Jesus introduces a characteristic of the new culture with the old thought system as a backdrop. Jesus foregrounds what has been obscured or negated by the old system. Below is a summary of these controversies.

10:2–12	Using Genesis 2:24 to refute the more relaxed view of the Pharisees, Jesus redefines the parameters governing divorce.
11:15–18	The narrator tells how the chief priests and scribes respond to the spellbinding effects of Jesus' teaching upon the crowds (the reader might assume that the teaching of the leaders did not have such an effect).
11:27–33	The three groups mentioned in Jesus' first passion prediction (8:31) question the source of Jesus' authority to act as he has in reference to the temple. Here Jesus creates the opportunity for the religious leaders to acknowledge his source of authority as divine. If the leaders answer that John's ministry is divinely ordained, they must admit that Jesus' authority is likewise divine. The reader already knows the source of Jesus' authority (1:2–11). As John Paul Heil points out, the reader should recognize that the episode serves to disclose "their [the leaders'] inadequacy to question his authority. . . . Jesus has thus masterfully exercised and demonstrated his own superior, divine authority over the Jewish leaders who stubbornly refuse to acknowledge and believe in the divine origin of John's baptism and hence of Jesus' authority."[10]
12:1–12	Jesus tells the parable of the Wicked Tenants to the leaders. Realizing that they are implicated by the parable, the leaders seek to arrest Jesus. While the readers should understand the referents in the parable and the fact that God himself is rejecting the old culture and replacing it with a new one, the extent of the leaders' insight is left in doubt. This episode is immediately followed by a series of dialogues between Jesus, the religious leaders, and the crowds in which Jesus demonstrates the inadequacy of the old system.
12:13–17	Jesus addresses the issue of taxes.
12:18–27	Jesus accuses the Sadducees of knowing neither God nor the Scriptures.

---

[10] John Paul Heil, *The Gospel of Mark as a Model for Action: A Reader-Response Commentary* (New York: Paulist, 1992), p. 233.

12:28–34   Jesus' definition of the law's essence challenges the
                  traditional structures of clean and unclean. The new
                  element here is the appearance of a scribe as an insider
                  in his positive evaluation of Jesus' teaching. Again the
                  status of insider is contingent upon insight into the
                  nature of the kingdom rather than position within or
                  conformity to the structures of the old system.

12:38–40   Jesus warns against the hypocrisy of the scribes who use
                  the system in order to enhance their own reputation
                  and material possessions while marginalizing those
                  (represented by the widow) for whom the law instructs
                  special care. The words "Beware of the scribes" remind
                  the reader of Jesus' earlier warning to the disciples:
                  "Beware of the yeast of the Pharisees and the yeast of
                  Herod" (8:15). All three parties are guilty of aborting
                  the essential nature of the law. In fact, in 10:46–12:40,
                  the entire range of Jewish leadership (chief priests,
                  scribes, elders, Pharisees, Herodians, and Sadducees)
                  engages Jesus in dialogue concerning basic
                  religio-ethical matters and is found wanting.

Redefining the New People of God in Terms of Insiders and Outsiders

As we suggested above, Jesus consistently reaches out to the disen-
franchised and marginalized of society. By presenting Jesus in such
situations, Mark depicts Jesus as challenging, even erasing, the old
boundaries that defined the insiders and outsiders among the people of
God. This redefinition of insider/outsider status is suggested rather
strongly when we compare Mark's treatment of the disciples with the
treatment of other key individuals in the narrative.

Peter and the Disciples.   Throughout the narrative Mark portrays the
disciples as comprehending neither the nature of Jesus' messiahship nor
the nature of discipleship within the redefined people of God.[11] By the
end of the narrative, Peter has accepted the possibility of Jesus' death
and even announces his own willingness to die with Jesus (14:31). But
when the moment of truth arrives, he and the other followers flee just as
Jesus had predicted. When the council interrogates Jesus, Peter proclaims

---

[11] Since a full treatment of this major motif would take us too far afield,
interested readers may consult the following references: Mark 4:10–13; 4:38–41;
5:30–31; 6:52; 7:17; 8:4; 8:14–21; 9:5–6; 9:10; 9:33–50; 10:13–16; 10:23–31;
10:35–41; 14:3–9.

publicly what the reader has suspected all along: "I do not know this man you are talking about" (14:71b). Peter fails to recognize that the religious leaders' treatment of Jesus fulfills Jesus' predictions in 13:9–13 and 8:34–38. Because Peter and the disciples are as incapable of understanding this parable as they have been of all the other parables, they show themselves to be outsiders. But three characters in Mark's narrative appear to have some insight into the nature of the new people of God. Two of these are paradigm outsiders who become insiders, while the third is a paradigm insider who also becomes an insider within the new people of God.

The Syrophoenician Woman. In 7:1–23 Jesus tells a parable concerning the definition of defilement to the crowd. The disciples fail to comprehend the significance of the parable as a redefinition of a category of clean and unclean. Their incomprehension elicits a rebuke from Jesus: "Then do you also fail to understand?" (7:18).

Immediately following this failure of the disciples, the reader encounters an episode underscoring the disciples' lack of understanding. A Syrophoenician woman (an ethnic outsider) readily solves Jesus' riddle concerning children, food, and dogs (7:24–30). The point of the episode seems to have nothing to do with faith but with insight (i.e., the ability to solve the riddling language of Jesus), for Jesus responds to the woman's solution, "For saying that, you may go—the demon has left your daughter" (7:29). The woman has more insight into the scope of Jesus' new culture than do the disciples.

The Roman Centurion. Here is another individual with insight into the defining quality of sonship and kingdom. The narrative highlights his reaction to Jesus' suffering and death by juxtaposing it with the reactions of the religious leaders and crowds. While the latter group misunderstands the significance of the events and Jesus' words (e.g., 15:16–20, 25–32, 33–36), the Roman centurion concludes, "Truly this man was God's Son!" (15:39b). It is not the statement itself, however, that should shock the reader, but the reason that the narrator gives for the centurion's assessment: "Now when the centurion, who stood facing him, saw that in this way he breathed his last . . ." (15:39a). To what does "in this way" refer? It could not refer to the splitting of the temple curtain, since this bit of insight is given to the reader alone. As the Roman centurion "stood facing him," he heard the cry of abandonment, "*Eloi, Eloi, lema sabachthani,*" and the "loud cry" (Mark 15:34–37). It is upon these two cries of abandonment and death that the centurion bases his claim. He has seen in the suffering of Jesus, in the absence of God, the essence of sonship. The centurion does not make his assessment in response to healings, exorcisms, or any teaching, but solely upon these cries of abandonment. Is this what the voice from heaven means when it silences Peter with "this is my Son, the Beloved; listen to him!" (9:7b)? No voice from God silences the centurion. There is only the sound of ripping flesh and temple curtain. The outsider has understood that Jesus' sonship is essentially defined in terms of suffering and death and that such insight is the mark of an insider. The reader has only to think on the disciples' inability to gain such an insight to recognize that they are in danger of becoming outsiders. Mark does not make such a conclusion explicit, but invites the reader to make the inference.

Joseph of Arimathea. The other person of insight is Joseph of Arimathea, a member of the Jewish council and a paradigm insider, a member of the very body that accuses Jesus of blasphemy and sedition. Joseph requests the body of Jesus with the intention of giving Jesus a proper burial. The narrator informs the reader that Joseph was "also himself waiting expectantly for the kingdom of God" (15:43b). Two things catch the reader's attention. First, the word "also" presupposes that someone else was "waiting expectantly" for the kingdom. The most likely referent is the group of women "looking on from a distance" (15:40-41). The narrator does not record their response to Jesus' death. Unlike the centurion, the women cannot see Jesus' face nor hear his shouts of abandonment. To respond with insight, the observer must see Jesus' face and hear his scream. If the above assessment is plausible, then the reader may assume that the women are closer to the kingdom than the disciples but have not arrived at the essential insight. Second, the plot pressures the reader to assume that Joseph's search for the kingdom leads him to Golgotha; i.e., he has found the kingdom in Jesus' death. Like the centurion (and perhaps the reader), Joseph has understood that the essence of the redefined people of God is found in suffering and death.

Conclusion: The Ending of Mark and the Predicament of the Reader

While this is the end of the story for Joseph, it is not for the readers, who must recall Jesus' three predictions of resurrection as well as the parable of the Buried Seed. The readers have been prepared for Jesus' resurrection by both the parable of the seed and Jesus' predictions. This brings us to Mark's controversial ending.

Jesus' address to his disciples in Mark 13 is calculated to prepare them for a time in which they would be responsible for perpetuating the new culture. Consequently, the reader must wonder about Jesus' promise to meet the disciples in Galilee (14:28) and the young man's reminder of such a meeting in 16:7. Is it possible for Jesus simultaneously to be absent and present with the disciples? Faced with this paradox, the reader suddenly realizes that the ending of Mark is not about the disciples in the story at all, but rather about the *readers-disciples*. Its focus is upon the readers who have struggled to **configure** the text's elements in a meaningful way. Whether or not the disciples ever solve the riddle of Jesus and his new culture is not the issue. The text does holds out the possibility of these outsiders becoming insiders (16:7) just as the young man at the tomb finds insider status after his failure in 14:51–52. But the reader cannot return to Galilee except by way of the text. The disciples were not able to understand the essence of the new people of God. The ending invites the readers not only to understand but to return to the Galilee of the text and to walk again through the text. Are the readers willing to become the living and dying embodiment of the kingdom's essence?

Mark's open ending is the quintessential gap to be filled by each reader. The invitation of the gap is to consider the possibility of a social reordering of reality based upon the unpredictable. This new way must be traveled in the absence of Jesus. The reader's faith must be that of the centurion and Joseph of Arimathea. The disciples and other characters in the story had Jesus as guide; the reader has the text.

REVIEW & STUDY

Key Terms and Concepts

Literary allusion	Intertextuality
Boundaries	Intercalation
Meaning assembly	*Paideia*
Narrative emplotment	Marginalization
Insider	Configure

Study Questions

1. Read the episodes of the feedings in Mark 6:30–44 and 8:1–10. Then read 2 Kings 4:42–44. Keeping in mind the suggestion that Jesus is reconstituting the people of God, what do you see as the significance of this allusion?

2. Read Mark through, giving special attention to the treatment of women. What role do you think the women play in the plot's point of view?

3. In Mark 4:11, Jesus tells the disciples that they have been given the secret of the kingdom of God. Have the disciples been given some information that the narrator has withheld from the reader? Reread chapters 1–3 to see if there is an occasion when the disciples receive such information. Now reread 4:1–12. What do you think the secret is?

4. In Mark 11:12–25 are the two intercalated episodes of the fig tree and the temple. Giving special attention to the narrator's comment in 11:13 ("for it was not the season for figs"), draw from the intercalation some inferences that you think are plausible.

5. Mark 14:53–15:47 contains numerous allusions to the Hebrew Bible. In a good reference Bible, look up these allusions. What do you think is the portrait of Jesus that the plot is asking the reader to recognize? Explain.

6. Find a recent book or journal article which deals with the social world of first-century Judaism. Read the appropriate portions and explain how such knowledge might influence your understanding of Mark's narrative.

7. We have mentioned briefly Mark's two motifs of incomprehension and insider/outsider. Read the Gospel through giving attention to any reference to clothing. What purpose do you think this possible motif serves in the narrative?

Suggestions for Further Reading

Anderson, Janice Capel and Stephen More, eds. *Mark and Method: New Approaches in Biblical Studies.* Minneapolis: Fortress, 1992.

Collins, Adela Yarbro. *The Beginning of the Gospel: Probings of Mark in Context.* Minneapolis: Fortress, 1992.

Eco, Umberto. *The Role of the Reader: Explorations in the Semiotics of Texts.* Bloomington: Indiana University Press, 1984.

Fowler, Robert. *Let the Reader Understand: Reader-Response and the Gospel of Mark.* Minneapolis: Fortress, 1991.

_____. "The Rhetoric of Direction and Indirection in the Gospel of Mark." *Semeia* 48 (1989): 115–34.

Iersel, Bas M. F. Van. "The Reader of Mark as Operator of a System of Connotations." *Semeia* 48 (1989): 83–114.

Iser, Wolfgang. *The Act of Reading: A Theory of Aesthetic Response.* Baltimore: Johns Hopkins University Press, 1978.

Kermode, Frank. *The Genesis of Secrecy.* Cambridge: Harvard University Press, 1979.

Kingsbury, Jack Dean. *The Christology of Mark's Gospel.* Minneapolis: Fortress, 1983.

Power, Mark Allan. *What Is Narrative Criticism?* Minneapolis: Fortress, 1990.

Resseguie, James L. "Reader-Response Criticism and the Synoptic Gospels." *Journal of the American Academy of Religion* 52 (1984): 307–24.

Robbins, Vernon K. *Jesus the Teacher: A Socio-Rhetorical Interpretation of Mark.* Minneapolis: Fortress, 1992.

Waetjen, Herman C. *A Reordering of Power: A Socio-Political Reading of Mark's Gospel.* Minneapolis: Fortress, 1989.

Weeden, Theodore. "The Heresy that Necessitated Mark's Gospel." In William Telford, ed. *The Interpretation of Mark.* Minneapolis: Fortress, 1985.

William, James G. *Gospel Against Parable: Mark's Language of Mystery.* Sheffield: Almond, 1985.

The Never-Ending Story

The hermeneutical task basically involves mediating between the text and a present situation. Traditional hermeneutics has placed heavy emphasis on the distinction between the original, objective meaning of the text in its historical situation and the interpretive application of that meaning to present situations. Approaches that emphasize the historical dimensions of the author's world as the locus of meaning tend to view meaning as something that the author has consciously placed within the text. Meaning for their author-centered approaches is just lying there, waiting to be scientifically excavated. The text is regarded as a purely analytical object reflecting the mind of the author. From this perspective, hermeneutics is a reproductive exercise. It is a recognition of the author's cognition, and the text becomes nothing more than a channel to the author's or early community's mind. At least implicit in this approach is the idea that revelation has occurred once and for all and is unrepeatable. Written revelation becomes objectified, static, final.

With the advent of New Criticism, the locus of meaning shifted to the autonomous text, freed from its historical moorings. Meaning resides within the structure of the text, independent of author, and the text alone legitimates an interpretation. But try as they may, the New Critics discovered that they could not completely dislodge the text from its originating circumstances. Understanding the rhetorical art of the original languages became crucial, as did recognizing the peculiarities of the biblical genres and their embedded literary forms. A familiarity with the conventional system of the text is indispensable, and this familiarity is possible only through historical research, especially through the comparative study of other similar texts.

We have also seen that reader-centered methods of interpretation have produced a paradigm change. The reader is no longer an innocent bystander passively succumbing to the irresistible influence of the text. Reading becomes an integral, if not primary, activity in the creation of meaning. The idea of the reader's artistic activity in the creation of meaning suggests that meaning is the product of the interaction between a present creating intellect and the literary representation of another. The world of the reader (at least at the level of ideology) becomes as important as (if not more important than) the world of the author. Readers are called upon to create a world from the building materials supplied by the text. In the process, however, readers import their understanding of the real world.

If the interpreter takes any of these interpretive thrusts in isolation (i.e., author-centered, text-centered, or reader-centered), consciously or unconsciously excluding the other two, hermeneutics becomes an unbalanced discipline. Hermeneutics is not a monologue; i.e., the author does not simply address readers through the medium of the text, the text does not alone speak to the reader, and the reader does not address only a silent text. Hermeneutics is a dialogue between the text, and reader, and the text and reader enter into a conversational covenant informed by the world of the author. It should be obvious to the reader that throughout this book I have implicitly prescribed a hermeneutical model that calls for integrating three worlds: the worlds of the author, text and reader. This approach rests upon a modified communication model in which the text and reader dialogue, and in which the world of the author offers preparatory, foundational information for the dialogue. If hermeneutics-is willing to bring to bear upon interpretation the scholarship of the differing critical approaches, the dialogue will inevitably be more informed, constructive, and pertinent.

While background studies into the world behind the text (the discovery of historical, ideological, traditional, social information) do not constitute interpretive ends within themselves, such studies do fulfill an important heuristic function within hermeneutics. The biblical texts did not generate themselves. While the author may not be present for questioning, the text certainly reflects the culture which gave it birth. This culture influenced the way in which the text itself speaks linguistically, conventionally, and ideologically. If methodologies such as source, form, and redaction criticism help to focus these influential forces, then they can certainly serve a preparatory function. Methods that attempt to get to the world behind the text are misused only when they fail to perpetuate the dialogue between the text and reader. They should inform the text/reader dialogue.

While the text may be the linguistic representation of an authorial object of consciousness, as an entity to itself, it begins to set its own agenda. It is a whole composed of parts. But the text is greater than the sum of its parts. We have suggested (chapter 4) that the language of literary texts is a special case of language. It is characterized by its rhetorical, metaphorical nature. If this observation is valid, then the connotative sense of the language is inexhaustible. In other words, language is unable to present completely what it represents. The words of the text individually and collectively continually reach beyond our interpretations. Consequently, any hermeneutic which searches for the final, absolute word expects something that language cannot yield. Should hermeneutics then concern itself with offering the definitive interpretation of texts? If hermeneutics supposes texts to be metaphorical and ultimately not sources of absolute knowledge, then texts will continue to escape our complete and final grasp. Yet as we saw in chapter 7, the text does impose restrictions upon interpretation. Perhaps we should refer to this paradoxically as a restricted infinity. While a metaphor can never be exhausted, it cannot mean just anything. It can mean an infinite number of things within parameters. The inexhaustibility of the text is similar to the number of points on a line segment between two end points. The interpretive methodologies focusing on the world of the text are more than instrumental in defining these parameters; they are rather absolutely essential. Without the insights of rhetorical criticism, New Criticism, and formalism, there simply is no context for a constructive dialogue between the text and reader. The text and reader might be speaking to each other, but it would be a language which the other cannot understand.

The metaphorical nature of the text has its counterpart in the person of the reader. Reader-response criticism, along with deconstructive criticism, has made modern readers aware of the metaphorical, rhetorical, non-objective nature, not only of the language of literary texts, but also of language in general. All readers live within a world represented by their words. Not only do we think in language, but we also evaluate, explain, and offer criticism of texts in language. When we move from the experience of reading to the task of conceptualizing that experience in language, we should not expect a precise correlation between the experience and the evaluation and description of it. Because readers bring to the text their own agendas, complete with communally approved methodology (Fish and the interpretive community), structures of faith, ideological presuppositions, and interpretive purposes, individual text/reader conversations vary. Meaning takes place somewhere within this conversation and can never exist apart from the interpretive context of the reader. Individual interpretations are not propositions, issues to be decided for or against. They are individual conversations with the text and are always situated within some context. Interpretation is relational and involves understanding the text in light of who we are, and understanding ourselves in light of the text.

The words on the page never change, and in one sense neither do the worlds of texts. But readers must always approach the textual world and make sense of it in relation to their own world, a world constantly in flux. If hermeneutics is to be perpetually pertinent, we must allow for this flux and recognize that texts are interpreted in time. Time, then becomes the "constant variable" within hermeneutics, the proverbial monkey wrench in the machinery of hermeneutics. The task of hermeneutics, therefore, can never be complete. If the ever-changing, never-ending character of hermeneutics tends to frustrate us at times, this frustration is counterbalanced by the possibilities that hermeneutics offers for personal growth.

Hermeneutics, then, is not an exercise whereby in some precise, scientific manner, we simply *reproduce* what lies in the text. It is rather a *productive* enterprise. It is undeniable that interpreters bring assumptions to the text. During the process of interpretation, however, the text itself may legitimate, deny, clarify, or modify those assumptions. This textual influence upon the reader is possible because while the text as signifier is inexhaustible, it does place parameters around interpretation, making one interpretation more or less plausible than another. The ideal, therefore, is a balance between interpretive dogmatism and individual solipsism. The discipline of hermeneutics should always seek to operate between these two limits. As Paul Ricoeur states,

> the logic of validation allows us to move between the two limits of dogmatism and skepticism. It is always possible to argue for or against an interpretation, to confront interpretations, to arbitrate between them and to seek agreement, even if this agreement remains beyond our immediate reach.[1]

The world of the text in this view is dynamic, a living organism, presenting itself differently on each reading. This also means that as readers we undergo continual change. When we read sacred texts we may have the sensation of experiencing God. But we are experiencing the Infinite through words. We experience the Word through words. But

---

[1] Paul Ricoeur, *Interpretation Theory: Discourse and the Surplus of Meaning* (Fort Worth: Texas Christian University, 1976), p. 79.

just as the Infinite can never be totally objectified in words, always transcending our finite definitions of God, perhaps the words themselves, at least in their totality, also always lie beyond our reach, escaping any final objective meaning. As the text discloses itself to us in ever-changing ways, perhaps we gain a vision of God who is not the "unmoved mover," the God of dogma, but the God who is dynamic, always relating to the changing world of humanity. If this is indeed the case, the experience of doing hermeneutics in not just a scientific discipline unrelated to the task of living; it is rather a continually life-changing and life-shaping experience. It can be an experience of God, and as such, it is redemptive.

Select Bibliography

Abrams, M. H. *A Glossary of Literary Terms.* New York: Holt, Rinehart & Winston, 1981.

Aichele, George. *The Limits of Story.* Philadelphia: Fortress Press, 1985.

Alter, Robert. *The Art of Biblical Narrative.* New York: Basic Books, 1981.

_____. *The Art of Biblical Poetry.* New York: Basic Books, 1985.

Alter, Robert and Frank Kermode, eds. *The Literary Guide to the Bible.* Cambridge: Harvard University Press, 1987.

Aune, David. *The New Testament in Its Literary Environment.* Philadelphia: Westminster Press, 1989.

Bailey, Cyril. *Phases in the Religion of Ancient Rome.* Westport: Greenwood Press, 1972.

Barr, James. *The Semantics of Biblical Language.* Oxford: Oxford University Press, 1961.

Barrett, C. K. *The New Testament Background: Selected Documents.* 2d ed. San Francisco: Harper & Row, 1987.

Beardslee, William A. *Literary Criticism of the New Testament.* Philadelphia: Fortress Press, 1970.

Beasley-Murray, George R. *Jesus and the Last Days: The Interpretation of the Olivet Discourse.* Peabody: Henrickson, 1993.

Berlin, Adele. *Poetics and Interpretation of Biblical Narrative.* Sheffield: Almond Press, 1983.

Bevan, E. "Hellenistic Popular Philosophy." In J. B. Bury et al., *The Hellenistic Age.* London: Cambridge University Press, 1925, pp. 79–107.

Biallas, Leonard J. *Myths, Gods, Heroes and Saviors.* Mystic, Conn.: Twenty-third Publications, 1986.

Bleicher, Josef. *Contemporary Hermeneutics.* London: Routledge and Kegan Paul, 1980.

Bornkamm, Günther. "The Theology of Rudolf Bultmann." In *The Theology of Rudolf Bultmann.* Edited by Charles W. Kegley. London: SCM, 1966.

Brown, Raymond E. "The Qumran Scrolls and the Johannine Gospel and Epistles." In *The Scrolls and the New Testament.* Edited by Krister Stendahl. Westport: Greenwood Press, 1975.

Braaten, Carl. *History and Hermeneutics*. Philadelphia: Fortress Press, 1966.

Bradley, David G. "The *Topos* as a Form in the Pauline Paraenesis." *JBL* 72 (1953), pp. 238–46.

Budick, Sanford and Wolfgang Iser, eds. *Languages of the Unsayable: The Play of Negativity in Literature and Literary Theory*. New York: Columbia University Press, 1989.

Bultmann, Rudolf. *Existence and Faith*. Edited and translated by Schubert Ogden. London: Hodder and Stoughton, 1961.

_____. *The History of the Synoptic Tradition*. Blackwell, 1963. Reprint. Peabody, Mass.: Hendrickson, 1993.

Burns, Gerald L. "Midrash and Allegory: The Beginnings of Scriptural Interpretation." In *The Literary Guide to the Bible*. Edited by Robert Alter and Frank Kermode. Cambridge: Harvard University Press, 1987.

Caird, G. B. *The Language and Imagery of the Bible*. Philadelphia: Westminster Press, 1980.

Caputo, John D. *Radical Hermeneutics: Repetition, Deconstruction, and the Hermeneutic Project*. Bloomington: Indiana University Press, 1987.

Carson, D. A. *Biblical Interpretation and the Church*. Nashville: Thomas Nelson, 1984.

Carter, Angela. *The Infernal Desire Machines of Doctor Hoffman*. London: Penguin Books, 1994.

Childs, Brevard. *Introduction to the Old Testament as Scripture*. Philadelphia: Fortress Press, 1979.

_____. *The New Testament as Canon: An Introduction*. Philadelphia: Fortress Press, 1985.

Clements, R. E. *Prophecy and Tradition*. Atlanta: John Knox Press, 1975.

Coetzee, J. M. *Foe*. London: Penguin Books, 1986.

Collins, Adela Yarbro. *The Beginning of the Gospel: Probings of Mark in Context*. Minneapolis: Fortress Press, 1992.

Conzelmann, Hans and Andreas Lindemann. *Interpreting the New Testament*. Translated by Siegfried S. Schatzmann. Peabody, Mass.: Hendrickson, 1988.

Cotterell, Peter and Max Turner. *Linguistics and Biblical Interpretation*. Downers Grove: InterVarsity Press, 1989.

Croatto, Severino. *Biblical Hermeneutics: Toward a Theory of Reading as the Production of Meaning*. Maryknoll: Orbis Books, 1987.

Culler, Jonathan. *On Deconstruction: Theory and Criticism after Structuralism*. Ithaca: Cornell University Press, 1986.

_____. *Structuralist Poetics: Structuralism, Linguistics and the Study of Literature*. Ithaca: Cornell University Press, 1986.

_____. *The Pursuit of Signs: Semiotics, Literature, Deconstruction*. Ithaca: Cornell University Press, 1986.

Damrosch, David. *The Narrative Covenant: Transformations of Genre in the Growth of Biblical Literature*. San Francisco: Harper & Row, 1987.

de Saussure, Ferdinand. *A Course in General Linguistics*. New York: McGraw-Hill, 1959.

Dibelius, Martin. *From Tradition to Gospel*. New York: Scribner's, n.d.

Dillon, J. *The Middle Platonists, 80 B.C. to A.D. 220*. Ithaca: Cornell University Press, 1977.

Doty, William G. *Letters in Primitive Christianity*. Philadelphia: Fortress Press, 1973.

Eagleton, Terry. *Literary Theory: An Introduction*. Minneapolis: University of Minnesota Press, 1983.

Eco, Umberto. *The Role of The Reader*. Bloomington: Indiana University Press, 1979.

Efird, James M. *The Old Testament Writings: History, Literature, Interpretation*. Atlanta: John Knox Press, 1982.

Farley, Margaret A. "Feminist Consciousness and Scripture." In *Feminist Interpretation of the Bible*. Edited by Letty M. Russell. Philadelphia: Westminster Press, 1985.

Fee, Gordon. *New Testament Exegesis: A Handbook for Students and Pastors*. 2d ed. Philadelphia: Westminster Press, 1993.

Fee, Gordon and Douglas Stuart. *How to Read the Bible for All Its Worth*. 2d ed. Grand Rapids: Zondervan, 1993.

Ferguson, Duncan. *Biblical Hermeneutics: An Introduction*. Atlanta: John Knox Press, 1986.

Ferguson, Everett. *Backgrounds of Early Christianity*. 2d ed. Grand Rapids: Eerdmans, 1993.

Ferguson, John. *Greek and Roman Religion: A Source Book*. Park Ridge, N.J.: Noyes Press, 1980.

Fisch, Harold. *Poetry with a Purpose: Biblical Poetics and Interpretation*. Bloomington: Indiana University Press, 1988.

Freyne, Sean. *Galilee, Jesus, and the Gospels: Literary Approaches and Historical Investigation*. Philadelphia: Fortress Press, 1988.

Frye, Northrop. *The Great Code: The Bible and Literature*. New York: Harvest/Harcourt, Brace and Jovanovich, 1982.

Furnish, Victor P. *Theology and Ethics of Paul*. Nashville: Abingdon Press, 1968.

Gabel, John and Charles Wheeler. *The Bible as Literature: An Introduction*. New York: Oxford University Press, 1986.

Gadamer, H. G. *Truth and Method*. New York: Seabury Press, 1975.

Gager, John G. *Kingdom and Community: The Social World of Early Christianity*. Englewood Cliffs: Prentice Hall, 1975.

Garry, Ann and Marilyn Pearsall, eds. *Women, Knowledge and Reality: Explorations in Feminist Philosophy*. Boston: Unwin Hyman, 1989.

Genette, Gérard. *Narrative Discourse*. Oxford: Oxford University Press, 1980.

Gottcent, John. *The Bible: A Literary Study*. Boston: Thayne Publishers, 1986.

Greenfield, Jonas C. "The Hebrew Bible and Canaanite Literature." In *The Literary Guide to the Bible*. Edited by Robert Alter and Frank Kermode. Cambridge: Harvard University Press, 1987.

Haight, Elizabeth. *Essays on the Greek Romances*. Port Washington, N.Y.: Kennikat Press, 1943.

Hassan, Ihab. *The Postmodern Turn: Essays in Postmodern Theory and Culture*. Columbus: Ohio State University Press, 1987.

Hayes, John and Carl Holladay. *Biblical Exegesis: A Beginner's Handbook*. Atlanta: John Knox Press, 1987.

Heidegger, Martin. *Being and Time*. Trans. by John Macquarrie and Edward Robinson. New York: Harper & Row, 1962.

Heil, John Paul. *The Gospel of Mark as a Model for Action: A Reader-Response Commentary*. New York: Paulist Press, 1992.

Hemer, C. J. *The Letters to the Seven Churches of Asia in Their Local Settings*. Sheffield: JSOT Press, 1986.

Hicks, R. D. *Stoic and Epicurean*. New York: Russell and Russell, 1962.

Hirsch. J. D., Jr. *Validity in Interpretation*. New Haven: Yale University Press, 1973.

Holland, Norman. *5 Readers Reading*. New Haven: Yale University Press, 1975.

Howard, R. J. *Three Faces of Hermeneutics*. Los Angeles: University of California Press, 1982.

Hutcheon, Linda. *A Poetics of Postmodernism: History, Theory, Fiction*. London: Routledge, 1988.

Inch, Morris A. and Hassell C. Bulloch. *The Literature and Meaning of Scripture*. Grand Rapids: Baker Book House, 1984.

Iser, Wolfgang. *The Act of Reading: A Theory of Aesthetic Response*. Baltimore: Johns Hopkins University Press, 1978.

_____. *The Implied Reader: Patterns of Communication in Prose Fiction from Bunyan to Beckett*. Baltimore: Johns Hopkins University Press, 1974.

_____. *Prospecting: From Reader Response to Literary Anthropology*. Baltimore: Johns Hopkins University Press, 1989.

_____. "The Reading Process: A Phenomenological Approach." In *Reader-Response Criticism: From Formalism to Post-Structuralism*. Edited by Jane Tompkins. Baltimore: Johns Hopkins University Press, 1980.

Japp, U. *Hermeneutik: Der theoretische Diskurs, die Literatur, und die Konstruktion ihres Zusammenhanges in den philologischen Wissenschaften*. Munich: Fink, 1977.

Johnson, Luke T. *The Writings of the New Testament: An Interpretation.* Philadelphia: Fortress Press, 1986.

Jülicher, Adolf. *Die Gleichnisreden Jesu.* Vol. 1. Tübingen: J. C. B. Mohr, 1910.

Kee, Howard Clark, Franklin W. Young, and Karlfried Froelich. *Understanding the New Testament.* 4th ed. Englewood Cliffs: Prentice-Hall, 1983.

Keegan, Terrance J. *Interpreting the Bible: A Popular Introduction to Biblical Hermeneutics.* New York: Paulist Press, 1986.

Keesey, Donald, ed. *Contexts for Criticism.* Mountain View, Calif.: Mayfield Publishing Co., 1987.

Kennedy, George A. *Classical Rhetoric and Its Christian and Secular Tradition from Ancient to Modern Times.* Chapel Hill: University of North Carolina Press, 1980.

_____. *New Testament Interpretation through Rhetorical Criticism.* Chapel Hill: University of North Carolina Press, 1984.

Kingsbury, Jack. *The Christology of Mark's Gospel.* Minneapolis: Fortress Press, 1983.

Klassen, William. "Coals of Fire: Sign of Repentance or Revenge?" *NTS* 9 (1962–63), pp. 337–50.

Koester, Helmut. *Introduction to the New Testament.* Vol. 1. New York: Walter De Gruyter, 1982.

Kort, Wesley A. *Modern Fiction and Human Time: An Essay in Narrative and Belief.* Gainesville, Fla.: University Presses of Florida, 1986.

_____. *Story, Text, and Scripture: Literary Interests in Biblical Narrative.* University Park, Penn.: Pennsylvania State University Press, 1987.

Kraemer, Ross Shepard. *Her Share of the Blessings: Women's Religions among Pagans, Jews, and Christians in the Greco-Roman World.* Oxford: Oxford University Press, 1992.

Krentz, E. *The Historical Critical Method.* Philadelphia: Fortress Press, 1975.

Ladd, George E. *A Theology of the New Testament.* Grand Rapids: Eerdmans, 1974.

LaSor, William, David Hubbard, and Frederic Bush. *Old Testament Survey.* Grand Rapids: Eerdmans, 1982.

Lategan, Bernard and Willem Vorster. *Text and Reality: Aspects of Reference in Biblical Texts.* Philadelphia: Fortress Press, 1985.

Lesky, Albin. *History of Greek Literature.* New York: Thomas Y. Crowell, 1966.

Lightfoot, J. B. *St. Paul's Epistle to the Philippians.* Reprint. Peabody: Hendrickson, 1993.

Lohfink, Gerhard. *The Bible, Now I Get It: A Form Critical Handbook.* New York: Doubleday, 1976.

Longman, Tremper, III. *Literary Approaches to Biblical Interpretation*. Grand Rapids: Zondervan, 1987.

Louis, Kenneth Gros with James Ackerman and Thayer S. Warshaw. *Literary Interpretations of Biblical Narratives*. Nashville: Abingdon Press, 1974.

Lyotard, Jean-François. *The Postmodern Condition: A Report on Knowledge*. Translated by Geoof Bennington and Brian Massumi. Minneapolis: University of Minnesota Press, 1993.

Mack, Burtan. *A Myth of Innocence: Mark and Christian Origins*. Philadelphia: Fortress Press, 1988.

Malherbe, A., ed. *The Cynic Epistles*. Missoula: Scholars Press, 1977.

Malina, Bruce J. *The New Testament World: Insights from Cultural Anthropology*. Atlanta: John Knox Press, 1981.

Mann, Thomas W. *The Book of the Torah: The Narrative Integrity of the Pentateuch*. Philadelphia: John Knox Press, 1988.

Martin, Luther. *Hellenistic Religions*. New York: Oxford University Press, 1987.

Martin, Ralph. *New Testament Foundations*. 2 vols. Grand Rapids: Eerdmans, 1978.

Martin, Wallace. *Recent Theories of Narrative*. Ithaca: Cornell University Press, 1986.

McKnight, Edgar V. *Meaning in Texts*. Philadelphia: Fortress Press, 1978.

_____. *Post-Modern Use of the Bible: The Emergence of Reader-Oriented Criticism*. Nashville: Abingdon Press, 1988.

_____. *The Bible and the Reader*. Philadelphia: Fortress Press, 1985.

Meeks, Wayne. *The Moral World of the First Christians*. Philadelphia: Westminster Press, 1986.

Merlan, P. *From Platonism to Neoplatonism*. 2d ed. Hague: Nijhoff, 1960.

Merleau-Ponty, Maurice. *Consciousness and the Acquisition of Language*. Translated by Hugh J. Silverman. Evanston: Northwestern University Press, 1973.

Mickelsen, A. Berkeley. *Interpreting the Bible*. Grand Rapids: Eerdmans, 1963.

Morgan, Robert with John Barton. *Biblical Interpretation*. New York: Oxford University Press, 1988.

Murray, Gilbert. *Five Stages of Greek Religion*. Garden City: Doubleday, 1955.

Neusner, Jacob. *Invitation to Midrash: A Teaching Book*. San Francisco: Harper & Row, 1989.

_____. *Midrash in Context: Exegesis in Formative Judaism*. Philadelphia: Fortress Press, 1983.

_____. *What Is Midrash?* Philadelphia: Fortress Press, 1987.

Neyrey, Jerome. "The Idea of Purity in Mark's Gospel." *Semeia* 35 (1986).

Norris, Christopher. *The Truth about Postmodernism*. Oxford: Blackwell, 1993.

Patte, Daniel. *What Is Structural Exegesis?* Philadelphia: Fortress Press, 1976.

Perrin, Norman. *What Is Redaction Criticism?* Philadelphia: Fortress Press, 1969.

Petersen, Norman. *Literary Criticism for New Testament Critics*. Philadelphia: Fortress Press, 1978.

Pritchard, J. B., ed. *Ancient Near Eastern Texts Relating to the Old Testament*. Princeton: Princeton University Press, 1969.

Pryke, John. "'Spirit' and 'Flesh' in the Qumran Documents and Some New Testament Texts." *RQ* 5 (1965), pp. 345–60.

Ramm, Bernard. *Hermeneutics*. Grand Rapids: Baker, 1961.

Ray, William. *Literary Meaning: From Phenomenology to Deconstruction*. New York: Basil Blackwell, 1984.

Rhoads, David. "Social Criticism: Crossing Boundaries." *Mark and Method*. Edited by Janice Chapel Anderson and Stephen D. Moore. Minneapolis: Fortress Press, 1992.

Richesin, Dale and Brian Mahan, eds. *The Challenge of Liberation Theology: A First-World Response*. Maryknoll: Orbis Books, 1981.

Ricoeur, Paul. "Biblical Hermeneutics." *Semeia* 4 (1975), p. 81.

———. *Essays on Biblical Interpretation*. Philadelphia: Fortress Press, 1980.

———. *Interpretation Theory: Discourse and the Surplus of Meaning*. Fort Worth: Texas Christian University Press, 1976.

———. *The Conflict of Interpretation*. Evanston: Northwestern University Press, 1974.

Robbins, Vernon K. *Jesus the Teacher: A Socio-Rhetorical Interpretation of Mark*. Minneapolis: Fortress Press, 1992.

Robertson, David. *The Old Testament and the Literary Critic*. Philadelphia: Fortress Press, 1977.

Robinson, James M. "The Historicality of Biblical Language." In *The Old Testament and Christian Faith*. Edited by Bernhard Anderson. New York: Harper & Row, 1963.

Roetzel, Calvin J. *The Letters of Paul: Conversations in Context*. Atlanta: John Knox Press, 1982.

Rosenberg, Joel. *King and Kin: Political Allegory in the Hebrew Bible*. Bloomington: Indiana University Press, 1986.

Rudolph, Kurt. "Mystery Religions." In *The Encyclopedia of Religion*. Vol. 7. Edited by Mircea Eliade. New York: Macmillan, 1987.

Rudwick, M. J. S. and E. M. B. Green, "The Laodicean Lukewarmness." *ExpT* 69 (1957–58), pp. 176–78.

Ruether, Rosemary Radford. "Feminist Interpretation: A Method of Correlation." In *Feminist Interpretation of the Bible*. Edited by Letty M. Russell. Philadelphia: Westminster Press, 1985.

_____. *Sexism and God Talk: Toward a Feminist Theology*. Boston: Beacon Press, 1983.
Russell, Letty M., ed. *Feminist Interpretation of the Bible*. Philadelphia: Westminster Press, 1985.
Ryken, Leland. *The Literature of the Bible*. Grand Rapids: Baker, 1987.
_____. *Words of Delight: A Literary Introduction to the Bible*. Grand Rapids: Baker, 1987.
_____. *Words of Life: A Literary Introduction to the New Testament*. Grand Rapids: Baker, 1986.
Sakenfeld, Katharine Doob. *Faithfulness in Action: Loyalty in Biblical Perspective*. Philadelphia: Fortress Press, 1985.
_____. "Feminist Uses of Biblical Materials." In *Feminist Interpretation of the Bible*. Edited by Letty M. Russell. Philadelphia: Westminster Press, 1985.
Sanders, Jack. "The Transition from Opening Epistolary Thanksgiving to Body in the Pauline Corpus." *JBL* 81 (1962), pp. 352–62.
Sanders, James A. *Canon and Community*. Philadelphia: Fortress Press, 1984.
Sands, P. C. *Literary Genius of the New Testament*. New York: Oxford University Press, 1932.
Savran, George W. *Telling and Retelling: Quotation in Biblical Narrative*. Bloomington: Indiana University Press, 1988.
Schubert, Paul. *Form and Function of the Pauline Thanksgivings*. Berlin: Alfred Töpelmann, 1939.
Schüssler Fiorenza, Elisabeth. "A Feminist Biblical Hermeneutics: Biblical Interpretation and Liberation Theology." In *The Challenge of Liberation Theology: A First-World Response*. Edited by L. Dale Richesin and Brian Mahan. Maryknoll: Orbis Books, 1981.
_____. *Bread Not Stone: Introduction to a Feminist Interpretation of Scripture*. Boston: Beacon Press, 1985.
_____. *Jesus: Miriam's Child, Sophia's Prophet*. New York: Continuum, 1994.
_____. "The Will to Choose or to Reject: Continuing Our Critical Work." In *Feminist Interpretation of the Bible*. Edited by Letty M. Russell. Philadelphia: Westminster Press, 1985.
Shuler, Philip. I. *A Genre for the Gospels: The Biographical Character of Matthew*. Philadelphia: Fortress Press, 1982.
Soskice, Janet Martin. *Metaphor and Religious Language*. Oxford: Oxford University Press, 1985.
Soulen, Richard. *Handbook of Biblical Criticism*. 2d ed. Atlanta: John Knox Press, 1981.
Stambaugh, John and David Balch. *The New Testament in Its Social Environment*. Philadelphia: Westminster Press, 1986.

Stegner, William R. *Narrative Theology in Early Jewish Christianity.* Louisville: Westminster/John Knox Press, 1989.

Sternberg, M. *The Poetics of Biblical Narrative.* Bloomington: Indiana University Press, 1985.

Stuart, Douglas. *Old Testament Exegesis.* Philadelphia: Westminster Press, 1980.

Talbert, Charles. *Literary Patterns, Theological Themes and the Genre of Luke–Acts.* SBLMS 20. Missoula: Society of Biblical Literature and Scholars Press, 1974.

Taylor, Vincent. *The Formation of the Gospel Tradition.* London: Macmillan, 1960.

Tenney, Merrill C. *New Testament Times.* Grand Rapids: Eerdmans, 1975.

Tillich, Paul. *A History of Christian Thought.* New York: Simon and Schuster, 1968.

Todorov, Tzvetan. *Symbolism and Interpretation.* Ithaca: Cornell University Press, 1986.

Tompkins, Jane P., ed. *Reader-Response Criticism: From Formalism to Post Structuralism.* Baltimore: Johns Hopkins University Press, 1980.

Tucker, Gene. *Form Criticism of the Old Testament.* Philadelphia: Fortress Press, 1971.

Tuckett, Christopher. *Reading the New Testament: Methods of Interpretation.* Philadelphia: Fortress Press, 1987.

Van der Woude, A. S. *The World of the Old Testament.* Grand Rapids: Eerdmans, 1989.

Van Til, Cornelius. *The New Hermeneutic.* Nutley: Presbyterian and Reformed Publishing Co., 1977.

Waetjen, Herman C. *A Reordering of Power: A Socio-Political Reading of Mark's Gospel.* Minneapolis: Fortress Press, 1989.

Walhout, Clarence, Roger Ludin, and Anthony Thiselton. *The Responsibility of Hermeneutics.* Grand Rapids: Eerdmans, 1985.

Weinfeld, Moshe. "Ancient Near Eastern Patterns in Prophetic Literature." *VT* 27 (April, 1977).

_____. *Deuteronomy and the Deuteronomic School.* Oxford: Oxford University Press, 1972.

Wright, Addison G. *The Literary Genre Midrash.* Staten Island, N.Y.: Alba House, 1967.

Index of Modern Authors

Abrams, M. H.   xxii
Alter, R.   70, 103, 106–8, 115
Aune, D.   121, 133–34

Bailey, C.   51
Barr, J.   20
Barrett, C. K.   50
Barthes, R.   4
Barton, J.   157
Beardsley, M.   xxi
Benjamin, D.   61
Berlin, A.   90, 93–94
Bevan, E.   44
Bornkamm, G.   188
Braaten, C.   ix
Bradley, D. G.   141
Brown, R. E.   57
Bultmann, R.   188, 202
Burns, G.   132
Bush, F.   102

Caputo, J.   xxvi
Childs, B.   205–6
Clements, R. E.   111
Conzelmann, H.   128
Cotterell, P.   10–11, 20, 167

Damrosch, D.   37, 38, 40–41
de Man, P.   229
de Saussure, F.   211–12
Delling, G.   24
Derrida, J.   227–29
Dibelius, M.   202
Dillon, J.   44
Doty, W. G.   138, 139, 141
Drury, J.   236

Eagleton, T.   4–5, 36, 188
Eco, U.   180–82

Farley, M.   222–23
Fee, G. D.   21, 34, 118, 134
Ferguson, D.   xx, 190
Ferguson, E.   36, 44, 49, 54–56
Fish, S.   217
Freyne, S.   61
Furnish, V.   46–47

Gabel, J.   72, 74, 134, 135
Gadamer, H. G.   xx
Gager, J. G.   61
Genette, G.   87
Gilmore, G.   52
Gottwald, N.   60
Green, E. M. B.   32
Greenfield, J. C.   37, 40
Gunn, D.   xxii

Haight, E.   119
Hayes, J.   17, 69–70, 188, 203, 205
Heidegger, M.   187
Heil, J. P.   247
Hemer, C. J.   32
Hengel, M.   61
Hicks, R. D.   44
Hirsch, E. D., Jr.   ix, 30
Holladay, C.   17, 69–70, 188, 203, 205
Holland, N.   216
Hubbard, D.   102

Iser, W.   164–65, 216

Japp, U.   159
Johnson, L. T.   9, 22, 42, 121–22, 148
Jülicher, A.   127

Kee, H. C.   51
Keegan, T.   206
Keesey, D.   4, 196, 208, 209, 215
Kermode, F.   103, 239
Klassen, W.   168, 169–177
Koester, H.   36, 44, 52, 119, 120
Kuenen, A.   198

Ladd, G. E.   22, 25
LaSor, W. S.   102
Lategan, B.   158, 161, 180
Lesky, A.   120
Levi-Strauss, C.   214
Lightfoot, J. B.   47–48
Lindemann, A.   128
Long, B. O.   61
Longman, T.   xxiii

Mack, B.   242–43
Malherbe, A.   44, 61
Malina, B.   61
Martin, L.   51
Martin, R.   46
Martin, W.   179
Matthews, V.   61
McKnight, E. V.   xxiv, 8–9, 67, 71,
    151–52, 159, 163, 165–66, 178,
    195
Meeks, W. A.   44, 61
Merlan, P.   44
Merleau-Ponty, M.   162
Michel, O.   34
Mickelsen, B.   30, 72, 75
Morgan, R.   157, 195
Murray, G.   49

Neusner, J.   130
Neyrey, J.   61, 244

Osiek, C.   61, 62

Puskas, C.   153

Ransom, J. C.   xxiii
Rhoads, D.   244
Richards, I. A.   215
Ricoeur, P.   xx, 30, 161, 257

Robinson, J. M.   137
Rodd, C. S.   60
Roetzel, C.   138
Rohrbaugh, R.   61
Rosenberg, J.   xxii, xxiii, 10
Rosenblatt, L.   8
Rudolph, K.   52
Rudwick, M. J. S.   32
Ruether, R. R.   223, 224–25
Russell, L. M.   232
Ryken, L.   76, 77, 78, 89, 108–9,
    118, 135, 143, 146

Sakenfeld, K. D.   223, 225
Sanders, J. T.   136
Sanders, J. A.   205
Sands, P. C.   144
Savran, G. W.   98, 101
Schubert, P.   136
Schüssler Fiorenza, E.   223, 225–27
Shuler, P.   119
Soulen, R.   16
Sternberg, M.   87–88, 90, 178–79
Streeter, B. H.   200
Stuart, D.   34, 118, 134

Talbert, C.   119
Taylor, V.   202
Tenney, M. C.   50
Theissen, G.   61
Thompson, J. E. H.   56
Tillich, P.   45, 46
Tuckett, C.   201, 203
Turner, M.   10–11, 20, 167

Van der Woude, A. S.   198–200
Vermes, G.   130–31
von Rad, G.   112
Vorster, W. S.   158, 161, 180

Walhout, C.   3, 7, 103, 227–28
Weinfeld, M.   42, 200
Wellhausen, J.   198–99
Wheeler, C.   72, 74, 134, 135
Wilson, R.   60
Wimsatt, W.   xxi

Index of Scripture References

Genesis
1   199
1–11   40, 41
1:1–2:4a   199
2–3   224
2:4b–4:26   199
2:24   247
5:1–27   199
6:1–8   199
8:11b   91
9:1–17   199
11   97
11:1–9   199
11:10–27   199
12–50   97
12:1   102
12:1–4a   199
12:4–9   90
12:6–20   199
12:10–20   86
16   97
18:1–8   89
18:1–15   98
18:3–5   89
19:24   167
20   97
20:1–8   199
20:1–17   86
20:3   199
21   97
21:8–34   199
21:17   199
22:1–19   199
22:10   105
22:13   105
22:17   72
24:10–61   98

24:28–31   90
24:47–51   91
25   97
25:7–10   199
27   97
27:1–45   97
29   91
29:1–9   99
29:1–20   99
30   97
30:30–34   93
30:35–36   93
30:37–43   93
35:4   198
36   240
36:31–39   198
37   97
37–48   81
37:1–4   86
37:28   86
37:36   86, 88
39   239
39:1   86
39:10–23   86
39:12b   239
42   97
42:18–20   100
42:33–34   100
48   97
49:11   107

Exodus
1:22   124
2:14   92
2:15–21   98
2:24   92
2:25   92

3:3   92
3:6   56
3:10   112
7–10   124
12:1–13   238
22:1   104
24:8   238
24:10   129
34:29–34   125

Leviticus
4:7   105
4:18   105
8:15   105
10:2   167
18:6–8   72

Numbers
11:11–15   98
11:13   237
11:22   237
12:6b–8   237
21:18   130

Deuteronomy
12–26   199
18:15ff.   57
23:18   35
34:5–8   198

Judges
3   72, 76
4:6   94
4:8   94
4:14   94
6:1–8:35   156

11:35   89
13   98
14:2   92
14:3   92
15:18   92
16:28   92
17:6   97
18:1   97
19:1   97
21:25   97

Ruth
2:11   102

1 Samuel
1   98
1:26   94
11   158
17:43   34
18–20   93

2 Samuel
11   95–96
12:1–4   104
12:5–6   104
13:28   104
14:25–26   104
18:9   105
18:9–15   105
18:12a   105

1 Kings
1:40   71
1:50   105
2:25   105
14:11   35
16:4   35
22:17   86, 237
22:19–20   85
22:29–38   86

2 Kings
4   99
4:8–37   98
4:43   237

2 Chronicles
18:16   237

Esther
5:3b   238
7:2b   239

Job
6:2   106
14:1–2a   73
27   40
28:11   40
28:12   40
28:14   40
28:22   40, 74
28:23   40

Psalms
11:6   167
18:3   108
23   109
23:1   167
24:7–8   75
42:1   106
62:11   107
118:27   105
119   14–15
119:105   72

Proverbs
1:20   74
10:1   107
20:1   107
25:21–23   168

Song of Songs
4:2a   108
4:3b   106
4:12   108

Isaiah
1:11–17   41
2:4   166
5:1–7   112
6:8   112
7:14   131

13:14   237
14:4ff.   113
23:1ff.   113
28:23–29   113
40–55   113
53   151, 183
54:16   130
65:17–25   34

Jeremiah
6:20   41
7:22   41
26:17–19   111
44   86
50:6   237

Ezekiel
1:10   151
1:26–28   151
10:14   151
14:12–23   113
16:1–43   113
17:1–10   113
19:1ff.   113
19:1–14   113
21:13–23   113
23:1–27   113
26:19–21   113
27:2ff.   113
28:1–10   113
31:1–18   113
32:17–32   113
34:12   237
40:1–48:35   151

Daniel
4:10–12   243
7:9   151
7:13   151
7:22   151
8   148
8:19ff.   148
10:13   15
10:21   151
12:1   151
12:1ff.   56
12:2–3   151

Hosea
2   73
11:1a   74, 131

Joel
1:4–2:11   151

Amos
1:7   107
3:3ff.   113
5:1   113
5:21–25   41
8:2   15
8:10   107

Jonah
1:2–3   85
4:2   85

Micah
5:5   107
6:6–8   41

Zechariah
1:8   151
1:18–21   151
6:1–6   151
9:11   238
10:2   237
14:1–9   34

Malachi
4:1–6   34

Matthew
1–2   124
1:22–23   131
2:14–15   131
2:16   124
3:1–4:25   124
5–7   119, 124
5:13–14   167
5:18   123
5:21   122
5:22   31, 72
5:27   122

5:29   31
5:30   31
5:31   122
5:33   122
5:38   122
5:39   29
5:43   122
7:28–29   124
8:1–9:35   124
9:10–13   126
9:13   122
9:36–10:42   124
10   119
10:10   126
10:14   126
10:38   75
11:1   124
11:2–12:50   124
11:19   123
11:28–30   123
13   118, 119, 124
13:24ff.   128
13:54–17:21   124
14:1–16   119
17:1–4   124
17:22–18:35   124
18:18   126
18:20   55, 123
19:1   124
19:2–22:46   124
19:30   126
22:1–14   74
22:15–46   122
22:23–33   55
22:36   55
23:13   122
23:15   31
23:15–16   122
23:23   122
23:25   122
23:27   122
23:29   122
23:33   31
23:37   75
23:37–39   118
24:1–25:46   122
24:35   123
24:41   126

26:1   124
26:3–28:20   124
28:16–20   125

Mark
1:1–8:33   245
1:2–11   247
1:5   236
1:7   244
1:10–11   244
1:12–13   244
1:29–31   245
1:40–43   245
2:14   245
2:15–17   245
2:16–17   126
2:18–22   245
2:23–28   245
3:1–6   245
3:13–19   246
3:22–30   244
3:31–35   245
4   118, 242
4:1ff.   128
4:3–9   242
4:10   242, 243
4:10–13   128, 248
4:11   237
4:11–12   243
4:11–20   242
4:13–25   243
4:21–25   242, 243
4:26–29   242
4:30–32   242
4:38–41   248
5:21-1–43   240
5:25–34   245
5:30–31   248
5:35–43   245
6   240
6:7–12:3   244
6:7–30   242
6:21–23   238
6:22b   238
6:23b   238
6:30–44   236
6:52   248

7:1–23   245, 249
7:3   59
7:17   248
7:18   249
7:24–30   245, 249
7:27–28   35
7:29   249
7:31–37   245
8:1–13   237
8:4   248
8:14–21   248
8:15   248
8:21   246
8:22–26   245
8:26   245
8:27–33   204
8:31   246, 247
8:34–38   249
8:34–9:1   246
8:35   126
9:5–6   248
9:7b   250
9:10   248
9:33–50   248
10:2–12   247
10:13–16   248
10:23–31   248
10:35–41   248
10:45   52
10:46–12:40   248
11:1–11   241
11:12–14   241
11:12–25   241
11:13   242
11:15–18   247
11:15–19   241
11:20–25   241
11:22–25   242
11:27–33   241, 247
11:27–34   241
12:1–12   247
12:13–17   247
12:18–27   247
12:28–34   248
12:38–40   248
13   251
13:9–13   249
14:3–9   248

14:12   238
14:22–25   238
14:24   238
14:28   251
14:31   248
14:51b   239
14:51–52   251
14:52   239, 240
14:71b   249
15:16–20   249
15:25–32   249
15:33–36   249
15:34–37   249
15:39a   249
15:39b   249
15:40–41   250
15:43b   250
16   240
16:7   251

Luke
1:46–55   129
1:68–79   129
2:14   129
2:29–32   129
5:29–32   126
5:36   126
7:12   159
8:24   24
9:18–22   204
11:8   165
11:9–10   129
13:34–35   118
14:15–24   29
17:22–24   127
24:27   76

John
1:1–3   57
1:9   46
2   118
3:16   75
3:29   99
4:1–4   92
7:1–10   157
15:15   49
21   201

Acts
2:16–21   131
15:10   123
24:2–3   145

Romans
1–2   201
1:13   138
1:29–31   139
2:21–22   144
3:3   24
3:25–26   201
5:3–5   145
6:2–14   144
6:6   24
6:14c–7:6   144
6:15   144
7:1   145
7:7   144
7:13   144
8:31–32   145
8:38–39   146
9:14   144
9:19   144
9:30   144
10:5–13   132
10:9   143
11:25   138
11:36   47
12:2   25
12:9–13   138
12:14–21   168
12:20   167
13   141
15:14–33   138

1 Corinthians
1:1–3   136
1:4–9   136
1:10   137
1:10–17   22, 138
1:28   24
2:14–3:3   22, 25
3:1   25
3:9b   144
4:10   24, 77
4:14–21   138

5:10–11 139, 142
6:9–10 142
6:19a 144
9:24 145
9:25 47
10:1 138
10:1–11 132
11:3 138
12:1 22, 138
12:11 25
12:11–13 25
12:12–26 23
12:15–21 144
12:17–19 23
12:21–30 23
12:23b–25 23
12:31 15
12:31 165
13:1–8a 24
13:4–8a 24
13:8–12 22
14:1 22
14:34–35 224
15:28 47
15:33 143
15:51 234
16:22 139

2 Corinthians
1:3 137
1:8 138
1:8–2:12 138
4:8 15–16
6:14 139
6:6–7 139, 142
6:8ff. 47
10:3 47
11:23–28 142
12:10 142
12:14–13:13 138
12:15 47

Galatians
1:10–2:21 138
1:11 138
1:16 165
3:28 224

4:12–20 138
5:19–23 139, 143
5:9 143
6:16 139
6:17 139

Ephesians
1:9 53
1:16 24
2:15 24
3:6 53
3:8–9 53
4:4–6 145
5 224
5:16 143
5:21–22 166
5:21–6:9 60, 142
6:14–17 143

Philippians
1:12 138
1:12–26 138
2:19–24 138
3:2 34–35
3:3 76
4:11–12 47
4:8 47, 139, 142

Colossians
3:12–14 142
3:18–4:1 60, 142

1 Thessalonians
2:1 138
2:17–3:13 138
4:9–12 49
4:9–5:11 141
4:13 138
4:13–18 139
5:8 47
5:23 139
5:27 139

1 Timothy
2:1–15 142
2:13–14 224
3:16 143, 151

5:1–21 142

Titus
1:7–8 142
2:1–10 142

Philemon
8 47
21f. 138

Hebrews
1:5–14 132
5:4–6 132
7:11–22 132

James
1:4 25
1:13 166
1:15 145
2:18–22 144
3:6 31
3:17 142

1 Peter
1:13 47
2:4–8 132
2:13–3:8 60
4:3 142

2 Peter
1:5–7 145
1:5–8 142
2:13–3:7 142
2:17b 144

1 John
4:18 25

3 John
15 49

Revelation
2:16 149
3:4 149
3:14–21 32
4:2–9 151

4:6–8   151
5:6–14   151
6:1–8   149, 151
7:9   151
9:1–11   151
9:13   151
9:20–21   142

12   52
12:1–5   149
12:3   151
12:7   151
13:1   151
13:8   151
17:3   151

17:7   151
17:12   151
17:16   151
19:14   151
20:4–6   151
21:2–22:5   151
22:15   35